Whatever Happened *to* Sunday Dinner?

A year of Italian menus with
250 recipes that celebrate family

STROMBOLI

4 CUP SIFTED FLOUR   RIND OF LEMON
6 EGGS.   "   " ORANGE
4 TBSP. BUTTER
Make well in flour add Eggs + etc
and mix - Knead 15 min well, do not
use much flour on the board. Put in bowl
cover with damp Cloth. take a little at a time
roll like a pencil - let dry - cut small
Pour Crisco in Pan enough to cover bring to boil.
Fry and put on paper towers (add a little Salt in Crisco.

---

in the same pan fry
1 lb Filbert Nuts
flavor, or water
lower flame when clear
(this in 3 batches) add
when honey is absorbed
and sprinkle with

Recipe For: _____
From the kitchen of: _____
Ingredients: 1 head cauliflower
            6 t butter
            2 t flour
            3 T sour cream
            3 T Parmigian
            1/4 t salt. 1/8
            Chopped fresh or

Steam cauliflower 4 -
5 minutes. Heat all other
ingredients together.

Califlour   Bontempi

2 eggs -   1st boil califlour then seperate
garlic   flourttes - then grease B dish
salt + pepper   then put them in Pan - then mix
1/4 C oil   + beat 2 eggs + the rest + put
tomatoes   on top - then grate mozarelli +
onion   put on top - also cheese then
parsly   Bake for 1/2 hr.
mozzarelli
grated
                Fedora
1 1/2 C raisins - 1 1/2 C appricot - cherries - mix
add flr + mix with your hands - now cream
1 C short - 1 C sug - 4 eggs - 2 C flr - 1/4 t soda
1/2 t salt - 1 C apple sauce - 1/4 C rum
(325 - 3 1/2 hrs or 2 1/4 hrs.)

         Stuff Tomatoes (about 6)
fry onion in oil - then 6 anchovies - 1 Teaspers
then add 1/2 C bread crumbs - or cubes - parsly
regona - nutmeg - mix up - then Stuff tomatoes
salt + peppers - grated cheese on top + oil.
315 - Bake 15 to 20 min.

Marinated Lamb Chops.
1/2 C oil - oregana - limon - alici paste - rub after
you turn them - in oven - marinate for at least 6 hrs.

Sweet Cheese Fritters.
6 graham crackers - confect sug - 4 Tflrs - 1/4 C almonds slivers - 1/2 Container ricotta - 2 or 3 eggs. mix
up - vanilla or cherry or rum.

Marenge for Le
6 eggs whites
drizzle Seegar 1
teme - Beat - Beat -
2 ltsp for egg wh
1/4 tls of cream of

---

half f
water:
t 375° and Bake
45 minutes

Whatever Happened *to* Sunday Dinner?

A year of Italian menus with
250 recipes that celebrate family

Lisa Caponigri

Food Photography by Guy Ambrosino

STERLING EPICURE
New York

STERLING EPICURE
New York

An Imprint of Sterling Publishing
387 Park Avenue South
New York, NY 10016

© 2012 by Lisa Caponigri
Photographs © 2012 by Guy Ambrosino
Food styling by Kate Winslow

ISBN 978-1-4027-8482-8 (hardcover)
ISBN 978-1-4027-9443-8 (ebook)

Library of Congress Cataloging-in-Publication Data

Caponigri, Lisa.
  Whatever happened to Sunday dinner? : a year of Italian menus, with more than 250 recipes, that
celebrate family / Lisa Caponigri ; photographs by Guy Ambrosino.
    p. cm.
  ISBN 978-1-4027-8482-8 (hardback)
 1. Cooking, Italian. 2. Dinners and dining. 3. Cookbooks. I. Title.
 TX723.C2835 2012
 641.5945--dc23
                              2011035569

Distributed in Canada by Sterling Publishing
c/o Canadian Manda Group, 165 Dufferin Street
Toronto, Ontario, Canada M6K 3H6
Distributed in the United Kingdom by GMC Distribution Services
Castle Place, 166 High Street, Lewes, East Sussex, England BN7 1XU
Distributed in Australia by Capricorn Link (Australia) Pty. Ltd.
P.O. Box 704, Windsor, NSW 2756, Australia

For information about custom editions, special sales, and premium and corporate purchases, please
contact Sterling Special Sales at 800-805-5489 or specialsales@sterlingpublishing.com.

Manufactured in the United States of America

2 4 6 8 10 9 7 5 3 1

www.sterlingpublishing.com

This book is dedicated to my grandmother
Catherine Lione Franco, who, through her example, instilled
in me a love of Italian cooking, an unconditional love of
family, and the belief that your glass is always half full.

Grazie infinite, nana.

contents

MENU 4   22

tortini di pomodori
tomato tarts

pasta con salsicce e broccolini
pasta with sausage and broccolini

medaglione di agnello con prosciutto
medallions of lamb, italian style

insalata mista alla siciliana
sicilian mixed salad

coppa italiana
italian parfaits

MENU 5   28

carciofi marinati
marinated artichokes

pasta con tonno e capperi
pasta with tuna and capers

tonno alla siciliana
tuna steaks in olive oil and garlic

fagiolini in tegame alla italiana
green beans with mozzarella and tomatoes

bocca di dama
mouth of a lady, almond and fruit cake

MENU 6   34

pizza rustica
rustic pizza

uova in cestino di pasqua
easter eggs in a basket

agnello ripieno
stuffed leg of lamb

spinaci alla parmigiana
spinach parmesan

i casateddi di margherita
margherita's ricotta turnovers

MENU 7   40

pomodorini ripieni di pesto
cherry tomatoes stuffed with pesto

paglia e fieno
spinach and egg fettuccine in cheese sauce

salmone alla italiana
salmon, italian style

finocchio gratinato
baked fennel parmesan

torta di pinoli
pine nut loaf cake

MENU 8   46

tortino di asparagi
asparagus torte

pasta pomodoro con vodka
pasta in vodka sauce

petti di pollo alla sostanza
chicken breasts in butter

carote glassate alla marsala
glazed carrots in marsala wine

meringue al cioccolato
meringue with chocolate

MENU 9   52

pasta sfoglia con salmone
puff pastry with smoked salmon

pasta ai quattro formaggi
baked four-cheese pasta

polpetti di vitello con salsa verde
veal balls with green sauce

zucchini ripieni
stuffed zucchini

pesche al forno
baked amaretto peaches

MENU 10   58

fettine di zucchine
zucchini rounds

pasta con sugo della domenica
pasta with sunday gravy

carne in sugo di pomodoro
meat from sunday gravy

bietola saltati
sautéed swiss chard

torta di mandorla
almond cake

MENU 11   64

crostini di formaggi
toasted cheese rounds

pasta al ragu della nonna caponigri
pasta with grandma caponigri's ragu sauce

pollo fritto
fried chicken, italian style

insalata di antipasti
antipasto salad

spumoni di fragole
strawberry spumoni

MENU 12   70

crostini con formaggio di capra e ficchi
toasts with goat cheese and figs

pasta con sugo di vitello
pasta with veal sauce

saltimbocca
veal scallopine stuffed with prosciutto

fagiolini saltati
sautéed green beans

torta della nonna
grandmother's cake

MENU 13   76

bruschetta al pomodoro
bruschetta with tomato and basil

manicotti
stuffed tube pasta

peperoni ripieni
lisa's famous stuffed peppers

insalata verde
classic green salad

torta di ricotta della nonna franco
nana's ricotta cake

MENU 14   82

crostini con pesto di olive nere
toasts with black olive paste

spaghetti al limone
lemon spaghetti

agnello arrosto con rosmarino e aglio
roast leg of lamb with rosemary and garlic

scarola della nonna
nana's escarole

pesche in vino bianco
peaches in white wine

MENU 15   86

prosciutto con melone
prosciutto with melon

polpetti alla lisa
lisa's famous meat-a-balls

pollo al forno della nonna
nana's baked chicken

insalata tre colori
tri-color salad

torta al cioccolato, caffè e nocciola
espresso and hazelnut chocolate cake

MENU 16   92

pecorino romano con miele e pepe
pecorino romano with honey and black pepper

polenta con funghi
polenta with mushrooms

salsicce grigliate
grilled sausage

spinaci saltati
sautéed spinach

torta di vino e noci
wine and nut cake

MENU 17   96

mozzarella fritta
fried mozzarella

pasta alla ligure
pasta with green beans, potatoes and basil pesto

pollo alla milanese
chicken in breadcrumbs

zucchini parmigiano
zucchini parmesan

budino di ricotta
ricotta cheese pudding

MENU 18   102

crostini con aioli di peperoni rossi
toasts with red pepper aioli

spaghetti alla siciliana con canciova e mudicca
spaghetti with anchovies and breadcrumbs

rotolini di sogliola
sole rollups

carciofi ripieni
stuffed artichokes

torta di arancio
orange cake

MENU 19   108

bruschetta siciliana
sicilian bruschetta with mixed olives

pasta ai frutti di mare
pasta with shellfish

vitello tonnato
veal in tuna sauce

pomodori ripieni
tomatoes stuffed with breadcrumbs

maritozzi
roman sugar cake with fruit and nuts

MENU 20   114

torta di mascarpone
mascarpone cheese torte with basil pesto and sun-dried tomatoes

spaghetti con caccio e pepe
spaghetti with cheese and black pepper

pollo cacciatore
hunter's chicken

insalata verde
green salad

torta della mamma con rhum
my mom's rum cake

MENU 21   120

caponata
sicilian eggplant appetizer

torta di maccheroni
macaroni and meat pie

pesce ripieno di finocchio
baked whole fish with fennel

frittata di verdure
vegetable omelet

sfogliatelle
ricotta turnovers

MENU 22   126

panini napolitani
neapolitan anchovy and cheese sandwiches

lasagne al forno
real italian lasagne

pollo alla vesuvio
chicken vesuvio

porri arrostiti
roasted leeks

zabaglione con fragole
italian custard with strawberries

MENU 23   132

peperoni arrotolati e ripieni
sicilian rolled peppers

zuppa di farro
barley soup

dentice alla livornese
red snapper in chunky tomato sauce

tortino di patate e prosciutto
potato and prosciutto casserole

granita al caffè
coffee ice

MENU 24   138

rotolo di mozzarella con prosciutto
mozzarella roll with prosciutto

farfalle con prosciutto, panna e piselli
bow–tie pasta with prosciutto, cream and peas

petti di pollo alla panna
chicken breasts in cream

spinaci saltati
sautéed spinach

panna cotta con lamponi
cooked cream with berries

MENU 25   142

arancini
rice balls

pasta alla puttanesca
pasta in tomato sauce with black olives and anchovies

vitello milanese
veal scallopine in breadcrumbs

insalata di pere, gorgonzola e nocciole
pear, gorgonzola and hazelnut salad

torta di grappa e pere
grappa and pear cake

MENU 26   148

involtini di melanzane
eggplant rollups

pasta alla norma
pasta with eggplant

pollo alla contadina
farmer's chicken with zucchini and tomatoes

cavolfiori gratinati
cauliflower in parmesan sauce

torta di mele
apple cake

MENU 27   154

salumi varie
antipasto platter of italian cured meats

pasta al boscaiola
woodman's pasta with mushroom sauce

carne di maiale con finocchio
pork tenderloin with fennel

funghi alla vittoria
mushrooms victoria

ciliege in chianti
cherries in chianti

MENU 28   160

tortino di funghi e cipolla
onion and mushroom torte

risotto con verdure
arborio rice with sautéed vegetables

manzo marinato
marinated flank steak

insalata siciliana
sicilian coleslaw

torta di frutta secca della nonna
grandma franco's fedora

MENU 29   166

crostini con pesto di ceci
toasts with chickpea paste

risotto con zucca e parmigiano
arborio rice with squash and parmesan

petti di pollo alla modenese
chicken breasts with mortadella

insalata fantasia
fantasy salad

uve con mascarpone
grapes in mascarpone cheese

MENU 30   172

polenta fritta con funghi e formaggio
fried polenta with mushrooms and cheese

pasta alla checca
pasta with cherry tomatoes, garlic and basil

cappesante ripieni di pesto
scallops stuffed with basil pesto

insalata di arancio, finocchio e cipolla rossa
orange, fennel and red onion salad

limoni ripieni
lemons filled with cream

MENU 31   178

fritelle di melanzane
eggplant fritters

torta di pasta siciliana
sicilian pasta torte

pollo ripieno di finocchio con patate al forno
fennel-stuffed chicken with oven-fried potatoes

i cannoli della nonna
the one, the only, nana's cannoli

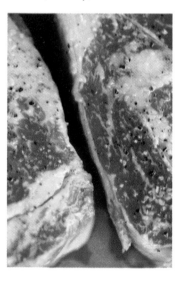

MENU 32   184

calamari fritti
fried squid

pasta con salmone affumicato e panna
pasta with smoked salmon and cream

involtini di pesce spada
swordfish rollups

finocchio e patate gratinate
fennel and potato cheese casserole

panforte
italian fruit cake

MENU 33   190

peperoni arrostiti con mozzarella e pesto
roasted peppers with mozzarella and basil pesto

risotto alla milanese
arborio rice with saffron

manzo in barolo
beef in barolo wine

cipolline agrodolce
sweet and savory cipolline onions

pinolata
pine nut cake

MENU 34   196

crostini di melanzane arrostite
toasts with roasted eggplant

gnudi di spinaci alla ricotta e parmigiano
spinach and cheese dumplings

baccalà all'italiano
cod, italian style

insalata mista con noce, pomodori secchi e gorgonzola
mixed greens with walnuts, sun-dried tomatoes and gorgonzola

mele al forno
baked apples in filo dough

MENU 35   202

crostini fiorentini
florentine toasts with chicken liver paste

tagliatelle al porcino
egg pasta with porcini mushrooms

bistecca alla fiorentina
florentine t-bone steak

funghi trifolati
sautéed mushrooms

zuccotto
dome-shaped chocolate mousse cake

MENU 36   208

verdure marinate
marinated vegetables

linguine con vongole alla nonna
nana's linguine with clam sauce

gamberi marinati alla siciliana
sicilian marinated shrimp

caprese al forno
baked caprese salad with tomato and mozzarella

castanaccio
chestnut cake

MENU 37   214

spiedini di mozzarella
mozzarella on skewers

pasta all'arrabbiata
pasta with spicy tomato sauce

salsicce e peperoni con patate
nana's classic sausage and peppers with potatoes

insalata verde con finocchio
green salad with fennel

crostata di gelato
spumoni pie bombe

MENU 38   220

crostini di olive verdi
toasts with green olive paste

peperonata
pepper stew over arborio rice

spiedini di manzo
beef on skewers

cavolfiori bontempi
grandma franco's cauliflower
bontempi

crostata di marmellata
marmalade tart

MENU 39   226

torta al formaggio bianco
white cheese torte

risotto con funghi
arborio rice with mushrooms

branzino in sale
sea bass in salt

*insalata di rucola, pere e
parmigiano*
arugula, pear and parmesan
salad

tiramisu
italian mascarpone cake

MENU 40   232

fritelle di zucchini
zucchini fritters

gnocchi con burro e salvia
gnocchi with butter and sage

baccalà alla siciliana
cod, sicilian style

insalata di funghi
mushroom salad

torta bassa di cioccolata
flourless chocolate cake

MENU 41   238

crostini ai tre funghi
three-mushroom toasts

*spaghetti con pesto alla
trapanese*
spaghetti with pesto, trapani style

arista al limone
roast pork with lemon

insalata del fattore
farmer's salad

cassata siciliana
sicilian sponge cake with ricotta

MENU 42   244

funghi ripieni
stuffed mushrooms

pasta e fagioli
pasta and white beans

tagliata con rucola e limone
sliced rib-eye steak with arugula
and lemon

*pere cotte in vino bianco con
pistachio e mascarpone*
poached pears in white wine
with pistachio and mascarpone
cream

MENU 43   250

bruschetta alla rucola
bruschetta with arugula

*gnocchi con gorgonzola e
pinoli*
potato dumplings with gorgonzola
and pine nuts

vitello alla marsala
veal scallopine in marsala wine

pomodori alla emiliana
stuffed tomatoes, emilia-romagna
style

*pere cotte con menta e
parmigiano-reggiano*
minted poached pears with
parmesan

MENU 44   256

crostini con gorgonzola
toasts with gorgonzola

*lasagne con funghi e
formaggi*
mushroom and cheese lasagne

stracotto
pot roast, tuscan style

*insalata di rucola con
parmigiano*
arugula salad with parmesan

affogato di caffè
ice cream drowned in coffee

MENU 45 262

crostini con ricotta e pepe nero
toasts with ricotta and black pepper

gnudi bianchi
ricotta dumplings

spiedini di arista con pane
roast pork skewers with bread

patate con rosmarino
rosemary potatoes

budino al cioccolato
italian chocolate pudding

MENU 46 268

panini di bietola
swiss chard stem sandwiches

gnocchi alla romana
baked potato dumplings with polenta and cheese

agnello scottaditto marinato della nonna franco
grandma franco's marinated lamb chops

pomodori arrostiti con aglio
roasted plum tomatoes with garlic

crostata di ricotta
ricotta pie

MENU 47 274

filo ripieno di formaggio e pomodori
filo dough stuffed with cheese and sun-dried tomatoes

minestra di pasta e ceci
pasta and chickpea soup

polpettone alla siciliana
sicilian meatloaf

cavollini di bruxelles saltati
sautéed brussels sprouts

biscotti italiani varie
cookie tray

MENU 48 280

crostini con prosciutto e miele
toasts with prosciutto and honey

conchiglie di pasta ripiene
stuffed pasta shells

petto di vitello ripieno con uvette e pinoli
veal breast stuffed with raisins and pine nuts

patate al forno
oven-roasted potatoes

salame al cioccolato
chocolate salami

MENU 49 286

pizzette
small pizzas

maccheroni con ricotta
macaroni with ricotta

petti di pollo con pomodori arrostiti e aglio
chicken breasts with sun-dried tomatoes and garlic crust

bietola alla romana
swiss chard, roman style

crema di amaretto
amaretto decadence

MENU 50 292

cuore di palmo al balsamico
hearts of palm in balsamic vinegar

minestrone
italian vegetable soup

petti di pollo aglio e olio
chicken in oil and garlic

piselli con prosciutto
peas with prosciutto

crostata di tartufo alla nocciola
hazelnut truffle pie

MENU 51 298

grissini con erbe e prosciutto
breadsticks with herbs and prosciutto

lasagne verde
spinach lasagne

braciole della nonna
nana's braciole

cipolline al forno
baked cipolline

monte bianco
chestnuts with cream

MENU 52 304

biscotti di parmigiano
parmesan wheels

timballo
sicilian timbale

filetto di manzo grigliata
grilled beef tenderloin

verdure siciliane arrostiti
roasted sicilian vegetables

strufoli della nonna
nana's strufoli

introduction

I am a second-generation Italian-American and, like many Italian-Americans, I grew up with the tradition of Sunday dinner. Sunday was for gathering, preparing, cooking, eating, sharing, talking, laughing. Some of my happiest memories are of sitting around my Nana Franco's big dining room table with my immediate family, my cousins, aunts, uncles, family friends, and whoever else happened to be visiting. Every Sunday was a time to disconnect from the rest of the world and reconnect with family and friends.

Sitting down to eat was the final phase of the day. For me, the experience began much earlier in the day, as I was my grandmother's "official helper" in the kitchen. Thanks to my parents, I grew up with a love of all things Italian and spent a great deal of my childhood in Italy. This thrilled my nana and she made her own personal contribution to my education— teaching me how to prepare the dishes she had learned to make from her mother and grandmother.

My grandmother, as well as my father, have passed on. I now have three children of my own, growing up faster than I could have

left: *My mother, grandparents and me, Laguna Hills, California*

imagined. The world moves so quickly, and there are so many demands on our time. But Sunday dinner is still sacred to my family. It is a day to plan together, cook together, dream together. As we chop, stir, set places at the table, sit, drink, eat, we talk about the week that has passed and the week that is to come. Sunday dinner is irreplaceable, the meeting place of memories that will last a lifetime.

You say, "That's fine for you, Lisa. But Sunday dinner isn't a tradition for my family. There's no way I can get everyone to the table for a relaxed meal every Sunday."

That's why I wrote this book. Inside its covers you'll find 52 Sunday dinner menus in the Italian tradition: an antipasto (usually

Sesame seeds cookies (Mrs Bea)
1½ lb flour
½ lb shortning
¼ lb sugar
3 eggs less one egg white for rolling
½ cup milk
1½ tbsp baking powder
1 tsp vanilla
Blend all together
take small amount of dough

and roll in Beat one egg
white with little water.
moisten the dough and
roll on seeds Bake 350°
cherry cookies - ½ c crisco - ¼ c sugar
1 yolk - 1 tsp flavoring. flour
beat egg white with little
water - mix dough all together with
enough water make little balls roll in
egg white then in grated almonds
place cherry in center & bake

— SALTIMBOCCA —
For 8 Scallopini, you need 8 very thin
slices of Ham (PROSCIUTTO) Top each
Scallopini with a slice of Ham, pound
the two together with a meat Mallet
working into the veal side a mixture
of 1 teaspoon grated lemon rind, ½ tsp
sage & ¼ tbs salt Roll up with ham inside
Fasten together with picks Saute in butter till brown
on all sides. Serve immediately. — Nov

Scallopini al Marsala
Pound each scallopini with Mallet for 8 scallopini
2 tbs flour ½ tsp salt ½ tsp paprika sauté in olive oil & butter
until browned on one side only. Turn add to the
pan ½ cup Marsala and ¼ water. Simmer until tender
Spoon the sauce over the meat to serve. Garnish
with water cress, cream sherry, & Marsala
2 scallopini per person

Lemon Pudding.
2 Eggs — 1 Lemon - Grated Rind & juice
1 Cup Milk - ¼ C. Sifted Flour
Butter —
eggs & beat yolks well
of the juice so the
up to a lemon color)
ingredients in order given

Califlour   Bentempi
2 eggs-   1st boil califlour then seperate
garlic   flourettes - then grease B dish
salt + pepper then put them in Pan - then mix
¼ C oil   + beat 2 eggs + the rest + put
tomatoes   on top - then grate mozzarelli
onion   put on top - also
parsly   Bake for ¼ hr
mozzarelli
grated   Fedora
1½ C raisins - 1½ C appricot
add flr + mix with your hand
1 C short - 1 C sug - 4 eggs -
½ t salt - 1 C apple sauce -
(325 - 3½ hrs or 2¼ hrs.)
Stuff Tomatoes (about
fry onion in oil - then 6 anch
then add ½ C bread crumbs.
regona - nutmeg - mix up - then
salt + pepers - grated cheese a
315 - Bake 15 to 20 min.
Marinated Lamb Chops.
½ C oil - oregana - limon - alive
you turn them - in oven - mar
Sweet Cheese Fritters.
6 graham crackers - confe
monds slivers - ½ container ri
up - vanilla or cherry or rum.

Guido, Felicia and me, cooking at home, South
Bend, Indiana

a crostini to pass at the table), a primo (first course: this is almost always a pasta, but it can also be a risotto, polenta, or a soup), a secondo (call it the main course) served with a single contorno (side dish), and, finally, dessert. Every menu is different, not a single recipe is repeated. Do you have to make every menu as I have planned it? Certainly not. Though many of these menus are thematic for me, there is no reason why you can't switch around recipes or drop a course, if you prefer. But remember, the goal isn't just to eat, it's to linger and relax.

With that in mind, here are five tips for making Sunday dinner a weekly reality in your home:

Make Sunday a priority. Schedule Sunday dinner into your family calendar as you would soccer practice, ballet lessons, school meetings. Take inventory of the activities you usually do on Sunday and shift them off to other days of the week. By making clear to your family that Sunday is your day to spend together, you are showing your children, in the most meaningful way possible, that eating with them, being with them, is important to you.

Plan ahead. On Sunday night, after you have enjoyed your first wonderful family dinner together, look ahead to the next weekend and decide what you want to make. It will only take five minutes. Write down the items you'll need to pick up at the store during the week. By planning ahead, you'll wake up Sunday morning relaxed and ready to go.

Decide the menu and assign the chores together. It's important to get the whole family involved in the preparation and serving of the meal. Once you decide on a menu, divide up the tasks—chopping, baking, setting the table. Sunday morning, set up workstations in the kitchen, so that everyone has their spot. In this way, dinner doesn't become a mom-centric accomplishment but rather something you all do together as a family.

Keep the menu simple. Sunday dinner doesn't have to be elaborate, just delicious. Cooking for your family should never be a chore; it should be a pleasure. You'll see that my recipes reflect this conviction. Though our Sunday dinners consist of multiple courses, the dishes, almost without exception, go together quickly and easily, and many can be prepped to some degree (or even entirely) ahead of time.

Let go and have fun. Remember, Sunday dinner is a good thing—it's not meant to be one more task to stress out about. It should be the highlight of your week, your time to talk, laugh, and revel in the love of your family.

Buon appetito and salute, and here is to making delicious memories!

—*Lisa Caponigri*

MENU

1

crostini con cannellini e pesto
crunchy toasts with white bean purée and basil pesto

....

pasta alla amatriciana
pasta with italian bacon and tomato sauce

....

vitello alla piccata
veal in lemon sauce

....

broccolini saltati
sautéed sicilian broccolini

....

zuppa inglese
trifle with lemon pudding and pound cake

This menu says, "Let's cook together and eat together!"
The cannellini appetizer reminds me of when I was little;
my mother would use legumes in every way imaginable—
in soup, with pasta, or as a side dish. This is another twist
on this versatile, creamy white bean.

4

crostini con cannellini e pesto

crunchy toasts with white bean purée and basil pesto

Cannellini beans are ubiquitous in Italian cooking. Here they are worked into a creamy, garlicky spread that is paired with pesto for a great crostini topping.

- 1 CAN (15 OUNCES) CANNELLINI BEANS (PREFERABLY IMPORTED ITALIAN; THEIR SKINS ARE THINNER AND EASIER TO DIGEST)
- ¼ CUP EXTRA-VIRGIN OLIVE OIL
- 3 TABLESPOONS FRESH LEMON JUICE
- 3 CLOVES GARLIC, PEELED
- SEA SALT
- PINCH OF FRESHLY GROUND BLACK PEPPER
- 1 LOAF THIN ITALIAN BREAD, SLICED ON THE DIAGONAL INTO 12 TO 15 SLICES
- 1 JAR (4 OUNCES) PESTO

Preheat the oven to 400F.

Put the beans, olive oil, lemon juice, garlic, salt to taste, and pepper in a blender, and process into a smooth purée.

Toast the bread slices in the oven or on a grill.

Spread one side of each of the bread slices with the bean purée and top with a dab of pesto.

pasta alla amatriciana

pasta with italian bacon and tomato sauce

Named for the town of Amatrice in the Lazio region, this tomato sauce is made extra-special with the addition of the rich flavor of pancetta and the heat of red pepper flakes.

- 2 POUNDS SPAGHETTI OR BUCATINI
- ½ CUP EXTRA-VIRGIN OLIVE OIL
- 1 POUND THICKLY SLICED PANCETTA, CUT INTO BITE-SIZE PIECES
- 1 RED ONION, CHOPPED
- 3 CLOVES GARLIC, CHOPPED
- 2 CUPS LISA'S CLASSIC TOMATO SAUCE (PAGE 89)
- 1½ TEASPOONS RED PEPPER FLAKES
- SEA SALT
- FRESHLY GROUND BLACK PEPPER
- 1 CUP SHREDDED PECORINO ROMANO

Bring a large pot of salted water to a boil. Add the pasta and cook until al dente (if using spaghetti, cook for 7 minutes; if using bucatini, cook for 6 minutes).

Meanwhile, in a large skillet over medium-high heat, heat the olive oil. Add the pancetta, onion, and garlic and cook, stirring, until the onion is transparent, taking care not to burn the garlic. Add the tomato sauce and red pepper flakes, and season with salt and black pepper.

Put aside 1 cup pasta cooking water and drain the pasta. Transfer the pasta to the skillet and toss to coat with the sauce. Let simmer with the sauce for 2 minutes. Add the cheese and stir to combine. Transfer to a large serving bowl and serve.

vitello alla piccata
veal in lemon sauce

*Tender, delicate veal in a velvety lemon sauce—
this is my daughter Felicia's favorite dish. Actually,
piccata is a misnomer here, as the sauce is not
at all piccante (which means "sharp" or "hot").
Rather, it is a lemon sauce that becomes creamy
once you add the white wine and cook it down.*

1½–2	**POUNDS THINLY SLICED VEAL**
1	**CUP ALL-PURPOSE FLOUR**
½	**STICK (4 TABLESPOONS) UNSALTED BUTTER**
1	**CUP EXTRA-VIRGIN OLIVE OIL**
	JUICE OF 2 LEMONS
1	**CUP WHITE WINE**
3	**TABLESPOONS CHOPPED FRESH ITALIAN PARSLEY**
2	**CLOVES GARLIC, CHOPPED**
2	**TABLESPOONS CAPERS (OPTIONAL)**
	SEA SALT
	FRESHLY GROUND BLACK PEPPER

One at a time, place the pieces of scallopine
between two pieces of waxed paper and pound
with a meat mallet until thin.

Preheat the oven to 200F.

Spread the flour over a large flat plate. Dredge
the veal in the flour, coating well on all sides,
and tap off any excess. Set the dredged pieces
on a tray.

Melt 3 tablespoons of the butter in the olive oil
in a large heavy skillet over medium heat. When
the butter foams, turn the heat up to high and
cook a few pieces of veal at a time (don't crowd
the skillet), about 1 minute per side, until just
golden. Transfer the cooked veal to a warm
platter in the oven to keep warm.

When all the veal is cooked, add the lemon juice,
white wine, and remaining 1 tablespoon butter
to the skillet. Deglaze the skillet by scraping
up and dissolving all the browned bits stuck to
the bottom of the pan. Stir in the parsley, garlic,
and capers (if using). Season with salt and
pepper, and spoon the sauce over the veal. Serve
immediately.

broccolini saltati
sautéed sicilian broccolini

*Sometimes sold as baby broccoli, broccolini is
a cross between broccoli and Chinese broccoli.
Requiring next to no prep, broccolini is an
excellent choice when entertaining.*

6–8	**BUNCHES BROCCOLINI**
⅓	**CUP PINE NUTS**
½	**CUP EXTRA-VIRGIN OLIVE OIL**
5	**CLOVES GARLIC, THINLY SLICED**
1	**TEASPOON RED PEPPER FLAKES**
½	**CUP GOLDEN RAISINS**
	SEA SALT

Trim the stems of the broccolini and discard.
Steam or parboil the broccolini in boiling water
for about 2 minutes.

Preheat the oven to 350F. Toast the pine nuts on
a small baking sheet until golden but not brown.
Transfer to a small bowl.

Meanwhile, in a large skillet, heat the olive oil
over medium-high heat, add the garlic, and cook
until soft (be careful not to let it brown). Add
the broccolini and cook until it is tender but still
crisp, about 5 minutes, stirring a few times. Add
the red pepper flakes, raisins, and salt to taste.
Add the toasted pine nuts and stir for 1 minute.

zuppa inglese

trifle with lemon pudding and
pound cake

*Whenever my mother had a special dinner party, I
knew there would be zuppa inglese for dessert. It
is elegant and makes for a dramatic presentation
when served in a footed glass trifle dish. You
can assemble it in the morning and keep it
refrigerated right up until you are ready to serve it.*

2 **CUPS LEMON PUDDING, STORE-BOUGHT OR
HOMEMADE**

1 **POUND CAKE, STORE-BOUGHT OR HOMEMADE,
CUT INTO 2-INCH SQUARES**

¼ **CUP RUM OR BRANDY (OPTIONAL)**

1 **CUP HIGH-QUALITY STRAWBERRY JAM**

2 **CUPS HULLED AND SLICED STRAWBERRIES,
(½ CUP RESERVED FOR DECORATION)**

ZEST OF 1 LEMON, FINELY GRATED

**FRESH WHIPPED CREAM TO GARNISH,
SWEETENED TO TASTE**

Spread a ½-inch layer of lemon pudding over
the bottom of the trifle dish. Arrange a layer
of pound cake squares over the pudding and
moisten them with some of the rum. Spread
a thin layer of strawberry jam over the pound
cake, then add a layer of sliced strawberries.
Spread a ½-inch layer of lemon pudding over
the strawberries and sprinkle with some of the
lemon zest. Add another layer of pound cake
squares and continue layering in same manner
with rum, jam, strawberries, pudding and zest
until the bowl is full. Top with whipped cream
and decorate with sliced strawberries.

**"una mamma
italiana
è un regalo
da dio."**

an italian
mother is a gift
from heaven.

MENU

2

SERVES 8 TO 10

sformato di prosciutto
prosciutto soufflé

pasta alla carbonara
pasta with eggs and bacon

arista al forno
roast pork

carciofi alla romana
baked artichokes, roman style

macedonia
fruit salad

I call this menu "Roman Holiday," as it brings back so
many wonderful memories of my life in Rome as a child.
I close my eyes, feel my father's hand in mine, and recall
the smell of roast pork, the signature dish of this great city,
wafting from the trattorie as we walked through the streets.
The food of Rome is hearty, comforting, and delicious—
Italy at its best.

sformato di prosciutto

prosciutto soufflé

What a wonderfully elegant way to start your dinner! Make sure everyone is seated at the table as you pull the soufflé from the oven so they can admire it in all its golden, puffy glory.

- ½ STICK (4 TABLESPOONS) UNSALTED BUTTER
- ½ CUP ALL-PURPOSE FLOUR
- 1 CUP WHOLE MILK
- 2 LARGE EGG WHITES
- 2 LARGE EGGS, SEPARATED
- ½ POUND IMPORTED PROSCIUTTO, THINLY SLICED AND CUT INTO BITE-SIZE PIECES
- 1 CUP GRATED PARMIGIANO-REGGIANO
- SEA SALT
- FRESHLY GROUND BLACK PEPPER

Preheat the oven to 350F. Butter and lightly flour a 2-quart soufflé dish.

In a large saucepan, melt the butter over medium heat. Add the flour and whisk until smooth. Gradually add the milk, whisking all the while to keep lumps from forming, and cook until the mixture thickens to the point that it coats the back of a wooden spoon. Remove from the heat.

In a large bowl, using an electric mixer, whip the 4 egg whites until soft peaks form.

Add the prosciutto, egg yolks, and Parmigiano-Reggiano to the white sauce and stir to combine. Gently fold in the beaten egg whites. Season to taste with sea salt and pepper.

Pour the mixture into the prepared soufflé dish and bake for 40 minutes, until it is fluffy and golden on top. Serve immediately (it will begin to deflate as soon as it's taken out of the oven).

pasta alla carbonara

pasta with eggs and bacon

The recipe for this simple yet wonderfully satisfying dish is from my favorite hole-in-the-wall trattoria in Rome, "Osteria da Edmondo."

- 1 STICK (8 TABLESPOONS) UNSALTED BUTTER
- ¼ CUP EXTRA-VIRGIN OLIVE OIL
- 1 POUND THICK-SLICED BACON OR PANCETTA, CUT INTO 1-INCH PIECES
- 1 HEAD GARLIC, SEPARATED INTO CLOVES AND CHOPPED
- 2 POUNDS SPAGHETTI
- 6 LARGE EGGS
- 2 CUPS GRATED PECORINO ROMANO
- FRESHLY GROUND BLACK PEPPER

Bring a large pot of salted water to a boil.

Meanwhile, melt the butter in a large skillet. Add the olive oil. Add the bacon and garlic and cook until the bacon is very crisp, taking care not to burn the garlic. Remove the bacon and garlic from the skillet, using a slotted spoon, and drain on paper towels.

Add the pasta to the boiling water and cook until al dente, about 8 minutes.

Meanwhile, in a large serving bowl, beat together the eggs, cheese, and pepper to taste. Stir in the bacon and garlic.

Drain the pasta and add to the bowl. Toss until the pasta is well coated with the egg and cheese mixture and serve immediately.

arista al forno

roast pork

Be sure to sear the pork well before putting it into the oven to roast—a golden brown crust adds layers of flavor.

1 **BONELESS PORK LOIN (ABOUT 4 POUNDS)**
2 **CLOVES GARLIC, SLICED**
1 **TEASPOON SEA SALT**
2 **TABLESPOONS FENNEL SEEDS**
   FRESHLY GROUND BLACK PEPPER
1 **TABLESPOON EXTRA-VIRGIN OLIVE OIL**
1 **CUP WHITE WINE**

Preheat the oven to 375F.

Keep the pork loin intact and leave a little of the belly flap.

In a small bowl, combine the garlic, salt, and fennel seeds. Rub the mixture into the meat on all sides, and season with pepper. Wrap the belly flap around the roast. Tie the roast every 1 ½ inches with kitchen string.

Heat the olive oil in a large skillet over medium heat. Brown the roast on all sides in the hot oil and transfer to a roasting pan.

Roast for 30 minutes. Add the wine to the pan and baste the roast with it. Continue to roast, basting a few more times, until the meat feels firm when pressed, about another 30 minutes, or until an instant-read thermometer inserted into the pork reads 155F to 160F.

Remove the pan from the oven and let the pork rest for 5 minutes. Turn the pork over and baste with the pan juices. Remove the string, cut the roast into thick slices, and arrange on a serving platter.

> **"ci sono italiani e poi ci sono italiani."**
>
> **there are italians and then there are italians.**

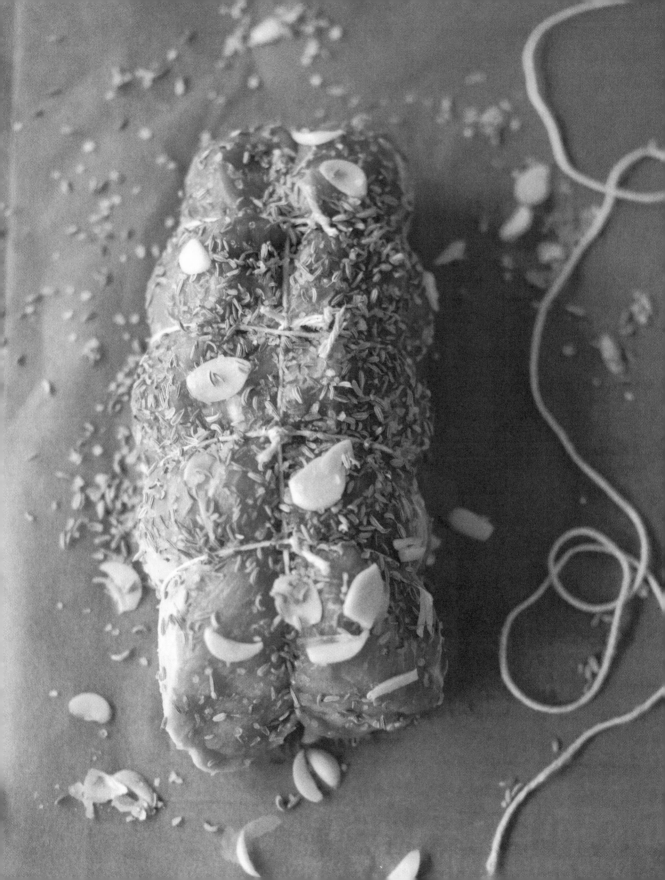

carciofi alla romana

baked artichokes, roman style

I like to use baby artichokes for this recipe because they're so tender, but it's equally delicious prepared with imported Italian artichoke hearts, which usually come in a jar. Just rinse them well before using.

¾	CUP EXTRA-VIRGIN OLIVE OIL
24	BABY ARTICHOKES
1	CUP FRESH ITALIAN BREADCRUMBS (PAGE 79)
½	CUP CHOPPED FRESH ITALIAN PARSLEY
4	CLOVES GARLIC, MINCED
	SEA SALT
	FRESHLY GROUND BLACK PEPPER
½	CUP FRESH LEMON JUICE

Preheat the oven to 325F. Coat the bottom of a square baking dish just big enough to hold the artichokes standing upright with 2 tablespoons of the olive oil.

Remove the outer leaves from the artichokes and trim the stems so the artichokes will stand upright. Set them in the prepared baking dish.

In a medium bowl, combine the breadcrumbs, parsley, garlic, salt and pepper to taste, and lemon juice. Spread the mixture over the artichokes and drizzle the top with the remaining olive oil. Bake until the artichokes are tender, about 25 minutes.

macedonia

fruit salad

In Italy, bananas are considered a morning fruit and aren't usually added to Macedonia, but Italian Americans tend to include them.

	JUICE OF 2 LARGE SWEET ORANGES
	JUICE OF 1 LEMON
2	BANANAS (OPTIONAL)
4	APPLES
2	PEARS
2	PEACHES
6	APRICOTS
1	CUP MIXED SEEDLESS BLACK AND GREEN GRAPES
1	TABLESPOON SUGAR

In a large serving bowl, combine the orange and lemon juices.

As you prep the fruit, add it to the citrus juices to keep it from browning: if using the bananas, peel them, then cut into small pieces; core and slice the apples and pears; pit and slice the peaches and apricots; cut the grapes in half.

Toss all the fruit together with the juice mixture, add the sugar, and serve.

MENU

3

SERVES 8 TO 10

foglie di salvia fritte
deep-fried sage leaves

....

capellini agrodolce
sweet and savory angel hair pasta

....

filetto di sogliola oreganata
fillet of sole with oregano

....

asparagi arrostiti
broiled asparagus

....

torta siciliana
orange and lemon tart

This menu reminds me of cooking with my nana. Her use of golden raisins and pine nuts was a tribute to her mysterious island, Sicily, where this Arab and Greek sweet and savory combination is so popular. As we cooked together, not only did nana share her recipes with me; she also taught me the history of her beloved Sicily.

16

foglie di salvia fritte

deep-fried sage leaves

Stuffed with salty anchovies, these crispy fried sage-leaf "sandwiches" are a uniquely tasty way to kick off a meal.

- 1   CUP EXTRA-VIRGIN OLIVE OIL
- 2   LARGE EGGS
- ½   TEASPOON SEA SALT
- ½   CUP ALL-PURPOSE FLOUR
- 4   ANCHOVY FILLETS, EACH CUT INTO 6 PIECES (24 PIECES)
- 48   FRESH SAGE LEAVES

Heat the olive oil in a deep skillet to 350F.

Meanwhile, in a large, shallow bowl, beat the eggs with the salt. Place the flour on a flat plate.

Place each piece of anchovy on a sage leaf. Top with the remaining leaves. Dip the sage leaf "sandwiches" in the beaten eggs to coat fully and dredge in the flour, tapping off any excess.

Fry the sage sandwiches in the hot oil in batches until golden brown on both sides. Using a slotted spoon, remove them from the oil and drain on paper towels before serving.

capellini agrodolce

sweet and savory angel hair pasta

With its inclusion of raisins, olives, and orange pieces, this pasta course is Sicilian through and through, and a delicious change of pace.

- 1   CUP PINE NUTS
- 2   POUNDS CAPELLINI
- 2   CLOVES GARLIC, CHOPPED
- ½   CUP PITTED CURED SICILIAN BLACK OLIVES
- ½   CUP GOLDEN RAISINS
- 1   ORANGE, PEELED, SEEDED, AND CUT INTO BITE-SIZE PIECES
- ½   CUP EXTRA-VIRGIN OLIVE OIL
- ½   CUP FRESH ORANGE JUICE

Preheat the oven to 300F.

Toast the pine nuts on a baking sheet for 4 to 5 minutes until golden.

Bring a large pot of salted water to a boil. Add the capellini and cook until al dente, 2 to 3 minutes.

Meanwhile, in a large serving bowl, combine the toasted pine nuts, garlic, olives, raisins, orange, olive oil, and orange juice.

Drain the capellini, add it to the bowl, and toss to combine with the other ingredients. Serve immediately.

filetto di sogliola oreganata

fillet of sole with oregano

The delicate sweetness of the sole provides a tasty backdrop for the cheesy, garlicky breadcrumb stuffing.

1	CUP FISH BOUILLON FROM A BOUILLON CUBE
1	CUP PLAIN BREADCRUMBS
½	CUP GRATED PARMIGIANO-REGGIANO
3	CLOVES GARLIC, MINCED
2	TABLESPOONS CHOPPED FRESH ITALIAN PARSLEY
1¼	TEASPOONS DRIED OREGANO
1	SPRIG FRESH ROSEMARY
4	FRESH SAGE LEAVES
1	TEASPOON SEA SALT
	FRESHLY GROUND BLACK PEPPER
4–6	TABLESPOONS EXTRA-VIRGIN OLIVE OIL
8	SOLE FILLETS (4 OUNCES EACH)
	LEMON WEDGES

Preheat the oven to 400F. Pour the bouillon into a 13- by 9-inch baking dish.

Combine the breadcrumbs, Parmigiano-Reggiano, garlic, parsley, oregano, rosemary, sage, salt, and pepper to taste in a medium bowl. Add as much of the olive oil, 1 tablespoon at a time, as needed to get a mixture with a moist, sandy texture.

Sprinkle the smooth side of the fillets with an even coating of the seasoned crumbs. Roll up the fillets and arrange them side by side, seam side down, in the baking dish with the bouillon. Bake until the breadcrumbs are golden and the fillets are just cooked through, about 20 minutes.

Transfer the fillets to a warm serving platter and arrange lemon wedges all around. Cover loosely with aluminum foil to keep warm.

Pour the liquid from the baking dish into a small saucepan. Bring to a boil and continue to boil until thickened and creamy. Serve the sauce on the side with the fillets.

asparagi arrostiti

broiled asparagus

This is the simplest of side dishes but always a hit.

2	POUNDS ASPARAGUS
5	TABLESPOONS EXTRA-VIRGIN OLIVE OIL
	SEA SALT
½	CUP GRATED PARMIGIANO-REGGIANO

Snap the bottoms off the asparagus stems where they naturally break. Steam the asparagus for 3 to 4 minutes until just tender. Immediately shock in cold water.

Arrange the asparagus in a single layer in large shallow baking dish and drizzle with the olive oil. Toss to coat. Season to taste with salt, and sprinkle with the Parmigiano-Reggiano. Broil 3 minutes. Serve warm.

torta siciliana

orange and lemon tart

This citrus-sparked tart makes a refreshing—though rich—end to the meal.

CRUST

- 1½   **CUPS ALL-PURPOSE FLOUR**
- ½   **TEASPOON SEA SALT**
- 1   **STICK (8 TABLESPOONS) COLD UNSALTED BUTTER, CUT INTO PIECES**

FILLING

- 1   **LARGE ORANGE**
- 2   **LEMONS**
- 6   **LARGE EGGS**
- 1   **CUP GRANULATED SUGAR**
- ½   **TEASPOON SEA SALT**
- ½   **CUP HEAVY CREAM**
- 1   **MEDIUM ORANGE, THINLY SLICED, FOR GARNISH CONFECTIONERS' SUGAR**

In a large bowl, combine the flour and salt. Add the butter and, using a pastry knife, cut it into the flour until the mixture forms coarse crumbs. Mix in 3 to 4 tablespoons ice water, 1 tablespoon at a time, until the dough is moist and holds together. Shape the dough into a disk, wrap in plastic, and refrigerate for 30 minutes.

On a lightly floured work surface, roll the dough out to a 14-inch disk. Transfer to an 11-inch tart pan (preferably one with a removable bottom) and fit the dough into the pan. Cover with plastic wrap and refrigerate 15 minutes.

Preheat the oven to 375F.

Line the tart with pie weights, rice, or dried beans. Bake for 15 minutes, until golden. Remove from the oven.

Meanwhile, grate ¾ teaspoon zest from the orange and ½ teaspoon zest from one of the lemons. Squeeze ¼ cup juice from the orange and ¼ cup juice from the lemons.

In a large bowl, whisk together the eggs, granulated sugar, salt, orange zest and juice, and lemon zest and juice. Whisk in the cream. Pour the filling into the partially baked tart shell. Set the tart on a baking sheet to catch any overflow. Bake until the crust is golden brown, about 30 minutes. Transfer to a rack and cool completely. Serve at room temperature.

When ready to serve, remove the side of the pan. Artfully arrange the orange slices on top and sprinkle with the confectioners' sugar.

MENU

4

SERVES 8 TO 10

tortini di pomodori
tomato tarts

pasta con salsicce e broccolini
pasta with sausage and broccolini

medaglione di agnello con prosciutto
medallions of lamb, italian style

insalata mista alla siciliana
sicilian mixed salad

coppa italiana
italian parfaits

Ever since my children were small, they loved crunching up the amaretto cookies and sprinkling them over the creamy mascarpone cheese, layer after layer, to make Coppa Italiana. It's the perfect dessert for the little ones. In fact, this whole menu is perfect for the youngest members of the family.

tortini di pomodori

tomato tarts

Start your meal with the colors of the Italian flag—puff pastry topped with bright red slices of ripe tomato and given a final garnish of fresh basil leaves right before going to the table.

- 2 SHEETS REFRIGERATED PUFF PASTRY
- 3 CLOVES GARLIC, CHOPPED
- ⅔ CUP EXTRA-VIRGIN OLIVE OIL, PLUS EXTRA FOR DRIZZLING
- ½ POUND PROSCIUTTO DI PARMA, THINLY SLICED AND CHOPPED INTO 1-INCH PIECES
- ½ TEASPOON FRESHLY GROUND BLACK PEPPER
- 10 FIRM ROMA TOMATOES, SLICED ¼ INCH THICK
- 1 TEASPOON FRESH THYME LEAVES
- ½ CUP FRESH BASIL LEAVES

Preheat the oven to 375F. Grease a large baking sheet.

Cut ten 4-inch circles from the sheets of puff pastry using an upside-down coffee cup. Place the pastry circles on the prepared baking sheet.

In a food processor or blender, combine the garlic, olive oil, prosciutto, and pepper. Process just 5 to 7 seconds into a rough purée. Spread the mixture evenly over the pastry circles. Arrange the tomato slices attractively on top of each circle. Drizzle with some olive oil and sprinkle with thyme. Turn up the edges of each tart. Bake for 15 minutes or until edges are golden and crisp.

Chop the basil, mix with a little olive oil, and drizzle over the tarts.

pasta con salsicce e broccolini

pasta with sausage and broccolini

I first enjoyed this dish on the island of Sardinia, where it was served to me with homemade sausage and the pasta della casa, ear-shaped orecchiette.

- 2 POUNDS ITALIAN SAUSAGE
- 2 POUNDS RIGATONI, PENNE, OR ORECCHIETTE
- 1 CUP EXTRA-VIRGIN OLIVE OIL
- 6 CLOVES GARLIC, CRUSHED INTO A PASTE
- 3 POUNDS BROCCOLI RABE, STEMS TRIMMED AND CUT INTO 1-INCH PIECES
- 1 TEASPOON RED PEPPER FLAKES
- 1 TEASPOON SEA SALT
- ½ STICK (4 TABLESPOONS) UNSALTED BUTTER
- 1 CUP GRATED PECORINO ROMANO

Remove the sausages from their casings and crumble. In a large skillet over high heat, brown the sausage. Transfer the sausage to paper towels to drain. Wipe the fat out of the pan.

Bring a large pot of salted water to a boil. Add the pasta and cook until al dente (if using rigatoni or orecchiette, cook for 8 minutes; if using penne, cook for 9 minutes).

Heat the olive oil and garlic in the wiped-out skillet over medium-high heat until the garlic is golden. Add the broccoli rabe, red pepper flakes, and salt and cook for 5 minutes, stirring a few times. Add the sausage and butter and cook over high heat for 5 minutes, stirring a few times.

Drain the pasta, reserving 1 cup of the cooking water, and transfer the pasta to the skillet. Mix well, adding the water if the pasta seems too dry. Pour into a large warm serving bowl, sprinkle the cheese all over the top, and serve.

medaglione di agnello con prosciutto

medallions of lamb, italian style

Pan-seared lamb medallions are paired with a thin slice of salty prosciutto, then finished with a white wine reduction sauce.

1   STICK PLUS 2 TABLESPOONS (10 TABLESPOONS TOTAL) UNSALTED BUTTER

12   THIN SLICES PROSCIUTTO DI PARMA

12   SLICES WHITE BREAD, CRUSTS REMOVED

12   LAMB CHOPS, ABOUT 1 INCH THICK, CUT OFF THE BONE, BONE REMOVED

SEA SALT

FRESHLY GROUND BLACK PEPPER

1   CUP WHITE WINE

In a large skillet, melt 2 tablespoons of the butter over medium heat. Add the prosciutto slices and warm through for 2 minutes. Transfer to a plate and cover with aluminum foil.

With a 2-inch round biscuit cutter, cut a round out of each slice of bread. Discard the trimmings. Melt 2 tablespoons butter in the same skillet over medium heat. Add the bread rounds (you may need to do this in two batches) and brown until golden on both sides. Remove to a paper-towel–lined plate and keep warm in the oven on low or cover with aluminum foil.

In the same skillet, melt the remaining 6 tablespoons butter over medium heat. Add the lamb medallions and cook no more than 2 minutes per side. Season to taste with sea salt and pepper on both sides as you cook.

Place the bread rounds on a serving platter and top each with a slice of prosciutto. Place a lamb medallion on each.

Add the wine to the skillet, turn the heat to high, and deglaze the pan, scraping up all the browned bits stuck to the bottom. Cook for 2 to 3 minutes to reduce the wine slightly. Pour over the lamb and serve.

insalata mista alla siciliana

sicilian mixed salad

This refreshing salad is a wonderful mix of bitter, sweet, and peppery greens, crunchy fennel, and luscious ripe tomatoes.

1   SMALL HEAD BUTTER LETTUCE, LEAVES TORN INTO SMALL PIECES

2   HEADS RADICCHIO, CUT INTO LONG STRIPS

1   BUNCH WATERCRESS, STEMS REMOVED

2   FENNEL BULBS, TRIMMED OF STALKS, BULBS CUT INTO ⅛-INCH-THICK CRESCENTS

1   SMALL HEAD ENDIVE, CUT INTO LONG STRIPS

1   RED ONION, CUT IN HALF, THEN SLICED INTO ⅛-INCH-THICK HALF-MOONS

4   RIPE TOMATOES, CUT INTO QUARTERS, THEN CUT IN HALF AGAIN

1   TEASPOON SEA SALT

1   TABLESPOON RED WINE VINEGAR

2   TABLESPOONS EXTRA-VIRGIN OLIVE OIL

FRESHLY GROUND BLACK PEPPER

Place the lettuce, radicchio, watercress, fennel, endive, onion, and tomatoes in a large salad bowl.

Place the sea salt in a large serving or salad spoon. Pour the vinegar into the spoon and stir with a fork until the vinegar begins to absorb the salt. Toss onto the salad. Pour the olive oil over the salad, add pepper to taste, then toss everything together to coat with the vinegar and oil.

coppa italiana

italian parfaits

These personal parfaits are a scrumptious combination of espresso-flavored mascarpone lightened with whipped egg whites layered with biscotti di amaretto crumbs.

16	OUNCES MASCARPONE
½	CUP FRESHLY BREWED ESPRESSO
6	TABLESPOONS SUGAR
3	LARGE EGG WHITES
10	BISCOTTI DI AMARETTO, GROUND INTO CRUMBS
	DARK CHOCOLATE SHAVINGS

Have ready 8 parfait glasses or wine glasses.

In a large bowl, stir together the mascarpone, espresso, and sugar.

In a medium bowl using an electric mixer, beat the egg whites until they form stiff peaks. Gently fold them into the mascarpone mixture.

Layer the parfaits into the glasses, beginning with 2 tablespoons of mascarpone, then 1 teaspoon of amaretto cookie crumbs, repeating the layers till you get to the top. Give each parfait a final sprinkling of amaretto crumbs. Top with shaved chocolate.

MENU

5

SERVES 8 TO 10

carciofi marinati
marinated artichokes

pasta con tonno e capperi
pasta with tuna and capers

tonno alla siciliana
tuna steaks in olive oil and garlic

fagiolini in tegame alla italiana
green beans with mozzarella and tomatoes

bocca di dama
mouth of a lady, almond and fruit cake

Food memories never leave us. When I was raising my children in Tuscany, I had no trouble convincing them to eat their pasta. Seafood, however, was a different matter. Our favorite trattoria was like a second home to us. One evening the owner infused delicious tuna into the sweet tomato sauce, and this rustic menu became one of their favorites.

carciofi marinati

marinated artichokes

The satisfying texture and light, lemony flavor of artichokes are always a favorite on the antipasto table.

2   JARS (ABOUT 18 OUNCES EACH) ARTICHOKE HEARTS PACKED IN WATER

¾   CUP EXTRA-VIRGIN OLIVE OIL

½   TEASPOON DRIED ROSEMARY

⅛   TEASPOON CRUSHED RED PEPPER

2   TABLESPOONS FRESH CHOPPED BASIL

SEA SALT

FRESHLY GROUND BLACK PEPPER

Rinse the artichokes very well, but gently, under cold running water. Place them in a large serving dish and toss with the olive oil, rosemary, red pepper and basil. Add sea salt and pepper to taste. Allow to marinate for 30 minutes at room temperature.

pasta con tonno e capperi

pasta with tuna and capers

Salty capers combine with tuna and sweet tomatoes for a satisfying country-style sauce for spaghetti.

½   CUP EXTRA-VIRGIN OLIVE OIL

4   CLOVES GARLIC, FINELY CHOPPED

2   CANS (28 OUNCES EACH) CRUSHED TOMATOES (PREFERABLY SAN MARZANO)

2   POUNDS SPAGHETTI

SEA SALT

FRESHLY GROUND BLACK PEPPER

2   CANS (5 OUNCES EACH) TUNA PACKED IN OLIVE OIL (PREFERABLY FROM ITALY), DRAINED AND FLAKED

½   CUP CAPERS, DRAINED

3   TABLESPOONS CHOPPED FRESH ITALIAN PARSLEY

In a medium saucepan heat the olive oil over medium heat. Add the garlic and cook, stirring, for 1 minute. Don't let it brown. Stir in the tomatoes. Let simmer, uncovered, until reduced to a medium-thick consistency, 25 to 30 minutes.

Meanwhile, bring a large pot of salted water to a boil. Add the spaghetti and cook for 7 minutes, until al dente.

Season the sauce to taste with sea salt and pepper. Stir in the tuna, capers, and parsley and simmer for 5 minutes.

Drain the spaghetti and place in a warm deep serving dish or bowl. Add the sauce and toss gently to mix. Serve immediately.

tonno alla siciliana
tuna steaks in olive oil and garlic

The key to tasty tuna, whether cooked on the grill, under the broiler, or on the stovetop, is to cook it fast and hot.

6	LEMONS, CUT IN HALF
	SEA SALT
	FRESHLY GROUND BLACK PEPPER
½	CUP FRESH LEMON JUICE
2	TABLESPOONS EXTRA-VIRGIN OLIVE OIL
⅓	CUP CHOPPED FRESH ROSEMARY LEAVES
2	TEASPOONS CHOPPED GARLIC
1	CUP ITALIAN BREADCRUMBS
8	CENTER-CUT AHI TUNA STEAKS (ABOUT 6 OUNCES EACH)

Preheat the oven to 400F. Place a piece of parchment paper on a baking sheet. Set the lemon halves on the baking sheet, cut side down. Sprinkle with sea salt and pepper and roast for 20 minutes, or until they begin to soften. Remove from the oven and let cool.

In a medium bowl, whisk together the lemon juice, olive oil, rosemary, and garlic. Place the breadcrumbs on a large flat plate.

Preheat the gas grill to high heat.

Brush the tuna steaks on both sides with the lemon-juice mixture. Dredge the tuna in the breadcrumbs on all sides. Grill the tuna 4 minutes per side for medium rare.

To serve, place the tuna steaks on a large platter and arrange the roasted lemon halves around them.

fagiolini in tegame alla italiana
green beans with mozzarella and tomatoes

The mozzarella melts just enough to provide a slightly gooey counterpoint to the crisp-tender green beans.

2	POUNDS GREEN BEANS, ENDS TRIMMED
6	TABLESPOONS EXTRA-VIRGIN OLIVE OIL
6	LARGE ROMA TOMATOES, CHOPPED
8	OUNCES FRESH MOZZARELLA CHEESE, CUT INTO BITE-SIZE PIECES
	SEA SALT
	FRESHLY GROUND BLACK PEPPER

Bring a large pot of salted water to a boil. Add the green beans and parboil until they are crisp-tender, 8 to 10 minutes. Drain the beans.

In a large skillet, heat the olive oil over medium heat. Add the tomatoes and cook, stirring, 2 to 3 minutes. Add the green beans and mozzarella and stir just until the cheese begins to melt. Transfer to a platter and season to taste with sea salt and pepper.

bocca di dama

mouth of a lady, almond and fruit cake

This almond-flavored cake, rich with eggs, is luscious without being too sweet. The almonds provide a buttery flavor and a crunchy texture.

1	CUP ALMONDS
2	CUPS SUGAR
1	LARGE EGG, LIGHTLY BEATEN
7	LARGE EGGS, AT ROOM TEMPERATURE
3	LARGE EGG YOLKS, AT ROOM TEMPERATURE
1¾	CUPS PASTRY FLOUR OR CAKE FLOUR
½	TEASPOON GRATED LEMON ZEST
¼	TEASPOON GROUND CINNAMON
¼	CUP CHOPPED CANDIED ORANGE PEEL
	POWDERED SUGAR FOR GARNISH (OPTIONAL)

Preheat the oven to 375F. Butter and flour a deep 12-inch cake pan.

Place the almonds in a small saucepan and barely cover with water. Bring to a boil, remove from the heat, drain, and let cool. Once they are cool enough to handle, squeeze the almonds out of their skins. Dry the almonds well, chop, then pound into a paste using a mortar and pestle. (This can also be done in a blender.) Transfer the almond paste to a small bowl. Add ¼ cup of the sugar and the lightly beaten egg and mix until a smooth paste forms.

Place the room-temperature eggs and egg yolks and the remaining 1¾ cups sugar in the top of a double boiler over simmering water (don't let the water boil and don't let it touch the bottom of the top boiler). Beat the eggs and sugar with a wooden spoon until the mixture is lukewarm. Remove the top boiler to the counter and continue to beat until the mixture is yellow and very thick. Add the almond mixture. Sprinkle in the flour a little at a time, mixing well after each addition. Add the lemon zest, cinnamon, and candied orange peel and mix in thoroughly.

Pour the batter into the prepared cake pan. (It shouldn't fill the pan more than two thirds full; this cake will rise significantly.) Bake for 40 minutes, or until golden. Transfer the cake to a rack to cool for at least 20 minutes. Flip the cake onto a platter and flip again onto another platter so the top of the cake is exposed. Sprinkle with powdered sugar, if desired, and serve at room temperature.

> ## "nella vita, chi non risica, non rosica."
>
> ### in life, he who risks nothing, gains nothing.

MENU

6

pizza rustica
rustic pizza

uova in cestino di pasqua
easter eggs in a basket

agnello ripieno
stuffed leg of lamb

spinaci alla parmigiana
spinach parmesan

i casateddi di margherita
margherita's ricotta turnovers

I can see nana rolling out the dough for Pizza Rustica on Easter morning while all her grandchildren and great-grandchildren scurried around the kitchen, anxious to pour the sprinkles on the colorful Easter Eggs in a basket.

pizza rustica

rustic pizza

This is my maternal grandmother's recipe and it is the traditional antipasto for our Easter dinner. Rich and creamy, it is stuffed with prosciutto, sausage, spinach, and three kinds of cheese.

PASTRY DOUGH

- 3½ CUPS ALL-PURPOSE FLOUR
- 1 TEASPOON SEA SALT
- 1½ STICKS (12 TABLESPOONS) COLD UNSALTED BUTTER, CUT INTO PIECES
- 4 TABLESPOONS COLD VEGETABLE SHORTENING, CUT INTO PIECES
- 3 LARGE EGGS
- 1 EGG, BEATEN, FOR EGG WASH ON TOP CRUST

FILLING

- 2 TABLESPOONS EXTRA-VIRGIN OLIVE OIL
- ½ POUND HOT ITALIAN SAUSAGE, REMOVED FROM CASINGS
- 1 TEASPOON MINCED GARLIC
- 2 BUNCHES (12 OUNCES EACH) FRESH SPINACH, WASHED WELL, HEAVY STEMS REMOVED AND COARSELY CHOPPED, OR 1 PACKAGE (10 OUNCES) FROZEN CUT-LEAF SPINACH, THAWED AND SQUEEZED DRY
- 4 LARGE EGGS
- 1 CONTAINER (15 OUNCES) RICOTTA
- ¾ POUND MOZZARELLA, SHREDDED
- ⅓ CUP PLUS 2 TABLESPOONS GRATED PARMIGIANO-REGGIANO
- ¼ POUND THINLY SLICED PROSCIUTTO, COARSELY CHOPPED

Make the pastry dough: Place the flour, salt, butter, and shortening in a food processor and process until the mixture resembles coarse meal. Blend in the eggs. With the machine running, add 1 tablespoon ice water at a time through the feed tube until a dough forms.

Remove the dough from the processor and form into a ball. Divide it into 2 pieces, one piece twice as big as the other. Flatten the dough pieces into disks. Wrap in plastic wrap and refrigerate until firm enough to roll out, about 30 minutes.

Meanwhile, make the filling: In a large skillet, heat 1 tablespoon of the olive oil over medium heat. Add the crumbled sausage and cook until golden brown, about 5 minutes, breaking the sausage up into small pieces. Add the garlic and cook until fragrant, about 1 minute. Transfer the mixture to a small bowl and let cool.

In the same skillet, heat the remaining 1 tablespoon olive oil over medium heat. Add the spinach and cook until it wilts and the juices evaporate, about 10 minutes, stirring often. Let cool to room temperature. Squeeze the spinach to remove as much liquid as possible.

In a large bowl, beat the 4 eggs together lightly to blend. Stir in the ricotta, mozzarella, and ⅓ cup of the Parmigiano. Add the sausage, spinach, and prosciutto and stir to mix.

Preheat the oven to 375F.

On a lightly floured work surface, roll out the larger piece of dough to a 17-inch circle. Fit the dough into a 9-inch springform pan. Trim the dough overhang to 1 inch. Spoon the filling into the crust. Roll out the remaining piece of dough to a 12-inch circle. Set the top crust over the filling. Pinch the edges of the top and bottom crusts together to seal. Crimp the edge decoratively. Brush the egg wash over the top. Cut three or four vents in the top crust. Sprinkle the remaining 2 tablespoons Parmigiano over the top.

Bake on the lower rack in the oven until the crust is golden brown, about 1 hour. Let stand 15 minutes. Release the pan side and transfer the pizza to a serving platter. Cut into wedges and serve.

uova in cestino di pasqua

easter eggs in a basket

This is so much fun for children. Colored (but not cooked) eggs are set on a length of sweet dough fashioned into a basket shape and then baked until the dough is golden and the eggs are hard-cooked. Our family traditionally makes them the night before Easter, then sets one on each dinner guest's plate the next day. We get down to the happy task of eating them on Pasquetta (literally, Little Easter), the Monday morning following Easter.

1	CUP SUGAR
1½	STICKS (12 TABLESPOONS) UNSALTED BUTTER
1	TEASPOON VANILLA EXTRACT
4	LARGE EGGS
4	CUPS UNBLEACHED ALL-PURPOSE FLOUR (APPROXIMATELY)
1	TABLESPOON BAKING POWDER
	PINCH OF SALT
½	CUP MILK (APPROXIMATELY)
12	MEDIUM EGGS, UNCOOKED, DYED VARIOUS PASTEL EASTER COLORS
1	LARGE EGG WHITE, BEATEN
	NONPAREILS (MULTICOLORED SPRINKLES)

In a large bowl, cream together the sugar and butter. Thoroughly beat in the vanilla and 4 eggs, one at a time.

In a medium bowl, sift together the flour, baking powder, and salt. Add to the butter mixture and mix well. Pour in the milk. Combine just until the mixture forms dough. The dough will be very soft. If it's too sticky, add a little more flour; if it's too dry, add a little more milk. Cover and let rest for 10 minutes at room temperature.

Preheat the oven to 400F. Line 2 cookie sheets with parchment paper.

Divide the dough into 12 equal pieces. Using the palms of your hands, roll each piece into a cigar shape about 12 inches long. Cut off two 1-inch pieces from each cigar.

On the parchment, arrange the cigars into U shapes, placing them about 2 inches apart on the baking sheets. Slightly turn out the top of each U. Set a colored egg horizontally at the bottom of each U. With your palms, roll out the 1-inch pieces of dough so they are long enough to crisscross over the eggs. Pinch the crisscross pieces to the dough.

Brush the dough with the egg white and sprinkle with the nonpareils. Bake until the dough is golden brown, about 20 minutes. The eggs, of course, will hard-cook in the oven. Let cool. Store in an airtight container.

agnello ripieno
stuffed leg of lamb

I continue my parents' tradition of serving this lamb at Easter. The Pecorino gives a peppery bite to the flavor of the lamb.

1	BONELESS LEG OF LAMB (6 POUNDS)
	SEA SALT
	FRESHLY GROUND BLACK PEPPER
¾	CUP FRESH BREADCRUMBS
¼	CUP EXTRA-VIRGIN OLIVE OIL
3	TABLESPOONS MINCED GARLIC
½	CUP GRATED PECORINO ROMANO
3	TABLESPOONS MINCED FRESH ITALIAN PARSLEY
1½	CUPS WHITE WINE

Preheat the oven to 375F. Set a rack in a roasting pan.

Pat the lamb dry with paper towels and season with sea salt and pepper.

In a small skillet, cook the breadcrumbs with the olive oil over medium heat until golden brown. Transfer to a small bowl, add the garlic, Pecorino, parsley, and salt and pepper to taste and stir to mix well.

Spread the mixture over the cut side of the lamb, roll the lamb up, and tie it in several places with kitchen string. Set on the rack in the roasting pan, pour in the wine, and roast until the meat is medium rare, 1 to 1½ hours, basting every 30 minutes, until a meat thermometer reads 135 – 140F. for medium rare.

Let the lamb stand 10 minutes. Carve into ¼-inch-thick slices and arrange on a warm platter.

spinaci alla parmigiana
spinach parmesan

A rich, cheesy Easter indulgence!

2	POUNDS SPINACH, WASHED WELL, HEAVY STEMS REMOVED, AND CHOPPED
½	STICK (4 TABLESPOONS) UNSALTED BUTTER
½	TEASPOON SEA SALT
¼	TEASPOON FRESHLY GRATED NUTMEG
3	LARGE EGGS, LIGHTLY BEATEN
6	TABLESPOONS GRATED PARMIGIANO-REGGIANO

Bring 2 cups water to a boil in a large saucepan. Add the spinach and cook for 5 minutes. Drain and finely chop.

In a medium skillet, melt the butter over medium heat. Add the spinach, salt, and nutmeg and cook for 4 minutes, stirring. Shut off the heat but keep the pan on the burner. Add the eggs to the skillet, sprinkle with the Parmigiano, and stir for 2 to 3 minutes, until the cheese starts to melt. Transfer to a warm serving dish and serve immediately.

i casateddi di margherita

margherita's ricotta turnovers

My grandmother's cousin Margherita has been making these ricotta turnovers for seventy years. As light as air, they are the perfect ending to this menu.

PASTRY DOUGH

- 4 **CUPS ALL-PURPOSE FLOUR**
- 4 **STICKS (1 POUND) UNSALTED BUTTER, SOFTENED**
- 1 **TABLESPOON GRANULATED SUGAR**
- 1 **CUP SOUR CREAM**
- 1 **TEASPOON ALMOND EXTRACT**

FILLING

- 1 **CONTAINER (15 OUNCES) RICOTTA**
- 1 **CUP CONFECTIONERS' SUGAR**
- 1 **LARGE EGG**

- 1 **LARGE EGG YOLK, BEATEN**
- 3 **TABLESPOONS GRANULATED SUGAR**
- ½ **TEASPOON GROUND CINNAMON**

Make the pastry dough: In a large bowl, mix together the flour and butter. Add the granulated sugar, sour cream, and almond extract and mix well. Cover the dough and set in a warm place for 30 minutes.

Make the filling: In a medium bowl, mix together well the ricotta, confectioners' sugar, and egg.

Preheat the oven to 400F.

Roll a handful of the dough out to ⅛-inch thickness (to resemble thin pie dough) on a lightly floured work surface. Use a round 5-inch cookie cutter to cut out a circle. (If you don't have a cookie cutter that size, improvise with a coffee can or a food-storage container.)

Place 1 tablespoon of the filling in the center of the round. With your finger, spread some of the egg wash around the edge of the circle. Fold the round in half over the filling and seal the edge with a floured fork. Repeat with the remaining dough and filling. Place the filled turnovers on a large baking sheet, leaving approximately two inches between them. Prick them with a fork to vent.

Mix together the granulated sugar and the ground cinnamon in a cup. Brush the tops of the turnovers with the beaten egg yolk, and sprinkle with the sugar mixture. Bake for 15 to 18 minutes until puffed and golden brown.

MENU

SERVES 8 TO 10

pomodorini ripieni di pesto
cherry tomatoes stuffed with pesto

··

paglia e fieno
spinach and egg fettuccine in cheese sauce

··

salmone alla italiana
salmon, italian style

··

finocchio gratinato
baked fennel parmesan

··

torta di pinoli
pine nut loaf cake

One of my first loves was a sweet Italian American boy who shared my passion for cooking. Later on, he became a well-known Italian caterer in my hometown and shared his secret for pesto-stuffed cherry tomatoes with me. These tomatoes can be prepared ahead of time and refrigerated until needed.

pomodorini ripieni di pesto

cherry tomatoes stuffed with pesto

Don't use grape tomatoes to make this—they won't stand upright and the filling will spill out.

PESTO

- 1   **CUP FRESH BASIL LEAVES**
- 3–4   **CLOVES GARLIC, PEELED**
- 5   **TABLESPOONS PINE NUTS**
- ½   **TEASPOON SEA SALT, OR TO TASTE**
- ½   **CUP EXTRA-VIRGIN OLIVE OIL, PLUS ADDITIONAL AS NEEDED**
- ½   **CUP GRATED PECORINO ROMANO**

- 1   **POUND CHERRY TOMATOES**

Place the basil leaves, garlic, pine nuts, salt, olive oil, and Pecorino in a food processor or blender and process until smooth. If the pesto is too thick for your taste, add a little more olive oil.

Cut the tops off the tomatoes. With a small spoon (I use an espresso spoon), scoop out the seeds and pulp, taking care not to puncture the skin. Fill the tomatoes with the pesto and serve at room temperature.

paglia e fieno

spinach and egg fettuccine in cheese sauce

Warm and comforting, this creamy pasta, with its combination of regular and spinach fettuccine, has been a favorite of my children forever. Panna da cucina, a cooking cream with a long shelf life, is now available in specialty stores in some areas of the United States, but heavy cream works just as well.

- 1   **STICK (8 TABLESPOONS) UNSALTED BUTTER**
- 1   **CUP HEAVY CREAM OR PANNA DA CUCINA**
      SEA SALT
      FRESHLY GROUND BLACK PEPPER
- 1   **POUND FRESH SPINACH FETTUCCINE**
- 1   **POUND FRESH PLAIN FETTUCCINE**
- 1½   **CUPS GRATED PARMIGIANO-REGGIANO, PLUS ADDITIONAL FOR GARNISH**

Put a large pot of salted water on to boil.

Meanwhile, in a large skillet, melt the butter. Slowly add the cream to the melted butter and bring to a simmer for about 4 minutes; don't let the cream come to a boil. Season to taste with sea salt and pepper.

Add the fettuccine to the boiling water and cook until al dente, about 2 minutes. Drain.

Transfer the cream mixture to a large warm pasta bowl. Add the Parmigiano. Add the fettuccine and toss until evenly coated with the cream and cheese. Serve immediately, garnishing each serving with a little more cheese.

salmone alla italiana

salmon, italian style

When I cook salmon, I want its natural flavor to shine through, not be covered by a strong-flavored sauce. Here it gets nothing but an olive-oil and garlic treatment.

- 1 WHOLE SALMON (APPROXIMATELY 4 POUNDS), CLEANED AND CUT IN HALF (TO FORM 2 LARGE FILLETS)
- 10 CLOVES GARLIC, CHOPPED
- ¾ CUP EXTRA-VIRGIN OLIVE OIL
  SEA SALT

Preheat the oven to 350F.

Rinse each salmon half under cold running water. Place the fillets skin side down on a large sheet of aluminum foil. Sprinkle with the garlic, drizzle with the olive oil, and season with sea salt to taste.

Tent the foil over the salmon so there are 3 to 4 inches between the foil and the fish; make sure to completely enclose the fish. Bake until the salmon flakes when gently prodded with a fork, about 20 minutes.

finocchio gratinato

baked fennel parmesan

Fennel is a favorite vegetable in Italy; I wish it had greater popularity in this country. My grandmother would often slice the bulb thin and set it out with espresso, to be enjoyed as a post-dinner digestive.

- ¾ STICK (6 TABLESPOONS) UNSALTED BUTTER
- 4–6 FENNEL BULBS, TRIMMED OF STALKS, EACH BULB CUT INTO QUARTERS
- 1 CUP GRATED PARMIGIANO-REGGIANO

Preheat the oven to 400F. Put 3 tablespoons of the butter in a large baking dish and place in the oven until melted.

Arrange the fennel bulb quarters in the baking dish. Sprinkle with the Parmigiano and dot with the remaining 3 tablespoons butter. Bake until the fennel is tender but not mushy, about 30 minutes.

torta di pinoli

pine nut loaf cake

Buttery and luscious, this cake is full of the rich flavor of pine nuts.

- 2 **VANILLA BEANS**
- 2 **LEMONS**
- 6 **TABLESPOONS PINE NUTS**
- 2¼ **STICKS (18 TABLESPOONS) UNSALTED BUTTER, SOFTENED**
- 1¼ **CUPS SUGAR**
- 4 **LARGE EGGS**
- ¾ **CUP ALL-PURPOSE FLOUR**
- ¼ **TEASPOON SALT**

Preheat the oven to 350F. Grease an 8½ by 4½ by 2½-inch loaf pan.

Slice the vanilla beans in half lengthwise and scrape out the seeds.

Finely grate the zest from both lemons. Juice 1 of the lemons.

Chop 3 tablespoons of the pine nuts.

In a large bowl using an electric mixer, beat together the butter, sugar, and vanilla seeds until the mixture is light and fluffy. Stir in the eggs, adding them one at a time and mixing well after each addition. Fold in the flour and chopped pine nuts, and then stir in the lemon zest and juice.

Spoon the batter into the prepared loaf pan. Mix the whole pine nuts with the salt and sprinkle them over the top. Bake until a skewer inserted in the center of the loaf comes out clean, about 1 hour. Let cool completely before removing from the pan.

"nella vita, chi non risica, non rosica."

in life, he who risks nothing, gains nothing.

45

MENU

SERVES 8 TO 10

tortino di asparagi
asparagus torte

pasta pomodoro con vodka
pasta in vodka sauce

petti di pollo alla sostanza
chicken breasts in butter

carote glassate alla marsala
glazed carrots in marsala wine

meringue al cioccolato
meringue with chocolate

A little bit of wine or liqueur often shows up in Italian American cooking, and often we attribute our longevity to this. After all, one of my grandparents lived to be 98 and another 101! Although the classic vodka sauce in this menu is virtually unknown in Italy, it is an Italian American staple.

tortino di asparagi

asparagus torte

Frozen puff pastry is such a welcome convenience. Here it is the crispy foundation of a savory pastry topped with cheese and bright green spears of asparagus.

1	SHEET FROZEN PUFF PASTRY, THAWED
2	CUPS SHREDDED FONTINA OR GRUYÈRE CHEESE
1	POUND ASPARAGUS, BOTTOMS SNAPPED OFF
¼	CUP EXTRA-VIRGIN OLIVE OIL
	SEA SALT
	FRESHLY GROUND BLACK PEPPER

Preheat the oven to 400F. Arrange the puff pastry on a cookie sheet. Prick the pastry with the tines of a fork in several places. Bake for 15 minutes.

Remove the pastry from the oven and sprinkle evenly with the cheese. Arrange half the asparagus spears on the pastry pointing in one direction, their tips lined up with a short end of the pastry, the remainder in the other direction, their tips lined up on the other short end. This way, when the tortino is cut, everyone gets tips. Drizzle with the olive oil and season with sea salt and pepper. Bake until the pastry is golden brown, the cheese melted, and the asparagus bright green with some brown spots, about 15 minutes. Cut and serve.

"chi va piano, va sano e lontano."

he who goes slowly, goes a long way and arrives healthy.

pasta pomodoro con vodka

pasta in vodka sauce

I like to add prosciutto to my vodka sauce. The sauce gets its lovely zing from the red pepper flakes and vodka.

- 5 **TABLESPOONS UNSALTED BUTTER**
- 4 **LARGE CLOVES GARLIC, FINELY CHOPPED**
- ¼ **POUND THINLY SLICED PROSCIUTTO, CUT INTO THIN STRIPS**
- 1 **CAN (28 TO 36 OUNCES) PEELED ITALIAN TOMATOES, DRAINED AND COARSELY CHOPPED**
- ½ **TEASPOON RED PEPPER FLAKES**
- ¾ **CUP HEAVY CREAM**
- ½ **CUP VODKA**
  SEA SALT
  FRESHLY GROUND BLACK PEPPER
- 2 **POUNDS PENNE**
- 1 **CUP GRATED PARMIGIANO-REGGIANO**

In a large skillet over medium heat, melt the butter. Add the garlic and cook until golden, about 2 minutes, stirring a few times. Add the prosciutto and cook 1 minute. Add the tomatoes and red pepper flakes, stir to combine, and let simmer for 5 minutes. Add the cream and vodka and cook for 5 to 10 minutes more, making sure the sauce does not come to a boil, and season to taste with sea salt and black pepper.

Bring a large pot of salted water to a boil. Add the penne and cook until al dente, 7 minutes. Drain, add to the sauce in the skillet, and toss until well coated. Top with the cheese and serve immediately.

petti di pollo alla sostanza

chicken breasts in butter

This recipe comes from a trattoria hidden away on a small side street in Florence. It's all buttery goodness.

- 1 **STICK (8 TABLESPOONS) UNSALTED BUTTER**
- 8 **BONELESS, SKINLESS CHICKEN BREAST HALVES, AT LEAST ½ INCH THICK**
  SEA SALT
  FRESHLY GROUND BLACK PEPPER

Preheat the oven to 375F.

In a large skillet, melt the butter over medium heat. Season the chicken breasts with salt and pepper and add to the butter, sautéing until golden brown and crispy, 4 to 5 minutes per side.

Transfer the breasts to a large baking dish and bake for 20 minutes, until cooked through. Pour the butter remaining in the skillet over the chicken.

carote glassate alla marsala

glazed carrots in marsala wine

The honey and Marsala make this dish a natural match-up for the butter-crisped chicken breasts.

- 12   **CARROTS, SLICED INTO ⅛-INCH ROUNDS**
- ¼   **CUP EXTRA-VIRGIN OLIVE OIL**
-     **SEA SALT**
-     **FRESHLY GROUND BLACK PEPPER**
- 2   **TABLESPOONS SICILIAN HONEY**
- ¼   **CUP SWEET MARSALA**

Steam the carrots for 5 to 7 minutes.

In a large saucepan, heat the olive oil over medium heat. Add the carrots, season with salt and pepper, and cook for 5 minutes.

Transfer the carrots to a warm serving bowl, leaving behind as much of the oil as possible, and toss with the honey and Marsala.

meringue al cioccolato

meringue with chocolate

One of the happiest days of my life was when I discovered the pasticceria that made this meringue. Enjoy them as they are or top them with chocolate sauce.

- 8   **LARGE EGG WHITES**
- ½   **TEASPOON CREAM OF TARTAR**
- 2   **CUPS SUGAR**
- 1½   **TEASPOONS VANILLA EXTRACT**
- ¾   **CUP (6 OUNCES) UNSWEETENED COCOA POWDER**

Preheat the oven to 200F. Line two large baking sheets with parchment paper.

In a large bowl with an electric mixer, beat the egg whites with the cream of tartar until they are foamy. Add the sugar a little at a time, beating all the while. Add the vanilla and cocoa and beat until stiff, shiny peaks form.

Drop the meringue mixture onto the prepared baking sheet using a tablespoon, leaving approximately two inches between the meringues. Each meringue should be about 3 inches in diameter. Bake for 1 hour, until shiny, but be careful not to overbake, or they will be too chewy. Let the meringues cool completely. Store in an airtight container.

MENU

9

pasta sfoglia con salmone
puff pastry with smoked salmon

pasta ai quattro formaggi
baked four-cheese pasta

polpetti di vitello con salsa verde
veal balls with green sauce

zucchini ripieni
stuffed zucchini

pesche al forno
baked amaretto peaches

When my children were very small, we moved back to Italy. Mac and cheese was one of the few staples of the American diet that they missed, so I began to make pasta ai quattro formaggi—true comfort food. Although they missed America, they never again asked for American mac and cheese.

pasta sfoglia con salmone

puff pastry with smoked salmon

This is so elegant and so easy—baked pastry rounds spread with a little sweet butter, then crowned with smoked salmon and capers.

1 **PACKAGE (16 OUNCES) FROZEN PUFF PASTRY, THAWED**

½ **STICK (4 TABLESPOONS) UNSALTED BUTTER, SOFTENED**

8 **OUNCES THINLY SLICED SMOKED SALMON**

¼ **CUP ITALIAN CAPERS**

Using a 2-inch round cutter or espresso cup, cut rounds out of the puff pastry. Bake according to the package instructions. Remove from the oven and let cool.

Spread butter on each of the rounds. Top with smoked salmon and 2 capers, and serve immediately.

"la pazienza non è mai troppa!"

you can never have enough patience!

pasta ai quattro formaggi
baked four-cheese pasta

As far as I'm concerned, this is mac and cheese, Italian style! Instead of topping it with breadcrumbs, I use croutons cut from Italian bread.

CROUTONS

- 1   LOAF ITALIAN BREAD, CUBED
- ½   CUP EXTRA-VIRGIN OLIVE OIL
-      SEA SALT
-      FRESHLY GROUND BLACK PEPPER
- ¼   CUP VERY FINELY CHOPPED GARLIC MIXED WITH ½ TEASPOON SEA SALT

BESCIAMELLA

- 1   STICK (8 TABLESPOONS) UNSALTED BUTTER
- ¼   CUP (4 TABLESPOONS) UNBLEACHED FLOUR
- 3   CUPS WHOLE MILK
- ½   TEASPOON SEA SALT
- ¼   TEASPOON BLACK PEPPER
- ¼   TEASPOON GRATED NUTMEG

- 2   POUNDS RIGATONI
- 1   CUP SHREDDED FONTINA
- ¾   CUP CRUMBLED GORGONZOLA
- ½   CUP GRATED PECORINO ROMANO
- ½   CUP GRATED PARMIGIANO-REGGIANO

Make the croutons: Preheat the oven to 350F. Place the bread cubes, olive oil, salt, pepper, and garlic mixture in a large bowl and toss until the cubes are evenly coated with the oil and garlic. Pour the bread cubes onto a large baking sheet and arrange them in a single layer. Bake until the croutons are golden and crunchy, about 15 minutes.

Make the besciamella: Melt the butter in a medium saucepan over medium heat, add the flour, and stir until smooth. Slowly add the milk, whisking constantly to keep any lumps from forming. Stir until the mixture thickens to the point that it coats the back of a wooden spoon. You can add a little more milk if the sauce is too thick. Season with the salt, pepper, and nutmeg.

Make the pasta: Increase the oven temperature to 500F. Butter a 13 by 9-inch baking dish. Bring a large pot of salted water to a boil. Add the rigatoni and cook 2 to 3 minutes less than the package says for al dente.

Meanwhile, in a very large bowl, combine the four cheeses and besciamella. Drain the pasta and toss with the cheese mixture. Transfer to the prepared baking dish and sprinkle the croutons over the top. Bake until the cheeses are melted, 6 to 7 minutes.

polpetti di vitello con salsa verde

veal balls with green sauce

Lots of fresh parsley, garlic, capers, anchovies, and red wine vinegar give salsa verde (green sauce) its punch. Here it's paired with veal balls spiked with Parmigiano-Reggiano and prosciutto.

GREEN SAUCE

- 1   SLICE WHITE BREAD
- 2   TABLESPOONS RED WINE VINEGAR
- 2   CUPS LOOSELY PACKED FRESH ITALIAN PARSLEY LEAVES
- 2   CLOVES GARLIC, PEELED
- 2   ANCHOVY FILLETS
- 1   TABLESPOON CAPERS
- ½   CUP EXTRA-VIRGIN OLIVE OIL
-     SEA SALT
-     FRESHLY GROUND BLACK PEPPER

VEAL BALLS

- 2   POUNDS GROUND VEAL
- ½   POUND THINLY SLICED PROSCIUTTO, CUT INTO SMALL PIECES
- ½   CUP SHREDDED PARMIGIANO-REGGIANO
- ¼   CUP PLAIN BREADCRUMBS
- 1   LARGE EGG
- ½   TEASPOON SEA SALT
- ¼   TEASPOON FRESHLY GROUND BLACK PEPPER
- ½   STICK (4 TABLESPOONS) UNSALTED BUTTER

Make the green sauce: Remove the crust from the bread and tear the bread into pieces. Place in a small bowl and pour the vinegar over it. Let stand for 10 minutes. Transfer the bread and vinegar to a blender or food processor. Add the parsley, garlic, anchovies, capers, and olive oil and process until smooth. Scrape the sauce into a small bowl, season to taste with sea salt and pepper, and stir to mix.

Make the veal balls: Preheat the oven to 200F and put an ovenproof platter in the oven. In a large bowl, combine the veal, prosciutto, Parmigiano, breadcrumbs, egg, salt, and pepper until thoroughly mixed. Shape the mixture into balls, 2 inches in diameter.

Melt half of the butter in a large skillet over medium heat and cook half of the veal balls until browned on all sides and cooked all the way through, 10 to 12 minutes. Transfer the cooked veal balls to the oven to keep warm. Melt the remaining butter and cook the remaining veal balls in the same manner.

When all the veal balls are cooked, spread the green sauce on a platter and put the veal balls on top of the sauce.

zucchini ripieni

stuffed zucchini

This recipe is a real favorite of mine and a great way to make use of garden-fresh zucchini and tomatoes.

¼	CUP PLUS 2 TABLESPOONS EXTRA-VIRGIN OLIVE OIL
1	MEDIUM ONION, CHOPPED
8–10	ROUND ZUCCHINI
4	CUPS PLAIN BREADCRUMBS
1	CUP CHOPPED FRESH ITALIAN PARSLEY
3	CLOVES GARLIC, CHOPPED
3	RIPE MEDIUM TOMATOES, CHOPPED
	SEA SALT
	FRESHLY GROUND BLACK PEPPER
½	CUP GRATED PECORINO ROMANO

Preheat the oven to 350F. Pour 2 tablespoons of the olive oil into a large baking dish and tilt the dish to coat the bottom.

In a large skillet, heat the remaining ¼ cup olive oil over medium heat. Add the onion and cook, stirring a few times, until transparent. Transfer the onion to a large bowl and let cool.

Cut the tops off the zucchini and scoop out the insides, leaving a ¼-inch-thick shell. (If you can't find round zucchini, use the long zucchini; slice it lengthwise and scoop out the seeds, leaving ¼ inch of the meat of the zucchini on the sides and bottom.

Add the breadcrumbs, parsley, garlic, and tomatoes to the onion. Season to taste with sea salt and pepper. Mix well. Fill the zucchini with the mixture.

Set the zucchini in the prepared baking dish. Cover with aluminum foil and bake for 20 minutes.

Remove the foil and top with the Pecorino. Bake for another 10 minutes, until the cheese is melted.

pesche al forno

baked amaretto peaches

When I was in my twenties, I stayed on the Tuscan coast at a small, rustic pensione where the mother and daughter did all the cooking. One hot summer evening, the daughter brought out fresh peaches stuffed with crunchy amaretto cookies. I begged for the recipe and, after receiving her mother's permission, she shared it with me.

6–8	RIPE PEACHES, NOT PEELED
1	CUP CRUSHED AMARETTO DI SARONNO COOKIES
3	TABLESPOONS SUGAR
12–16	TEASPOONS AMARETTO DI SARONNO LIQUEUR
	WHIPPED CREAM FOR GARNISH

Preheat the oven to 350F.

Cut the peaches in half from top to bottom and remove the stones. Scoop out a little of the flesh around the hollow left by the stone. Set the peaches cut side up in a large baking dish. In a small bowl, combine the crushed cookies and sugar. Fill the hollows of the peaches with the mixture. Top each with 1 teaspoon Amaretto liqueur.

Bake until the peaches are soft, 20 to 30 minutes. Serve warm but not hot, topped with a dollop of whipped cream.

MENU

10

SERVES 8 TO 10

fettine di zucchine
zucchini rounds

....

pasta con sugo della domenica
pasta with sunday gravy

....

carne in sugo di pomodoro
meat from sunday gravy

....

bietola saltati
sautéed swiss chard

....

torta di mandorla
almond cake

My grandfather and his seven brothers never missed Sunday dinner at my Great-Grandma Franco's house, and I'm quite certain that it had something to do with her Sunday gravy. As I was growing up, Great-Grandma Franco's tradition was kept alive by making her recipe every Sunday. The key to her rich, velvety tomato sauce is the amount of time the meat simmers.

fettine di zucchine

zucchini rounds

Tender slices of zucchini get a delicious warm cheese topping lightened with whipped egg whites.

- 2 **POUNDS SMALL ZUCCHINI**
- 1 **STICK (8 TABLESPOONS) UNSALTED BUTTER**
- 4 **OUNCES FONTINA, GRATED**
- ⅓ **CUP (3 OUNCES) MASCARPONE**
- 2 **LARGE EGG WHITES, AT ROOM TEMPERATURE**
  SEA SALT
  FRESHLY GROUND BLACK PEPPER

Preheat the oven to 375F.

Trim the zucchini and cut on the diagonal into ¼-inch-thick slices. Arrange the slices in a large shallow baking dish or on a large baking sheet in a single layer.

In a medium saucepan over low heat, heat the butter, fontina, and mascarpone together until melted, stirring a few times. Remove from the heat.

In a medium bowl using an electric mixer, beat the egg whites until stiff peaks form. Fold the whipped egg whites into the cheese mixture. Let cool. Spread the mixture over the zucchini.

Bake for about 20 minutes, or until golden. Season to taste with sea salt and pepper and serve warm.

pasta con sugo della domenica

pasta with sunday gravy

Italian Americans, no matter where their families have come from in Italy, are united by one dish—Sunday gravy. It's two courses in one pot. Serve the pasta tossed with some of the meat-flavored tomato sauce. Then, as the secondo, serve the meats that have been simmering in the sauce, setting them out on a platter.

- ½ **CUP EXTRA-VIRGIN OLIVE OIL, PLUS ADDITIONAL AS NEEDED**
- 1 **RACK (ABOUT 3½ POUNDS) SPARE RIBS, CUT INTO INDIVIDUAL RIBS**
- 8 **LINKS SWEET ITALIAN SAUSAGE WITH FENNEL SEEDS**
- 4 **VEAL CHOPS ·**
  UNCOOKED MEATBALLS FROM LISA'S FAMOUS MEAT-A-BALLS (PAGE 88)
- 2 **LARGE ONIONS, CUT INTO QUARTERS**
- 8 **CLOVES GARLIC, PEELED**
- 6–8 **CUPS LISA'S CLASSIC TOMATO SAUCE (PAGE 89)**
- 2 **POUNDS RIGATONI OR ZITI**
- ½ **CUP FRESH BASIL LEAVES, CHOPPED**
- ½ **CUP FRESH ITALIAN PARSLEY LEAVES, CHOPPED**
  FRESHLY GROUND BLACK PEPPER
- 1 **CUP GRATED PARMIGIANO-REGGIANO**

In a large (at least 8-quart), heavy pot, heat the olive oil over medium heat. Working in batches, taking care not to crowd the pot, brown the spare ribs, sausages, and veal chops well on all sides, removing them to a tray as they are browned. If needed, you can add more oil to the pan in small amounts. Add the meatballs and brown them well on all sides. Remove to the tray with the other meat as they are browned.

Add the onions and garlic to the pot and cook, stirring, until the onions are lightly browned, about 4 minutes. Stir in the tomato sauce. Return all the meat to the pot. Bring the sauce to a boil, reduce the heat to a simmer, and cook until the sauce has thickened and the ribs are tender, at least 4 hours.

For the pasta course: Bring a large pot of salted water to a boil. Add the rigatoni and cook 2 minutes less than indicated on the package.

Meanwhile, stir the basil and parsley into the sauce and add pepper to taste.

Drain the pasta and return it to the pot. Add enough of the sauce to the pasta to lightly coat it. Transfer to a large platter and serve with a generous helping of Parmigiano.

For the meat course: Remove the meats from the gravy and arrange them on another platter. Drizzle with the sauce but don't drown them. Serve after the pasta.

bietola saltati
sautéed swiss chard

Cooked quickly in a little olive oil, this Swiss chard is redolent of garlic, with a little kick provided by the red pepper.

- 3 **BUNCHES SWISS CHARD**
- ¼ **CUP EXTRA-VIRGIN OLIVE OIL**
- 4 **CLOVES GARLIC, THINLY SLICED**
- 1 **TABLESPOON RED PEPPER FLAKES**
  SEA SALT

Wash the Swiss chard thoroughly. You don't need to dry it. Cut off only the ends of the stems, as the white part (though sometimes the stem can be red or yellow, depending on the type of Swiss chard you buy) of the stem is delicious and nutritious. Chop the chard roughly—not into small pieces but into pieces about 3 inches long.

In a large sauté pan over medium heat, heat the olive oil. Add the garlic and stir for 1 minute. Add the Swiss chard and stir gently for 2 to 3 minutes.

Transfer the chard to a large serving bowl and sprinkle with the red pepper flakes and sea salt to taste.

Note: After you serve the bietola, some of the flavored olive oil will remain in the bottom of the bowl. This is delicious to soak up with thick slices of Italian bread, as they do in Tuscany.

torta di mandorla

almond cake

Perfumed with the heady aroma of almonds, this very rich cake has a deceptively light crumbly texture provided by the whipped egg whites folded into the batter.

¼	**CUP SLICED ALMONDS**
⅓	**CUP NATURAL ALMONDS**
1¼	**CUPS ALL-PURPOSE FLOUR**
1½	**CUPS GRANULATED SUGAR**
9	**LARGE EGGS, SEPARATED**
	FINELY GRATED ZEST OF 1 LEMON
2	**TABLESPOONS CONFECTIONERS' SUGAR**

Preheat the oven to 325F. Butter a 10-inch Bundt pan.

On a cookie sheet, toast the sliced almonds until golden, approximately 8 minutes.

Grind the ⅓ cup of the natural almonds into a grainy paste using a mortar and pestle or a blender. Transfer to a large bowl and mix with the flour and 1 tablespoon of the granulated sugar.

In a medium bowl using an electric mixer, beat the egg yolks with the remaining granulated sugar until pale and thick. Stir into the almond mixture. Stir in the lemon zest.

Wash the beaters of the mixer and dry them well. In another large bowl using the mixer, beat the egg whites until they are fluffy, between soft and stiff peaks. Gently fold the whites into the batter.

Pour the batter into the prepared baking dish and bake until golden brown, 40 to 45 minutes. Sprinkle with the confectioners' sugar and toasted sliced almonds.

"a tavola,
si scordano
i guai."

at table, you forget
your worries.

MENU

| 11 |

SERVES 8 TO 10

crostini di formaggi
toasted cheese rounds

....

pasta al ragu della nonna caponigri
pasta with grandma caponigri's ragu sauce

....

pollo fritto
fried chicken, italian style

....

insalata di antipasti
antipasto salad

....

spumoni di fragole
strawberry spumoni

I never knew my paternal grandmother, but, luckily, I know her through her recipes, handwritten and passed down by my aunts to me. Food isn't just fuel; it's a link with our past, a link with the people we love, and an opportunity to continue our family traditions. My Grandma Caponigri's sauce is worth every minute of effort.

crostini di formaggi

toasted cheese rounds

The red onion adds just the right amount of bite to these cheesy-good crostini.

- ¾ CUP MASCARPONE
- ½ CUP SHREDDED MOZZARELLA
- ½ CUP GRATED PARMIGIANO-REGGIANO
- ½ CUP CHOPPED RED ONION
- 2 LOAVES THIN ITALIAN BREAD, EACH CUT INTO 12 SLICES ON THE DIAGONAL

Preheat the broiler.

In a medium bowl, combine the mascarpone, mozzarella, Parmigiano, and onion. Spread the mixture on the bread slices.

Set the slices on large baking sheets and place under the broiler until golden and bubbly. Serve warm.

pasta al ragu della nonna caponigri

pasta with grandma caponigri's ragu sauce

My father's mother, Lucia Caponigri, was born in the isolated, mountainous region of Basilicata in southern Italy. There she perfected her recipe for ragu before leaving her village with my grandfather for a life in America. They settled in Chicago, where they raised thirteen children, giving her lots of opportunity to make her famous ragu! The recipe makes plenty: it will sauce 6 to 8 pounds of pasta, but it freezes beautifully.

- 1 CUP EXTRA-VIRGIN OLIVE OIL
- 2 CUPS CHOPPED ONIONS
- 1 GREEN BELL PEPPER, SEEDED AND CHOPPED
- 2½ POUNDS GROUND VEAL
- 2½ POUNDS BULK ITALIAN SAUSAGE
- 2½ POUNDS GROUND BEEF SIRLOIN
- 2 CANS (28 OUNCES EACH) CHOPPED TOMATOES (PREFERABLY SAN MARZANO)
- 2 CANS (28 OUNCES EACH) CRUSHED TOMATOES (PREFERABLY SAN MARZANO)
- 1 CAN (12 OUNCES) TOMATO PASTE
- ¼ CUP SUGAR
- 3 CLOVES GARLIC, PEELED, EACH STUCK ON A TOOTHPICK
- 1 TABLESPOON CHOPPED FRESH BASIL
- 1 TABLESPOON IMPORTED OREGANO
- 1 TABLESPOON CHOPPED FRESH ITALIAN PARSLEY
- 1 TABLESPOON SEA SALT
- 2 BAY LEAVES
- 2 POUNDS SPAGHETTI OR PAPPARDELLE

In a very large skillet, heat the olive oil over medium heat. Add the onions and bell pepper and cook, stirring a few times, until the onions are transparent. Transfer the onions and bell pepper to a very large pot.

In the same oil, brown the veal, sausage, and sirloin over medium heat. Transfer to the pot using a slotted spoon. Add the chopped and crushed tomatoes, tomato paste, sugar, garlic, basil, oregano, parsley, salt, and bay leaves to the pot and stir to combine everything well. Cook for 6 to 8 hours over low heat. Remove the bay leaves and garlic cloves before serving.

Bring a large pot of salted water to a boil. Add the pasta and cook until al dente (if using spaghetti, 7 minutes; if using pappardelle, 4 minutes). Transfer 3 cups of the sauce to a large pasta bowl. Drain the pasta, add it to the bowl, and toss with the sauce.

pollo fritto
fried chicken, italian style

Fried chicken gets an Italian twist with a quick spritz of lemon juice before being dredged in flour and fried, then a garnish of fresh sage leaves fried until crisp in the leftover hot oil.

2	**CHICKENS, EACH CUT INTO 8 SERVING PIECES**
½	**CUP FRESH LEMON JUICE**
	SEA SALT
	FRESHLY GROUND BLACK PEPPER
3	**CUPS ALL-PURPOSE FLOUR**
4	**CUPS VEGETABLE OIL**
12	**FRESH SAGE LEAVES**
	LEMON WEDGES

Preheat the oven to 225F.

Rub the chicken pieces with the lemon juice and season with sea salt and pepper.

Place the flour in a sturdy brown paper bag. Add the chicken a few pieces at a time and shake to coat. Transfer to a tray.

Heat the vegetable oil in a large, deep skillet until very hot (use caution). Add a few pieces of chicken at a time to the oil and cook until golden on all sides and cooked through, 8 to 10 minutes per batch. Transfer the cooked pieces to a large baking dish and keep warm in the oven while you finish frying all the chicken.

When all the chicken has been cooked, add the sage leaves to the hot oil and fry for 2 minutes; don't allow the leaves to burn. Arrange the leaves over the chicken and squeeze the wedges of lemon over the top.

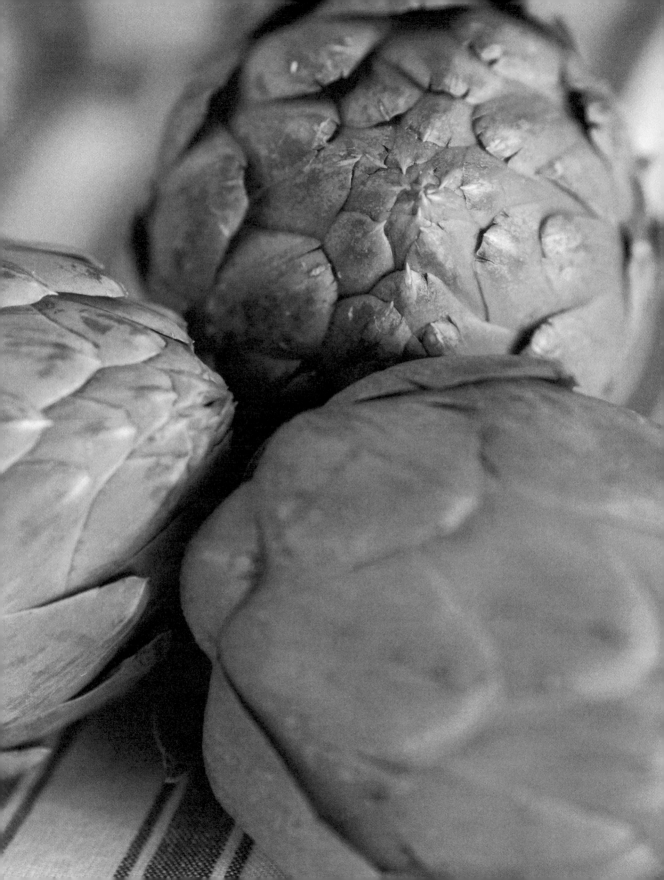

insalata di antipasti

antipasto salad

This Italian American favorite is always fun to serve. Feel free to improvise with other ingredients.

- 1 CUP MARINATED ARTICHOKE HEARTS, CUT IN HALF, OR QUARTERS IF LARGE
- 8 THIN SLICES GENOA SALAMI, EACH SLICE CUT INTO 4 PIECES
- 1 PIECE (¼ POUND) PROVOLONE CHEESE, CUBED
- 1 CUP PITTED BLACK OLIVES
- 1 RED ONION, CHOPPED
- 2 FENNEL BULBS, TRIMMED OF STALKS AND CHOPPED
- 1 HEAD ROMAINE LETTUCE, CHOPPED
- ¼ CUP EXTRA-VIRGIN OLIVE OIL
- 2 TABLESPOONS RED WINE VINEGAR
- SEA SALT
- FRESHLY GROUND BLACK PEPPER

In a large salad bowl, combine the artichoke hearts, salami, provolone, olives, onion, fennel, and romaine. Sprinkle with the olive oil and vinegar, season to taste with sea salt and pepper, and toss well.

spumoni di fragole

strawberry spumoni

This delicate whipped strawberry dessert is nothing like Italian-American spumoni ice cream. A traditional Italian use of fresh strawberries and whipping cream, it's name comes from the Italian "spuma" meaning foamy and, true to its name, this dessert is light as air.

- 1 QUART FRESH STRAWBERRIES
- 1½ TEASPOONS FRESH LEMON JUICE
- 3 TABLESPOONS GRANULATED SUGAR
- 2 CUPS HEAVY CREAM
- ½ CUP CONFECTIONERS' SUGAR

Hull the strawberries and crush them in a medium bowl. Strain them using a fine-mesh strainer or food mill. Add the lemon juice and granulated sugar to the purée and mix well.

In another medium bowl using an electric mixer, beat the heavy cream until stiff peaks form, slowly adding the confectioners' sugar as you beat. Fold the whipped cream into the strawberry purée.

Transfer the mixture to a 3-quart spumoni mold or any other dessert mold that can be frozen. Freeze for 1 to 2 hours (this is a creamy frozen dessert, not solid frozen). Cut into 8 to 10 portions to serve.

MENU

| 12 |

SERVES 8 TO 10

crostini con formaggio di capra e ficchi
toasts with goat cheese and figs

pasta con sugo di vitello
pasta with veal sauce

saltimbocca
veal scallopine stuffed with prosciutto

fagiolini saltati
sautéed green beans

torta della nonna
grandmother's cake

Torta della Nonna, literally "grandmother's cake," was a daily request of my daughter, Felicia, when she arrived home from school in Florence. So off we would go to the forno (oven) at our neighborhood bakery, where she would devour a slice of creamy goodness.

crostini con formaggio di capra e ficchi

toasts with goat cheese and figs

Contrasts always make for lively eating. Here the bite of goat cheese is paired with the sweet, deep richness of figs.

- 2 TABLESPOONS UNSALTED BUTTER
- ½ TEASPOON MINCED FRESH THYME
- ½ POUND FRESH OR DRIED FIGS, FINELY CHOPPED
- ½ TEASPOON SEA SALT
- ¼ TEASPOON FRESHLY GROUND BLACK PEPPER
- 2 LOAVES THIN ITALIAN BREAD, CUT DIAGONALLY INTO SLICES ½ INCH THICK
- 6 TABLESPOONS EXTRA-VIRGIN OLIVE OIL
- 8 OUNCES GOAT CHEESE, AT ROOM TEMPERATURE

Preheat the oven to 350F.

In a medium sauté pan, melt the butter. Stir in the thyme. Add the figs, salt, and pepper and heat until mixture is bubbly. Reduce the heat to a simmer and cook until most of the liquid has evaporated and the mixture has a texture almost like that of marmalade, 10 to 12 minutes. Transfer to a bowl.

Meanwhile, brush the bread slices on both sides with the olive oil. Place the slices in a single layer on baking sheets and bake for 7 minutes, or until golden.

To serve, spread goat cheese on each slice of toast and top with a little of the fig mixture.

pasta con sugo di vitello

pasta with veal sauce

Delicate veal and earthy porcini mushrooms make for a superlative pasta sauce.

- 1 CUP DRIED PORCINI MUSHROOMS
- 2 CUPS BEEF STOCK
- ½ CUP EXTRA-VIRGIN OLIVE OIL
- 1 WHITE ONION, CHOPPED
- 3 POUNDS BONELESS VEAL SHANK, CUT INTO 1-INCH CUBES
- 1 CUP WHITE WINE
-   SEA SALT
-   FRESHLY GROUND BLACK PEPPER
- 3 TABLESPOONS TOMATO PASTE
- 1 CAN (28 OUNCES) CRUSHED TOMATOES
- 2 POUNDS RIGATONI OR PENNE
- 1 CUP GRATED PARMIGIANO-REGGIANO

In a small bowl, soak the mushrooms in 1 cup of the beef stock for 30 minutes. Drain through a fine-mesh strainer over a bowl. Set aside the mushrooms and stock.

In a large skillet, heat the olive oil over medium heat. Add the onion and veal and cook, stirring a few times, until the veal is browned. Add the wine, season to taste with sea salt and pepper, and cook for 10 to 15 minutes over low heat. Stir in the tomato paste, crushed tomatoes, all the stock, and the mushrooms and gently simmer for 1 hour.

When ready to serve, bring a large pot of salted water to a boil. Add the pasta and cook until al dente.

Transfer the veal sauce to a large pasta bowl. Drain the pasta and toss well with the sauce. Sprinkle with the Parmigiano and serve.

saltimbocca

veal scallopine stuffed with prosciutto

You've got to love a dish that translates into "jumps in mouth," meaning it's so good you just can't wait to eat it. And what's not to like—thin veal cutlets rolled up with a slice of prosciutto and fresh sage leaves that are fried until crispy, then finished with a white-wine pan sauce.

12	**SLICES VEAL SCALLOPINE**
	SEA SALT
	FRESHLY GROUND BLACK PEPPER
24	**FRESH SAGE LEAVES**
12	**THIN SLICES PROSCIUTTO DI PARMA**
½	**CUP ALL-PURPOSE FLOUR**
1	**STICK (8 TABLESPOONS) UNSALTED BUTTER**
1	**CUP WHITE WINE**

Place the slices of veal between sheets of waxed or parchment paper and pound with a meat mallet or the end of a rolling pin until slightly flattened. Season on both sides with sea salt and pepper. Place 2 sage leaves and a slice of prosciutto on each veal slice and fold in half or roll up, securing the end with a toothpick.

Place the flour on a large flat plate and season with sea salt and pepper. Dredge each veal package in the flour, coating fully and tapping off any excess.

Melt the butter in a large skillet over medium heat. Cook the veal in 2 batches, browning for about 2 minutes per side. As they are cooked, transfer to a warm platter and tent with aluminum foil.

When all the veal has been cooked, pour the wine into the skillet and deglaze, scraping up the browned bits from the bottom of the pan. Cook over medium heat until the wine has reduced by half. Pour over the veal and serve.

fagiolini saltati

sautéed green beans

Be sure to cook the green beans just until al dente (crisp-tender) for the best flavor.

2	POUNDS THIN GREEN BEANS (HARICOT VERTS OR FRENCH BEANS)
¼	CUP EXTRA-VIRGIN OLIVE OIL
¼	CUP FRESH LEMON JUICE
	SEA SALT

Trim the ends from the beans. Bring a large pot of salted water to a boil. Add the beans and parboil for 4 to 5 minutes, just until they turn bright green and are crisp-tender. Drain and rinse under cold running water to stop the cooking.

In a large skillet over medium heat, heat the olive oil. Add the green beans and cook, stirring a few times, for 3 minutes, until heated through.

Transfer the beans to a large serving bowl and toss with the lemon juice. Season to taste with sea salt and serve.

"a poco
a poco,
tempo
al tempo."

little by little,
it all
gets done.

torta della nonna

grandmother's cake

This is my absolute favorite Italian dessert, a buttery crust filled with a creamy, delectable mixture of sweetened ricotta, eggs, and pine nuts and topped with more pine nuts, which get toasted as the torta bakes.

CRUST

2	CUPS ALL-PURPOSE FLOUR
3	LARGE EGGS
½	CUP SUGAR
¾	STICK (6 TABLESPOONS) UNSALTED BUTTER

FILLING

2	CUPS WHOLE-MILK RICOTTA
½	CUP PLUS 1 TABLESPOON SUGAR
¼	CUP FRESH LEMON JUICE
3	LARGE EGGS
1	CUP PINE NUTS
1	LARGE EGG WHITE

Make the crust: In a large bowl, combine the flour, eggs, sugar, and butter to form a smooth dough. On a lightly floured work surface, knead until very smooth. Don't refrigerate the dough; place it in a medium bowl, cover with a clean kitchen cloth, and let it set at room temperature for 30 to 40 minutes.

Make the filling: In a large bowl, combine the ricotta, ½ cup of the sugar, the lemon juice, the eggs, and ¾ cup of the pine nuts.

Preheat the oven to 350F.

On a lightly floured work surface, cut the dough in half. Roll out one half large enough to fit into a 9-inch pie plate. Sprinkle the remaining 1 tablespoon sugar over the crust. Pour the filling into the crust. Roll out the remaining dough until it is about an inch bigger than the plate. Place on top of the filling. Crimp the top and bottom crusts together with your fingers. Do not vent. Brush the top crust with the egg white. Sprinkle the remaining ¼ cup pine nuts over the top and press down slightly into the crust. Bake for 30 minutes, or until top is golden.

MENU

13

SERVES 8 TO 10

bruschetta al pomodoro
bruschetta with tomato and basil

....

manicotti
stuffed tube pasta

....

peperoni ripieni
lisa's famous stuffed peppers

....

insalata verde
classic green salad

....

torta di ricotta della nonna franco
nana franco's ricotta cake

One of the first dishes my nana taught me to make was stuffed peppers. Her trick was to roast the peppers in water in the oven first, which removes any bitter taste and makes this dish sweet and smoky.

bruschetta al pomodoro

bruschetta with tomato and basil

I like to make my own bread for bruschetta and crostini, but you can certainly use a bakery-bought loaf instead.

LISA'S RUSTIC ITALIAN BREAD

- 3 **CUPS BREAD FLOUR**
- 2 **TEASPOONS SUGAR**
- ½ **TEASPOON SALT**
- 1 **PACKAGE INSTANT ACTIVE YEAST**
- 1 **CUP WARM WATER (120F TO 130F)**
- 2 **TABLESPOONS OLIVE OIL**
  CORNMEAL
- 1 **LARGE EGG WHITE, BEATEN**

BRUSCHETTA

- 4 **RIPE TOMATOES, DICED**
- ¼ **CUP EXTRA-VIRGIN OLIVE OIL (APPROXIMATELY)**
  SEA SALT
  FRESHLY GROUND BLACK PEPPER
- 6 **FRESH BASIL LEAVES, CHOPPED**

Make Lisa's Rustic Italian Bread: In a large bowl, combine the flour, sugar, salt, and yeast and mix well. Add the warm water and olive oil and mix well.

Turn the dough out onto a lightly floured work surface. Knead the dough until smooth, about 10 minutes. Place the dough in a lightly oiled bowl and cover with plastic wrap and a clean kitchen towel. Let rise in a warm place (80F to 85F) for 30 to 40 minutes, until doubled in size.

Sprinkle an ungreased cookie sheet with cornmeal. Punch down the dough. Cover the dough with an inverted bowl on your counter for 15 minutes.

Shape the dough into a loaf about 12 inches long. Place the loaf on the prepared cookie sheet. Cover and let rise until doubled in size, 35 to 40 minutes.

Preheat the oven to 375F. With a sharp knife, make one deep lengthwise slash in the top of the loaf. Brush with the egg white, and bake 25 to 30 minutes, until golden on top. Allow bread to cool 30 minutes and slice into ½-inch slices. Brush with olive oil and toast in a 350F oven for 8 minutes.

Make the bruschetta: In a medium bowl, combine the tomatoes and olive oil and season to taste with sea salt and pepper. Spoon onto the toasted bread slices and top each one with chopped basil.

manicotti

stuffed tube pasta

This dish reminds me so much of my nana. Her food was never fancy, but it was always good. If you like, you can assemble the manicotti the night before and refrigerate. They'll take bit longer to heat through in the oven.

- 1 **POUND MANICOTTI SHELLS**
- 2 **POUNDS RICOTTA**
- 4 **LARGE EGGS**
- 3 **TABLESPOONS CHOPPED FRESH ITALIAN PARSLEY**
- 3 **TABLESPOONS CHOPPED FRESH BASIL**
- 1 **CUP GRATED PECORINO ROMANO**
  SEA SALT
  FRESHLY GROUND BLACK PEPPER
- 4 **CUPS LISA'S CLASSIC TOMATO SAUCE (PAGE 89)**

Bring a large pot of salted water to a boil. Add the pasta and cook at least 2 to 3 minutes less than directed on the package. Drain and rinse under cold running water until cool to the touch and leave in the colander.

Meanwhile, in a large bowl, beat by hand the ricotta, eggs, parsley, basil, and 1/2 cup of the Pecorino Romano. Season to taste with sea salt and pepper.

Preheat the oven to 400F. Pour 2 cups of the tomato sauce into a large baking dish and tilt the dish to evenly coat the bottom with sauce.

Gently fill the manicotti shells with the cheese mixture. (If you don't have a pastry bag—which works very well—use an espresso or other small, narrow spoon so you don't tear the shells.) As you fill them, place the shells in the prepared baking dish. The shells can touch one another, but they shouldn't overlap. When all the manicotti are filled, pour over the remaining 2 cups tomato sauce and sprinkle with the remaining 1/2 cup cheese. Bake until bubbly, about 20 minutes.

peperoni ripieni
lisa's famous stuffed peppers

I can't tell you how many times I've made this recipe! It's a real family favorite and easy to put together.

6	LARGE BELL PEPPERS: 2 RED, 2 YELLOW, 2 GREEN
1½	POUNDS GROUND BEEF SIRLOIN
1	WHITE ONION, CHOPPED
1	LARGE EGG
½	CUP ITALIAN BREADCRUMBS, HOMEMADE (RECIPE FOLLOWS) OR STORE-BOUGHT
1	CAN (6 OUNCES) TOMATO PASTE OR 1 TUBE (4 TO 6 OUNCES) ITALIAN CONCENTRATO DI POMODORO
4	CLOVES GARLIC, CHOPPED
4	ANCHOVY FILLETS, CHOPPED (OPTIONAL)
6	TABLESPOONS EXTRA-VIRGIN OLIVE OIL
2	LADLES LISA'S CLASSIC TOMATO SAUCE (PAGE 89)
¼	CUP GRATED PARMIGIANO-REGGIANO

Preheat the oven to 350F. Fill a large baking dish with 1/2 inch water.

Cut the peppers in half lengthwise and remove the stems, seeds, and white membranes. Place the peppers, cut side down, in the water-filled baking dish. Bake until the peppers are soft to the touch, about 10 minutes.

Meanwhile, in a large bowl, combine the ground beef, onion, egg, breadcrumbs, tomato paste, garlic, anchovies, and olive oil until well mixed.

Remove the peppers from the oven, drain off the water in the dish, and pat the peppers dry. Pour the tomato sauce into the dish and tilt to coat the bottom. Set the pepper halves, cut side up, in the dish. Spoon the filling into the peppers and bake for 55 minutes.

Spoon 1 tablespoon of tomato sauce from the bottom of the dish over each stuffed pepper half and sprinkle with Parmigiano-Reggiano. Return to the oven for 5 to 10 minutes to melt the cheese.

homemade italian breadcrumbs

Makes about 1½ cups

1	CUP BREADCRUMBS FROM STALE ITALIAN BREAD
½	TEASPOON SEA SALT
½	TEASPOON FRESHLY GROUND BLACK PEPPER
½	TEASPOON DRIED PARSLEY
½	TEASPOON GARLIC POWDER
¼	TEASPOON DRIED OREGANO
¼	TEASPOON DRIED BASIL
½	CUP PARMIGIANO-REGGIANO

Mix together all ingredients in a bowl.

insalata verde

classic green salad

The perfect side salad for a hearty menu like this one.

- **1** HEAD BUTTER LETTUCE
- **3** RIPE TOMATOES, CUT INTO WEDGES
- **2** CUCUMBERS, PEELED AND SLICED INTO ¼-INCH-THICK SLICES
- **¼** TEASPOON SEA SALT, PLUS ADDITIONAL TO TASTE
- **1** TABLESPOON BALSAMIC VINEGAR
- **3** TABLESPOONS EXTRA-VIRGIN OLIVE OIL
- **FRESHLY GROUND BLACK PEPPER**

Tear up the lettuce leaves and put them in a large salad bowl. Add the tomatoes and cucumbers and toss together.

To dress the salad, put the salt in a large soup or salad spoon, add the vinegar, and mix with a fork until the salt dissolves. Pour over the salad and toss. Pour the olive oil over the salad and toss again, seasoning with more salt and pepper to taste.

torta di ricotta della nonna franco

nana's ricotta cake

How many times did this cake end a meal at my grandparents' house? It brings back happy memories of Gramps regaling us with his stories of "the good ol' days," and nana saying, "Oh, Frank!"

- **1** BOX (18 ¼ OUNCES) YELLOW CAKE MIX
- **3** EGGS
- **1¼** CUPS WATER
- **⅓** CUP VEGETABLE OIL
- **1¾** CUPS RICOTTA
- **3** LARGE EGGS
- **¾** CUP GRANULATED SUGAR
- **1** TEASPOON VANILLA EXTRACT
- **CONFECTIONERS' SUGAR**

Preheat the oven to 350F. Grease a 13- by 9-inch glass baking dish.

Prepare the yellow cake mix according to the package directions with the eggs, water, and vegetable oil. Pour the batter into the prepared baking dish.

In a medium bowl, combine the ricotta and eggs, adding the eggs one at a time and mixing well after each addition. Add the granulated sugar and vanilla and mix well.

Pour the ricotta mixture over the cake batter. Bake until golden brown, about 1 hour. While still hot, sprinkle the top with confectioners' sugar. Let the cake cool before serving.

MENU

14

SERVES 8 TO 10

crostini con pesto di olive nere

toasts with black olive paste

....

spaghetti al limone

lemon spaghetti

....

agnello arrosto con rosmarino e aglio

roast leg of lamb with rosemary and garlic

....

scarola della nonna

nana's escarole

....

pesche in vino bianco

peaches in white wine

One of my favorite memories of raising my children in Italy was spending summers in the small village in Sicily where my grandmother was born, a stone's throw from the Mediterranean Sea, where days are warm, long, and lazy. This was my go-to menu: a refreshing dish with a no-cook sauce, lemon spaghetti, that satisfies and refreshes.

crostini con pesto di olive nere

toasts with black olive paste

Crispy slices of bread topped with a salty-savory spread of black olives kick off this Sicilian-inspired menu.

1	**CUP PITTED BLACK OLIVES**
2	**TABLESPOONS EXTRA-VIRGIN OLIVE OIL**
1	**TEASPOON FRESH LEMON JUICE**
	FINELY GRATED ZEST OF 1 LEMON
2	**TABLESPOONS UNSALTED BUTTER, SOFTENED (OPTIONAL)**
1	**BAGUETTE**

Finely chop the olives. Add the olive oil, or process the olives with the olive oil into a coarse paste in a blender. Add the lemon juice and zest. If you like, add the butter to give the paste a more delicate flavor. Stir or process just to combine.

Preheat the oven to 350F. Slice the bread in $1/2$-inch-thick slices and toast for 6 minutes in the oven.

Spread each bread slice with the paste and serve.

spaghetti al limone

lemon spaghetti

This dish is popular in Sicily, the land of lemons. Refreshing and light, it's the perfect choice for a summer Sunday dinner, particularly if you're dining al fresco.

2	**POUNDS SPAGHETTI**
1	**CUP EXTRA-VIRGIN OLIVE OIL, OR MORE AS NEEDED**
1	**CUP GRATED PARMIGIANO-REGGIANO**
1	**CUP FRESH LEMON JUICE**
2	**TABLESPOONS FINELY GRATED LEMON ZEST**
	SEA SALT
	FRESHLY GROUND BLACK PEPPER
$1/2$	**CUP HEAVY CREAM (OPTIONAL)**

Bring a large pot of salted water to a boil. Add the spaghetti and cook until al dente, 7 minutes.

Meanwhile, in a serving bowl large enough to accommodate the pasta, combine the olive oil, Parmigiano, and lemon juice and zest, and season to taste with sea salt and pepper.

Drain the pasta and transfer it to the serving bowl. Toss until well coated with the lemon sauce. If using cream, add it at this time. If the pasta seems dry, add a little more olive oil. Serve immediately.

agnello arrosto con rosmarino e aglio

roast leg of lamb with rosemary and garlic

My preference is to make this dish with New Zealand baby lamb, which I think is the most tender. Infused with garlic and rosemary, this lamb will melt in your mouth!

½	CUP EXTRA-VIRGIN OLIVE OIL
1	BONELESS LEG OF LAMB (4 TO 5 POUNDS)
6	CLOVES GARLIC, CHOPPED
	LEAVES FROM 4 SPRIGS FRESH ROSEMARY, CHOPPED
1	TABLESPOON SEA SALT
1	TEASPOON FRESHLY GROUND BLACK PEPPER
4	POUNDS SMALL WHITE POTATOES

Preheat the oven to 350F. Pour ¼ cup of the olive oil into a large roasting pan (at least 13 by 9 by 2½ inches). Set the leg of lamb in the pan.

In a measuring cup, combine the remaining ¼ cup olive oil and the garlic, rosemary, sea salt, and pepper. Brush the mixture generously all over the leg of lamb.

Arrange the potatoes around the lamb and bake the lamb about 15 minutes per pound for medium rare, 1 to 1½ hours. Every 30 minutes, baste the potatoes with the olive oil mixture in the pan.

Remove the lamb to a cutting board and let rest for 15 minutes. Slice the lamb and arrange on a large warm serving platter, scattering the potatoes around the lamb.

scarola della nonna

nana's escarole

Scarola, as my Sicilian grandmother called it, is delicious and good for you. Its bitter flavor is offset by the fresh taste of the lemon juice.

2	POUNDS ESCAROLE
½	CUP EXTRA-VIRGIN OLIVE OIL
4	CLOVES GARLIC, PEELED
	SEA SALT
	FRESHLY GROUND BLACK PEPPER
2	LEMONS, QUARTERED

Cut the stems off the escarole and wash the leaves thoroughly.

In a soup pot over medium heat, cook the olive oil, garlic and escarole, stirring occasionally to keep the escarole from sticking, until the escarole is wilted, 15 to 20 minutes.

Transfer the escarole to a large serving bowl, season to taste with sea salt and pepper, and squeeze the juice from the lemon wedges over the top. Serve immediately.

pesche in vino bianco

peaches in white wine

Juicy, sun-ripened peaches steeped in a pitcher of white wine—the perfect end to a summer meal!

1	BOTTLE (750 ML) ITALIAN WHITE WINE
6	RIPE PEACHES, PITTED AND CUT INTO ⅛-INCH-THICK WEDGES

Pour the wine into a large glass pitcher. Add the peaches, cover, and let steep at room temperature for 12 hours.

Serve the peaches and wine at room temperature in wine glasses with small spoons.

MENU

15

SERVES 8 TO 10

prosciutto con melone
prosciutto with melon

polpetti alla lisa
lisa's famous meat-a-balls

pollo al forno della nonna
nana's baked chicken

insalata tre colori
tri-color salad

torta al cioccolato, caffè e nocciola
espresso and hazelnut chocolate cake

My great-grandmother Franco was known for her meat-balls, and every Sunday she would get up bright and early to roll, fry, and simmer hundreds of them in tomato sauce for her large family. There was only one problem: my seven great-uncles would sneak into the kitchen and sample them. By dinner time my great-grandmother was left to wonder, "What happened to all my meatballs?"

prosciutto con melone

prosciutto with melon

This was a staple in my parents' house as I was growing up. It is so delicious and elegant, though I still remember the skeptical looks on the faces of my parents' non-Italian friends when it was served to them—but one bite was all it took to change their minds!

- 1 LARGE RIPE CANTALOUPE
- 12 THIN SLICES PROSCIUTTO DI PARMA OR SAN DANIELE

Cut the cantaloupe in half, cut off the rind, and remove the seeds. Slice each half into 6 wedges, for a total of 12.

Gently wrap each cantaloupe wedge with a slice of prosciutto, starting at the tip of the melon slice. Arrange on a tray and serve.

polpetti alla lisa

lisa's famous meat-a-balls

Since the tomato sauce is so long simmering and it's just as easy to make it with double the ingredients, make extra and freeze it to have on hand. You'll find that I call for this sauce throughout the book in many different types of preparations, so think about freezing it in 2- and 4-cup containers for ease of use.

LISA'S CLASSIC TOMATO SAUCE

- 6 CLOVES GARLIC, CUT IN HALF, GREEN SPROUTS REMOVED IF NECESSARY
- ½ CUP EXTRA-VIRGIN OLIVE OIL
- 4 CANS (28 OUNCES EACH) CRUSHED TOMATOES (PREFERABLY SAN MARZANO)
- 1½ TABLESPOONS SUGAR
- 1½ TEASPOONS DRIED ITALIAN OREGANO
- 1½ TEASPOONS CHOPPED FRESH BASIL
- ½ TEASPOON SEA SALT
- ½ TEASPOON FRESHLY GROUND BLACK PEPPER

MEATBALLS

- 2 SLICES ITALIAN BREAD
- ½ CUP MILK
- 1 POUND GROUND VEAL
- 1 POUND COARSE-GROUND SAUSAGE MEAT WITH FENNEL SEEDS
- 1 POUND GROUND BEEF SIRLOIN
- 3 LARGE EGGS
- 1 CUP CHOPPED ITALIAN PARSLEY
- 8 CLOVES GARLIC, MINCED
- ¾ CUP GRATED PECORINO ROMANO
- ¾ CUP GRATED PARMIGIANO-REGGIANO
- 1 TABLESPOON DRIED OREGANO
-   SEA SALT
-   FRESHLY GROUND BLACK PEPPER
- 1 CUP EXTRA-VIRGIN OLIVE OIL FOR FRYING

Make Lisa's Classic Tomato Sauce: In a large pot, heat the garlic in the olive oil over low heat for 3 minutes. Don't allow the garlic to brown. Add the remaining sauce ingredients and simmer over very low heat for 2 to 4 hours.

Meanwhile, make the meatballs: In a small bowl, soak the bread in the milk.

In a large bowl, combine the ground meat, eggs, parsley, garlic, cheeses, oregano, and sea salt and pepper to taste. Squeeze the excess milk from the bread and add the bread to the meat mixture, making sure everything is well combined.

With your hands, shape the mixture into meatballs 2 to 2¹/₂ inches in diameter. Place the meatballs on a tray as you make them.

Heat the olive oil in a large skillet over medium heat. In batches, brown the meatballs on all sides. Transfer to paper towels to drain.

Add the meatballs to the simmering tomato sauce and cook another 2 to 4 hours over very low heat.

pollo al forno della nonna
nana's baked chicken

No matter how many people showed up for dinner, my nana always seemed to have an extra pan of her baked chicken on hand. It's simple and satisfying.

4   TABLESPOONS EXTRA-VIRGIN OLIVE OIL, PLUS 6 TABLESPOONS FOR RUBBING THE CHICKENS

2   CHICKENS, EACH CUT INTO 8 SERVING PIECES

1½ CUPS ALL-PURPOSE FLOUR

1   TABLESPOON RED PEPPER FLAKES

SEA SALT

FRESHLY GROUND BLACK PEPPER

Preheat the oven to 375F. Pour 4 tablespoons of the olive oil into a large baking dish and tilt the dish to coat the bottom with the oil.

Lightly rub the chicken pieces with the remaining 6 tablespoons olive oil. Put the flour, red pepper flakes, and salt and black pepper to taste in a sturdy brown paper bag. Place 2 or 3 pieces of chicken at a time in the bag and shake to coat the chicken fully with the seasoned flour. Tap off any excess.

Arrange the dredged chicken pieces in the prepared baking dish in a single layer. Bake until fully cooked through, about 1 hour.

insalata tre colori

tri-color salad

This salad adds snap and color to the plate.

1 LARGE FENNEL BULB, TRIMMED OF STALKS, BULB CUT INTO ⅛-INCH-THICK SLICES

2 CARROTS, CUT INTO THIN ROUNDS

1 LARGE RED OR GREEN BELL PEPPER, SEEDED AND CUT INTO VERY THIN STRIPS

1 SMALL HEAD BIBB LETTUCE, LEAVES TORN INTO MEDIUM PIECES

2 RIPE MEDIUM TOMATOES, CUT INTO WEDGES

   SEA SALT

3–4 TABLESPOONS EXTRA-VIRGIN OLIVE OIL

1 TABLESPOON RED WINE VINEGAR

Place the fennel, carrots, bell pepper, lettuce, and tomatoes in a large salad bowl.

When ready to serve, season to taste with salt, add the olive oil and vinegar, and toss gently to coat the salad with the dressing.

torta al cioccolato, caffè e nocciola

espresso and hazelnut chocolate cake

When I was living in Florence, I was lucky to get a hold of this recipe from my favorite pasticceria (pastry shop). The key is its ground hazelnut crust.

3½ CUPS SHELLED HAZELNUTS

6 OUNCES BITTERSWEET CHOCOLATE (70% CACAO)

2½ STICKS (20 TABLESPOONS) UNSALTED BUTTER, PLUS MORE FOR GREASING THE PAN

½ CUP FRESHLY BREWED ESPRESSO OR ¼ CUP ESPRESSO POWDER DISSOLVED IN ¼ CUP BOILING WATER

6 LARGE EGGS, SEPARATED

1 CUP SUGAR

Preheat the oven to 350F. Butter a 10-inch round springform pan and line the bottom with parchment paper.

Place the hazelnuts on a baking sheet and roast until brown. Let cool. Rub off the skins (you can do this with a clean dish towel) and chop fine.

Break the chocolate into pieces. Place in the top of a double boiler (or in a glass or metal mixing bowl) set over gently simmering water. Add the butter and coffee and melt, stirring a few times until smooth. Let cool. Stir in the hazelnuts.

In a large bowl using an electric mixer, beat the egg yolks and sugar together until the mixture is pale and doubles in volume. Fold in the chocolate mixture. In another large bowl using the mixer (be sure to wash and dry the beaters well), beat the egg whites until stiff peaks form. Gently fold the whites into the batter.

Pour the batter into the prepared pan and bake until a cake tester inserted in the center comes out with a few crumbs on it, about 1 hour. Let cool in the pan for 15 minutes, and then remove the side of the pan.

MENU

16

SERVES 8 TO 10

pecorino romano con miele e pepe
pecorino romano with honey and black pepper

....

polenta con funghi
polenta with mushrooms

....

salsicce grigliate
grilled sausage

....

spinaci saltati
sautéed spinach

....

torta di vino e noci
wine and nut cake

When I was seventeen, I went to school in a walled medieval city on the Adriatic coast of Italy. One evening a professor of mine invited his students home for dinner. In dramatic fashion, he brought a huge white cloth to the table and unveiled a steaming mountain of polenta. Then he made a well with a ladle and poured tomato sauce, sausage, and mushrooms into it. I'll never forget it!

pecorino romano con miele e pepe

pecorino romano with honey and black pepper

Buy the best-quality Pecorino you can afford for this antipasto and, if you can find it, crystallized honey from Sicily.

- 1   **POUND PECORINO ROMANO, CUT INTO BITE-SIZE CHUNKS**
- ¼   **CUP SICILIAN HONEY**
-      **FRESHLY GROUND BLACK PEPPER, GROUND ONTO A PLATE**

Insert a toothpick into each chunk of Pecorino. Dip the chunks in the honey, roll them in the pepper, and set on a platter.

polenta con funghi

polenta with mushrooms

This dish makes for a dramatic presentation, the polenta spread out on a platter and the mushroom sauce poured in a well in the center.

- 2   **TABLESPOONS DRIED PORCINI MUSHROOMS (OPTIONAL)**
- ¼   **CUP EXTRA-VIRGIN OLIVE OIL**
- 1   **SMALL ONION, FINELY CHOPPED**
- 1½   **POUNDS BUTTON MUSHROOMS, SLICED**
- 2   **CLOVES GARLIC, FINELY CHOPPED**
- 3   **TABLESPOONS CHOPPED FRESH ITALIAN PARSLEY**
- 3   **RIPE MEDIUM TOMATOES, PEELED AND DICED**
- 1   **TABLESPOON TOMATO PASTE**
- ¼   **TEASPOON FRESH THYME LEAVES OR ⅛ TEASPOON DRIED THYME**
- 1   **BAY LEAF**
-      **SEA SALT**
-      **FRESHLY GROUND BLACK PEPPER**
- 2½   **CUPS POLENTA**
-      **SEVERAL SPRIGS ITALIAN PARSLEY FOR GARNISH**

If using them, place the dried mushrooms in a small cup and add warm water to cover. Let soak for 20 minutes. Remove the mushrooms using a slotted spoon and rinse them well in several changes of cool water. Pour the soaking water through a fine-mesh strainer to remove any sand. Set both aside.

In a large skillet, heat the olive oil over low heat. Add the onion and cook, stirring a few times, until soft and golden. Add the button mushrooms, increase the heat to medium high, and cook, stirring until the mushrooms are soft and the liquid evaporates. Add the garlic, parsley, and tomatoes and let simmer for 4 to 5 minutes. Stir in the tomato paste and thyme. Add the bay leaf, rehydrated mushrooms, and soaking water. Mix well and season to taste with sea salt and pepper. Reduce the heat to a simmer and cook for 15 to 20 minutes, until slightly thickened. Remove from the heat.

Meanwhile, in a large, heavy saucepan, bring 6¼ cups water to a boil. Add 1 tablespoon sea salt. Reduce the heat to a simmer and slowly add the polenta, stirring all the time. Continue until all the polenta has been added. Using a long-handled wooden spoon, reduce the heat to low, and stir until the polenta is a thick mass and pulls away from the side of the pan; this can take anywhere from 25 to 50 minutes, depending on the type of polenta. For the best results, never stop stirring the polenta until you remove it from the heat.

When the polenta is ready, gently reheat the mushroom sauce. Spoon the polenta onto a warm serving platter. Make a well in the center. Spoon some of the sauce in the well. Garnish with parsley sprigs. Serve at once, passing the remaining sauce in a separate bowl.

salsicce grigliate

grilled sausage

With such a hearty primo, keep your secondo simple, with grilled sausage. Feel free to use any type of fresh sausage you prefer.

12 LINKS SWEET ITALIAN SAUSAGES, WITH FENNEL SEEDS

Prepare a grill. Grill the sausages until cooked through, about 35 minutes, turning them every 10 minutes. Cut each link into thirds, arrange on a platter, and serve.

spinaci saltati

sautéed spinach

Spinach sautéed in olive oil with garlic provides balance to the richness of the sausage.

4 CLOVES GARLIC, SLICED

½ CUP EXTRA-VIRGIN OLIVE OIL

2 POUNDS FRESH SPINACH, WASHED WELL AND HEAVY STEMS REMOVED, OR FROZEN SPINACH, THAWED AND SQUEEZED DRY

SEA SALT

FRESHLY GROUND BLACK PEPPER

In a large skillet over medium heat, heat the garlic in the olive oil until soft but not brown. Add the spinach and cook, stirring, until wilted and heated through. Season to taste with sea salt and pepper.

Transfer to a warm serving dish and serve.

torta di vino e noci

wine and nut cake

This cake is delicious served topped with a spoonful of whipped cream.

2 STICKS (16 TABLESPOONS) UNSALTED BUTTER, SOFTENED

2 CUPS SUGAR

6 LARGE EGGS

3 CUPS ALL-PURPOSE FLOUR

1 TEASPOON BAKING POWDER

1 CUP RED WINE

¾ POUND SHELLED NUTS (WALNUTS WORK BEST), CHOPPED

Preheat the oven to 350F. Butter an 8-cup Bundt pan.

In a large bowl with an electric mixer, beat together the butter and sugar. Beat in the eggs, one at a time. Add the flour (all at once) and baking powder and mix well. Beat in the wine, and stir in the nuts.

Pour the batter into the prepared pan. Bake for 1 hour, or until golden on top.

MENU

17

mozzarella fritta
fried mozzarella

pasta alla ligure
pasta with green beans, potatoes and basil pesto

pollo alla milanese
chicken in breadcrumbs

zucchini parmigiano
zucchini parmesan

budino di ricotta
ricotta cheese pudding

When my son Guido was so young he couldn't even pronounce the word "mozzarella," he was already helping me make Mozzarella Fritta. Cooking together has always been one of my happiest family memories.

mozzarella fritta

fried mozzarella

Crunchy on the outside, smooth and stringy on the inside, this antipasto is fun to make and fun to eat.

- 2 **POUNDS MOZZARELLA**
- ½ **CUP ALL-PURPOSE FLOUR**
- 1 **CUP PLAIN BREADCRUMBS**
- 2 **LARGE EGGS**
- ¼ **TEASPOON SEA SALT**
- 1 **CUP EXTRA-VIRGIN OLIVE OIL**

Cut the mozzarella into 1-inch-thick slices, and then cut the slices into four 1-inch squares.

Spread the flour on a flat plate. Spread the breadcrumbs on another plate. Place the eggs in a large, shallow bowl and beat slightly with the sea salt.

In a large skillet, heat the olive oil over medium heat. While it heats, dredge the cheese squares in the flour, dip them in the eggs, and then dredge them in the breadcrumbs.

When the oil is hot, fry the cheese squares, about 3 minutes on each side, until the breadcrumbs turn golden. Serve immediately.

pasta alla ligure

pasta with green beans, potatoes and basil pesto

I first had this dish in a trattoria in the Liguria region of Italy, culinary home of pesto. The combination of pasta, potatoes, and pesto seems unlikely, but it works, creating a hearty primo pungent with the flavor of fresh basil.

PESTO

- 3 **CUPS LOOSELY PACKED FRESH BASIL LEAVES**
- ¾ **CUP EXTRA-VIRGIN OLIVE OIL**
- ¼ **CUP PINE NUTS**
- 3 **CLOVES GARLIC, PEELED**
- 1 **TEASPOON SEA SALT**
- **FRESHLY GROUND BLACK PEPPER TO TASTE**
- ½ **CUP GRATED PECORINO-ROMANO**

PASTA

- 1 **POUND GREEN BEANS, ENDS TRIMMED AND CUT INTO 2-INCH LENGTHS**
- 1½ **POUNDS POTATOES (PREFERABLY YUKON GOLD)**
- 2 **POUNDS PASTA, SUCH AS GEMELLI, FARFALLE, OR FUSILLI**
- **SEA SALT**
- **FRESHLY GROUND BLACK PEPPER**

Make the pesto: Put the basil, olive oil, pine nuts, garlic, salt, and pepper in a blender or food processor and process until smooth. Pour the mixture into a small bowl and stir in the Pecorino. Check the seasonings to taste.

Bring a large pot of salted water to a boil. Add the green beans and blanch until they turn bright green and are tender, approximately 10 minutes. Using a slotted spoon, remove the beans to a colander and run under cold water to keep them from cooking any further. Set aside.

While the beans are cooking, peel the potatoes. Once you've removed the beans from the pot of boiling water, add the potatoes and boil until they are soft and can be broken apart with a wooden spoon, approximately 20 minutes. Using a slotted spoon, transfer them to the colander.

Add the pasta to the boiling water and cook until al dente, 10 minutes.

Meanwhile, place the potatoes, green beans, and pesto in a large bowl. Drain the pasta and add to the bowl. Mix together with a wooden spoon. The potatoes should be broken up into chunks in a rustic fashion. If the mixture is too dry, add a little more olive oil. Season to taste with sea salt and pepper.

"a ogni uccello il suo nido e bello."

there's no place like home.

pollo alla milanese
chicken in breadcrumbs

This dish was a staple on my nana's table. She understood that there is good flavor in simplicity.

- 1 **CUP EXTRA-VIRGIN OLIVE OIL**
- 2 **CUPS PLAIN BREADCRUMBS**
- 6 **CLOVES GARLIC, CHOPPED**
- 2 **TABLESPOONS CHOPPED FRESH ITALIAN PARSLEY**
- 1 **TABLESPOON CHOPPED FRESH OREGANO**
- 8–10 **BONELESS, SKINLESS CHICKEN BREAST HALVES**
  LEMON WEDGES

Preheat the oven to 350F. Add 2 tablespoons of the olive oil to a large baking dish and tilt the dish to coat the bottom.

On a large flat plate, combine the breadcrumbs, garlic, parsley, and oregano. Lightly dredge the chicken in the mixture on both sides. Set the coated pieces on a tray.

In a large skillet, heat the remaining olive oil over medium heat. In batches, cook the chicken until golden brown on both sides. As they brown, transfer the pieces to the prepared baking dish and arrange in a single layer.

Bake the chicken until no longer pink in the center, about 30 minutes. Transfer to a platter and serve with lemon wedges.

zucchini parmigiano

zucchini parmesan

This is a Parmesan dish in its purest form—no tomato sauce, no mozzarella, just lots of grated Parmigiano-Reggiano and the garden-fresh flavor of the zucchini.

EXTRA-VIRGIN OLIVE OIL
8 ZUCCHINI, CUT INTO ⅛-INCH ROUNDS
2 CUPS GRATED PARMIGIANO-REGGIANO
SEA SALT

Preheat the oven to 300F.

In a medium skillet, add enough olive oil to cover the bottom of the pan and arrange as many zucchini rounds as will fit in the pan in a single layer. Cook over medium heat until golden on each side but not brown. Transfer the rounds to a paper-towel–lined plate to drain. Repeat with the remaining zucchini, adding more oil to the pan as needed.

In a 9-inch square baking dish, arrange a layer of zucchini, overlapping the rounds slightly. Sprinkle with Parmigiano and a dash of salt. Repeat the layers until the dish is full, ending with a final sprinkling of Parmigiano.

Bake until the top is golden, 20 to 30 minutes.

budino di ricotta

ricotta cheese pudding

This rich, creamy pudding is very simple and quick to make. It tastes superb topped with fresh red fruit such as strawberries, cherries, or raspberries that have been sprinkled with a liqueur or a high-quality balsamic vinegar. In fact, this would be a good time to use an aged balsamic vinegar, its delicate perfume and sweet-sour flavor pairing deliciously with the fresh fruit. (Be aware that this pudding contains raw eggs.)

18 OUNCES (ABOUT 2¼ CUPS) RICOTTA
½ CUP SUGAR
4 LARGE EGGS, SEPARATED
FINELY GRATED ZEST OF 1 LEMON
½ CUP FINELY CHOPPED CANDIED FRUIT
⅔ CUP GOLDEN RAISINS
1¼ CUPS HEAVY CREAM
3 TABLESPOONS STREGA LIQUEUR OR GALLIANO
⅔ CUP CRUSHED BISCOTTI DI AMARETTO

In a large bowl, beat together the ricotta, sugar, egg yolks, and lemon zest until light and fluffy. Add the candied fruit and raisins and beat again until well combined.

In a medium bowl using an electric mixer, beat the cream until firm peaks form, then fold the cream alternately with the liqueur into the ricotta mixture. Wash and dry the beaters of the mixer well.

In another medium bowl using the mixer, beat the egg whites until they hold stiff peaks. Gently fold the beaten whites into the ricotta mixture until thoroughly combined.

Spoon the mixture into individual dessert glasses or a large serving bowl, cover, and chill for 4 to 6 hours, until cold.

Right before serving, sprinkle the crushed biscotti di amaretto evenly over the top.

MENU

18

SERVES 8 TO 10

crostini con aioli di peperoni rossi
toasts with red pepper aioli

spaghetti alla siciliana con canciova e mudicca
spaghetti with anchovies and breadcrumbs

rotolini di sogliola
sole rollups

carciofi ripieni
stuffed artichokes

torta di arancio
orange cake

As we cooked together, my nana would tell me stories of her life. This menu reminded her of the time she first moved to America with her family. Life was difficult, and spaghetti with anchovies and breadcrumbs went a long way. Later, when she was raising her own children, she made this dish on many Friday nights. It's delicious, satisfying, and easy to prepare—typical Sicilian ingenuity.

crostini con aioli di peperoni rossi

toasts with red pepper aioli

The sweet-smoky flavor of this creamy red pepper spread is heavenly on crisp-baked crostini.

CROSTINI

12	SLICES (½ INCH THICK) CIABATTA BREAD
2	TABLESPOONS EXTRA-VIRGIN OLIVE OIL
	SEA SALT
	FRESHLY GROUND BLACK PEPPER
2	CLOVES GARLIC, PEELED

RED PEPPER AIOLI

2	CLOVES GARLIC, PEELED
½	CUP ROASTED RED PEPPERS, DRAINED AND PATTED DRY
⅓	CUP MAYONNAISE
2	TABLESPOONS EXTRA-VIRGIN OLIVE OIL
	SEA SALT
	FRESHLY GROUND BLACK PEPPER

Make the crostini: Preheat the oven to 400F. Brush the bread slices on both sides with the olive oil. Season to taste with sea salt and pepper. Bake the bread until crisp and golden, about 5 minutes. As soon as the toast slices cool enough that they can be handled, rub them on one side with the garlic cloves.

Make the red pepper aioli: Finely chop the garlic in the food processor. Add the peppers and blend until almost smooth. Blend in the mayonnaise. With the machine running, add the olive oil and blend until smooth. Remove the aioli to a small bowl and season to taste with sea salt and pepper.

Spread the aioli over the toast and serve.

spaghetti alla siciliana con canciova e mudicca

spaghetti with anchovies and breadcrumbs

This Sicilian dish shows the ingenuity of home cooks who learned to feed their families well with limited resources. Leftover bread is transformed into a flavor-packed sauce for spaghetti with the addition of anchovies, garlic, and red pepper flakes.

20	OIL-PACKED ANCHOVY FILLETS, DRAINED
½	CUP MILK
1½	CUPS COARSELY GROUND FRESH BREADCRUMBS (OR SUBSTITUTE GOOD QUALITY STORE-BOUGHT BREADCRUMBS)
1	CUP EXTRA-VIRGIN OLIVE OIL
4	CLOVES GARLIC, SMASHED TO A PASTE
½	TEASPOON RED PEPPER FLAKES (APPROXIMATELY)
2	POUNDS SPAGHETTI
¼	CUP COARSELY CHOPPED FRESH ITALIAN PARSLEY

In a shallow bowl, cover the anchovies with the milk and let soak for 10 minutes. (This reduces the saltiness of the fish.) Drain well and finely chop.

In a small, dry skillet, toast the breadcrumbs over medium heat until golden brown, about 4 minutes. Transfer the crumbs to a plate and let cool.

Heat the olive oil in a large skillet over medium heat. Add the garlic and cook until golden, about 2 minutes. Remove the pan from the heat and discard the garlic.

Add the red pepper flakes and anchovies to the skillet. Mash the anchovies against the side of the pan with a wooden spoon until a smooth purée forms. Cook the mixture over medium-low heat for 1 minute. Remove from the heat.

Bring a large pot of salted water to a boil. Add the spaghetti and cook until al dente, 7 minutes. Drain the pasta, reserving 3 tablespoons of the cooking water. Add the water to the anchovy sauce and warm over medium-low heat. Add the pasta to the skillet and toss to coat with the sauce.

Transfer the pasta to a warm serving bowl, toss with the breadcrumbs and parsley, and serve immediately.

Meanwhile, in a small skillet, melt the butter over medium heat. When it begins to foam, add the green onions, lemon zest, and red pepper flakes. Cook, stirring, for 3 minutes. Keep warm.

Transfer the stuffed fillets to a warm platter, pour the hot sauce over the top of them, and serve.

rotolini di sogliola
sole rollups

Delicate sole retains its moistness when rolled up with a parsley-garlic filling and served with a hot lemon-butter sauce.

- 4 **POUNDS SOLE FILLETS**
- 1 **CUP FRESH ITALIAN PARSLEY, CHOPPED**
- 3 **CLOVES GARLIC, MINCED**
  SEA SALT
  FRESHLY GROUND BLACK PEPPER
- 1 **STICK (8 TABLESPOONS) UNSALTED BUTTER**
- 3 **GREEN ONIONS, MINCED**
  GRATED ZEST OF 1 LEMON
- ¼ **TEASPOON RED PEPPER FLAKES**

Preheat the oven to 300F. Butter a large baking dish. Lay the sole fillets out flat on a work surface.

In a small bowl, mix together the parsley, garlic, and sea salt and black pepper to taste. Sprinkle a thin layer of this mixture over each fillet. Roll up each fillet and place in the prepared baking dish in a single layer, seam side down. Cover the dish with aluminum foil and bake for 30 minutes.

carciofi ripieni
stuffed artichokes

Stuffed artichokes was the very first contorno that my grandmother taught me to make. If you like, instead of making the breadcrumbs yourself with the bread slices, olive oil, parsley, and garlic, you can substitute 2 cups store-bought Italian breadcrumbs.

8	LARGE ARTICHOKES
1	LEMON, CUT IN HALF
4	SLICES WHITE BREAD
¾	CUP EXTRA-VIRGIN OLIVE OIL
¾	CUP FRESH ITALIAN PARSLEY LEAVES, CHOPPED
4	CLOVES GARLIC, CHOPPED
	SEA SALT
	FRESHLY GROUND BLACK PEPPER

Cut off the stems of the artichokes so you are able to stand them up. Remove and discard the tough outer leaves. Cut the sharp tips off the remaining leaves with scissors. Slice off about 1/2 inch from the top of each artichoke. Open the artichokes gently with your hands. Remove the fuzzy chokes with a knife or melon baller. Wash the artichokes under cold running water. Rub the lemon halves all over the cut portions of the artichokes to prevent discoloring. Set the artichokes, cut part down, on paper towels.

If you're making your own breadcrumbs, remove the crusts from the bread. Chop the bread into small pieces and place in a medium bowl. Add 1/2 cup of the olive oil and the parsley, garlic, and sea salt and pepper to taste. Mix together well.

Work the breadcrumbs between the leaves and into the centers of the artichokes. Stand the artichokes up in a saucepan just large enough to accommodate them. Pour 1 inch of water into the pan. Drizzle the remaining 1/4 cup olive oil over the artichokes. Cook the artichokes over medium heat, covered, for 40 to 60 minutes, depending on their size. The artichokes will turn bright green. If the water evaporates, add a little more. When the artichokes are cooked, you want to have 4 to 5 tablespoons sauce left in the pan. If you have too much liquid, remove the artichokes and boil it down.

Spoon the sauce over the artichokes and serve.

torta di arancio

orange cake

Dense and refreshing, this cake gets an extra flavor punch from the addition of rum.

- 1 **CUP CHOPPED MIXED CANDIED ORANGE AND LEMON PEEL**
- 2 **JIGGERS RUM**
- 1½ **STICKS (12 TABLESPOONS) UNSALTED BUTTER, SOFTENED**
- ¾ **CUP SUGAR**
- 3 **LARGE EGGS**
- ½ **TEASPOON GRATED ORANGE ZEST**
- 1 **CUP PASTRY FLOUR**
- ¾ **CUP ALL-PURPOSE FLOUR**

In a small bowl, soak the candied orange and lemon peel in the rum.

Preheat the oven to 400F. Line the side and bottom of a 10-inch springform pan with buttered parchment paper.

In a large bowl, beat together the butter and sugar until smooth and creamy. Add the eggs, one at a time, beating well after each addition. Stir in the orange zest. Add the steeped candied peels, as well as any of the remaining rum, and stir to incorporate.

On a sheet of waxed paper, sift the two flours together. Add to the batter and stir until smooth. Pour the batter into the prepared springform pan and bake for 45 minutes, or until golden on top. Transfer to a rack and let cool for 30 minutes before cutting.

"buon vino fa buon sangue!"

good wine makes good blood!

MENU

19

SERVES 8 TO 10

bruschetta siciliana
sicilian bruschetta with mixed olives

....

pasta ai frutti di mare
pasta with shellfish

....

vitello tonnato
veal in tuna sauce

....

pomodori ripieni
tomatoes stuffed with breadcrumbs

....

maritozzi
roman sugar cake with fruit and nuts

My daughter once dreadfully embarrassed my entire family
when she asked for veal in a fish restaurant in Sicily. I'm
still amazed we weren't expelled from the premises right
then and there! So, this menu combines veal and fish—to
make everyone happy. The tuna sauce, a classic in Italian
cuisine, can be made ahead of time.

bruschetta siciliana

sicilian bruschetta with mixed olives

Serve these delicious little slices of heaven with a good red Sicilian wine such as Nero d'Avola.

- ½ CUP PITTED SICILIAN BLACK OLIVES
- ½ CUP PITTED SICILIAN GREEN OLIVES
- ¼ CUP CHOPPED CARROTS
- 4 CLOVES GARLIC, ROASTED, UNPEELED, IN A 350F OVEN UNTIL SOFT, THEN SQUEEZED FROM THE PEEL
- 1 TABLESPOON CAPERS
- 1 TABLESPOON CHOPPED FRESH OREGANO
- 1 TABLESPOON CHOPPED FRESH ITALIAN PARSLEY
- 3 TABLESPOONS EXTRA-VIRGIN OLIVE OIL
- SEA SALT
- FRESHLY GROUND BLACK PEPPER
- 1 LOAF ITALIAN BREAD, SLICED IN ¼-INCH SLICES, TOASTED

Place the olives, carrots, garlic, capers, herbs, olive oil, and sea salt and pepper to taste in a blender or food processor and process until the olives are chopped.

Spread the mixture on toasted bread and serve.

pasta ai frutti di mare

pasta with shellfish

In this recipe, the frutti di mare (fruit of the sea) are shrimp and bay scallops, served with linguine in a garlicky white wine sauce. Simple and incredible!

- 2 POUNDS LINGUINE
- ¾ CUP EXTRA-VIRGIN OLIVE OIL
- 6 CLOVES GARLIC, FINELY CHOPPED
- 2 POUNDS MEDIUM SHRIMP, PEELED AND DEVEINED
- 2 POUNDS BAY SCALLOPS
- SEA SALT
- FRESHLY GROUND BLACK PEPPER
- 1 CUP WHITE WINE
- FINELY CHOPPED FRESH BASIL FOR GARNISH

Bring a large pot of salted water to a boil. Add the linguine and cook until al dente, 5 minutes.

Meanwhile, in a large skillet over medium heat, heat the olive oil. Add the garlic and cook, stirring, for 1 minute. Add the shrimp and scallops and cook, turning the seafood as needed, just until the shrimp turn bright pink. Season to taste with salt and pepper. Add the wine and simmer for 2 minutes.

Ladle out and save about a cup of the pasta cooking water. Drain the linguine, transfer it to the skillet, and cook for 1 minute, tossing it with the seafood. If the pasta seems dry, toss in a bit of the saved pasta cooking water to loosen. Transfer to a large warm pasta bowl and garnish with basil.

vitello tonnato
veal in tuna sauce

Tuna sauce for veal? Absolutely! It's a classic pairing—neutral, delicate veal topped with a lemony tuna sauce rich with eggs (be aware, this dish contains raw eggs) and salty from the addition of anchovies and capers. Be sure to use imported canned tuna from Italy packed in olive oil.

VEAL

- 1   **BONELESS LEG OF VEAL (2 POUNDS)**
- 10   **WHOLE BLACK PEPPERCORNS**
- 2   **BAY LEAVES**
- 1   **ONION, SLICED**
- ½   **TEASPOON SEA SALT**
- 3   **CUPS VEGETABLE STOCK**
- 1   **CUP DRY WHITE WINE**

TUNA SAUCE

- 1   **CAN (6 OUNCES) TUNA PACKED IN OLIVE OIL, WELL DRAINED**
- 6   **ANCHOVY FILLETS**
- 1   **CUP EXTRA-VIRGIN OLIVE OIL**
- 2   **LARGE EGG YOLKS**
- 1   **TABLESPOON FRESH LEMON JUICE**
-   **SEA SALT**
-   **FRESHLY GROUND BLACK PEPPER**
-   **LEMON WEDGES**
- 4   **TEASPOONS CAPERS**

Place the veal in a large pot with the pepper-corns, bay leaves, onion, and salt. Add the stock and wine. Bring to a boil. Reduce the heat to medium and simmer for 1 hour, covered, or until knife-tender.

Remove the veal from the stock, let it cool, then refrigerate until fully chilled, about 45 minutes.

Make the tuna sauce: In a small bowl using a fork, work the tuna and anchovies together until they have the consistency of a paste. Work in 2 tablespoons of the olive oil, and then the egg yolks. Transfer the mixture to a blender and process until smooth. Add the lemon juice. Slowly add the remaining olive oil, running the blender until the sauce is thick and smooth. Add sea salt and pepper to taste. Refrigerate the sauce until ready to use.

Slice the chilled veal into ¼-inch-thick slices and arrange on a serving platter, along with the lemon wedges. Pour the tuna sauce over the veal and top with the capers.

"patti chiari, amicizie lunghe."

clear agreements, long friendships.

pomodori ripieni

tomatoes stuffed with breadcrumbs

My mother always made these for us growing up and there was never a crumb left. Ripe tomatoes stuffed with crisp breadcrumbs, showered with Parmigiano, and run under the broiler until bubbly and golden—what's not to like?

- 2 CUPS ITALIAN BREADCRUMBS
- ½ CUP EXTRA-VIRGIN OLIVE OIL, PLUS MORE FOR DRIZZLING
- SEA SALT
- FRESHLY GROUND BLACK PEPPER
- 8 RIPE MEDIUM TOMATOES
- 1 CUP GRATED PARMIGIANO-REGGIANO

In a medium bowl, combine the breadcrumbs, olive oil, and sea salt and pepper to taste.

Cut the tops off the tomatoes and, with a spoon, scrape out the pulp. Discard the seeds. Chop the pulp and mix it into the breadcrumb mixture.

Preheat the broiler.

Fill each of the tomatoes with the breadcrumb mixture. Set the tomatoes in a broiler pan. Drizzle a little olive oil over the top of each one. Sprinkle with the Parmigiano. Broil the tomatoes until they are tender and the breadcrumbs and cheese are golden, about 6 minutes.

maritozzi

roman sugar cake with fruit and nuts

Maritozzi are individual cakes full of nuts, raisins, and candied orange peel and finished with a sugary glaze. They're also wonderful in the morning with a cappuccino.

- 1 PACKAGE ACTIVE DRY YEAST
- 2 CUPS PASTRY FLOUR, SIFTED
- ¼ TEASPOON SEA SALT
- 2 TABLESPOONS EXTRA-VIRGIN OLIVE OIL
- 3½ TABLESPOONS SUGAR
- 3 CUPS SEEDLESS RAISINS
- 1 TABLESPOON CHOPPED PINE NUTS OR WALNUTS
- 1 TABLESPOON FINELY CUT CANDIED ORANGE PEEL

In a small bowl, combine the yeast and 2 tablespoons lukewarm water and let stand for 5 minutes. Add another tablespoon of water and 2 tablespoons of the flour, mix well, and let stand in a warm place until doubled in size, about 15 minutes.

Pour the remaining flour onto a pastry board and form a well in the center. Place the risen dough, salt, olive oil, and 1 tablespoon water in the well. Knead it well to make a soft, pliable dough. Continue to knead until the dough no longer sticks to the board or your fingers. Sprinkle 2½ tablespoons of the sugar over the dough and work it in.

Sprinkle the dough with a little flour and shape it into a ball. Place it in a bowl, cover, and let stand in a warm place for 1 hour, until double in size.

Lightly flour the pastry board. Knead the raisins, nuts, and orange peel into the dough until they are well distributed. Roll the dough into a thick tube approximately 3 inches wide and 18 inches long and cut into 12 slices. Shape each slice into an egg shape. Set the dough eggs on a buttered baking sheet, cover, and let stand in a warm place until puffy, about 3 hours.

Preheat the oven to 450F. Bake the cakes for 7 minutes. While they are baking, mix together the remaining 1 tablespoon sugar and 1 teaspoon water. Remove the cakes from the oven and brush with the sugar mixture. Turn the oven off and return the cakes to the cooling oven for a few minutes. Serve warm or at room temperature.

MENU

20

SERVES 8 TO 10

torta di mascarpone
mascarpone cheese torte with basil pesto and sun-dried tomatoes

....

spaghetti con caccio e pepe
spaghetti with cheese and black pepper

....

pollo cacciatore
hunter's chicken

....

insalata verde
green salad

....

torta della mamma con rhum
my mom's rum cake

There's nothing like reliving memories with your children, and we do it all the time. This is one of the great menus that brings back images of our picnics in the olive groves of Tuscany on cool fall afternoons when we would see old Italian hunters on their way to la caccia (the hunt).

torta di mascarpone

mascarpone cheese torte with basil pesto and sun-dried tomatoes

This is an Italian twist on the popular combination of goat cheese, pesto, and sun-dried tomatoes—tart and creamy mascarpone taking the place of the goat cheese.

- 16 OUNCES MASCARPONE
- ½ CUP PESTO, STORE-BOUGHT OR HOMEMADE (PAGE 98)
- ¼ CUP OIL-PACKED SUN-DRIED TOMATOES, DRAINED AND CHOPPED
- TOASTED BREAD SLICES

Line a 2-cup mold with a piece of cheesecloth or plastic wrap so that it hangs over the edge of the mold. Spread one-third of the mascarpone in the bottom of the mold and press down to get out any air bubbles. Spread half the pesto over the mascarpone. Sprinkle with the chopped tomatoes. Spread half the remaining mascarpone over the tomatoes and top with the remaining pesto. Spread a final layer of mascarpone over the top.

At this point, you can serve the torta or refrigerate it for up to 24 hours. To unmold the torta, set a small plate on top of the mold and invert the plate and mold. Remove the mold and gently peel away the cheesecloth.

Serve with toasted bread slices.

spaghetti con caccio e pepe

spaghetti with cheese and black pepper

A Roman favorite, please give this unusual pasta preparation a try. Salty Pecorino and generous gratings of fresh black pepper combine for unforgettable flavor.

- 2 POUNDS SPAGHETTI
- 1 CUP GRATED PECORINO ROMANO
- 2 HEAPING TABLESPOONS FRESHLY GROUND BLACK PEPPER
- SEA SALT

Bring a large pot of salted water to a boil. Add the spaghetti and cook until al dente, 7 minutes.

Drain the pasta, reserving 3 tablespoons of the cooking water. Transfer the pasta to a large serving bowl and toss well with the reserved water and the cheese, pepper, and sea salt to taste. Serve immediately.

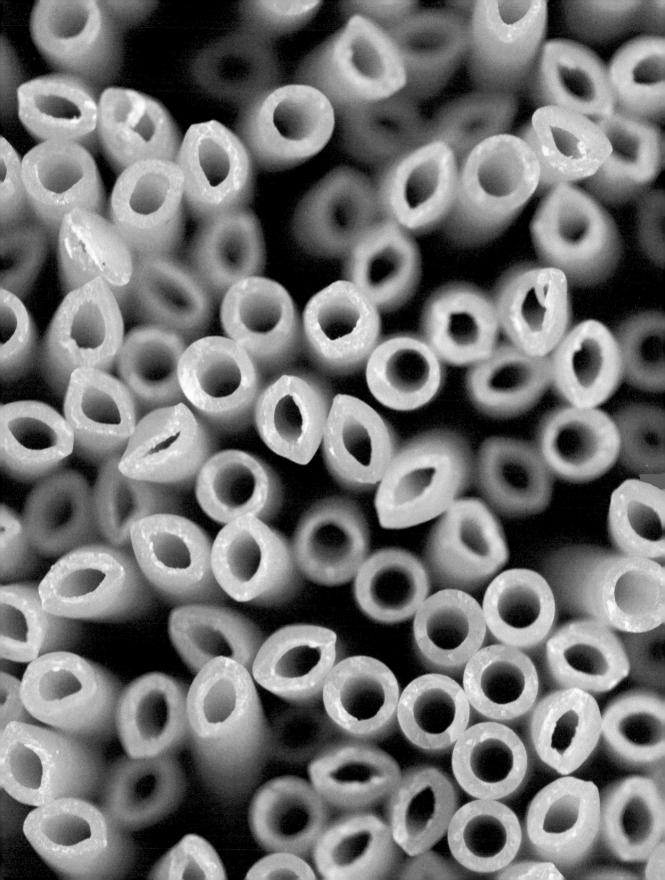

pollo cacciatore
hunter's chicken

Chicken cacciatore is rustic Italian cooking at its most satisfying. Any extra sauce can be frozen and used another day.

2–3	SMALL CHICKENS, EACH CUT INTO 8 SERVING PIECES
	SEA SALT
	FRESHLY GROUND BLACK PEPPER
1½	CUPS ALL-PURPOSE FLOUR
½	CUP EXTRA-VIRGIN OLIVE OIL
5	ONIONS, CUT IN HALF, THEN SLICED INTO PAPER-THIN HALF-MOONS
4	CLOVES GARLIC, CHOPPED
2	LARGE BELL PEPPERS, SEEDED AND CUT INTO STRIPS
1	CUP RED WINE
1	CAN (28 OUNCES) CHOPPED TOMATOES (PREFERABLY SAN MARZANO) WITH THEIR JUICE
2	CUPS SLICED BUTTON MUSHROOMS

Season the chicken with sea salt and pepper and dredge lightly in the flour.

Heat the olive oil in a deep 12-inch Dutch oven over high heat. Working in batches, brown the chicken on all sides, about 10 minutes per batch. Transfer the chicken to paper towels to drain.

Add the onions, garlic, and bell peppers to the skillet and cook over medium-high heat until the onions are translucent, about 2 minutes. Add the wine and deglaze the pan, scraping up any browned bits from the bottom. Reduce the wine for 3 minutes. Stir in the tomatoes. Return the chicken to the pan. Cover and simmer for 40 minutes.

Add the mushrooms and simmer, uncovered, until they are tender and the chicken is cooked all the way through, about another 15 minutes. Season with salt and pepper to taste.

insalata verde
green salad

This salad is the perfect counterpoint to the cacciatore—peppery, slightly bitter, and refreshing.

1	MEDIUM HEAD BIBB LETTUCE, SEPARATED INTO LEAVES AND CUT INTO STRIPS
1	HEAD GREEN ENDIVE, SEPARATED INTO LEAVES AND CUT INTO STRIPS
1	BUNCH WATERCRESS, HEAVY STEMS REMOVED
½	TEASPOON SEA SALT
¼	CUP BALSAMIC VINEGAR
¾	CUP EXTRA-VIRGIN OLIVE OIL
	FRESHLY GROUND BLACK PEPPER

Place the lettuce, endive, and watercress in a large salad bowl.

In a small bowl, dissolve the salt in the vinegar and let stand for 2 minutes. Pour over the greens and toss. Add the olive oil, toss again and season to taste with pepper.

torta della mamma con rhum

my mom's rum cake

This was my father's favorite cake. The rum gives the cake an irresistible flavor as well as keeping it moist.

CAKE

- 1 CUP CHOPPED PECANS
- 1 BOX (18 OUNCES) DUNCAN HINES BUTTER GOLDEN CAKE MIX
- 1 BOX (3.35 OUNCES) VANILLA PUDDING MIX
- ½ CUP LIGHT RUM
- 1 STICK (8 TABLESPOONS) UNSALTED BUTTER, SOFTENED, PLUS ADDITIONAL TO GREASE PAN
- 4 LARGE EGGS

GLAZE

- 1¼ STICKS (10 TABLESPOONS) UNSALTED BUTTER
- 1 CUP SUGAR
- ¼ CUP RUM

Preheat the oven to 325F. Butter and flour an 8-cup Bundt pan, tapping out any excess flour. Sprinkle the pecans over the bottom of the pan.

In a large bowl, stir together the cake mix and pudding mix. Add the rum, butter, eggs, one at a time, and ½ cup water and beat for 2 minutes. Pour the batter into the prepared Bundt pan. Bake for 50 to 60 minutes, until a toothpick or cake tester comes out clean. Transfer to a rack to cool for 1 hour. Flip onto a platter.

Make the glaze: Melt the butter in a medium saucepan. Add the sugar and stir until it dissolves. Stir in the rum and ¼ cup water. Boil, stirring, for 3 to 4 minutes.

Poke holes in the cake with a toothpick. Pour the glaze evenly over the cake and let stand 30 minutes before serving.

"finche c'è vita, c'è speranza."

as long as there's life, there's hope.

MENU

21

SERVES 8 TO 10

caponata
sicilian eggplant appetizer

....

torta di maccheroni
macaroni and meat pie

....

pesce ripieno di finocchio
baked whole fish with fennel

....

frittata di verdure
vegetable omelet

....

sfogliatelle
ricotta turnovers

Caponata was a constant on my nana's dinner table. It not only incorporates delicious vegetables, but can be used as an antipasto or as a sauce on pasta--either hot or cold. My nana's secret ingredient? Pitted Sicilian green olives (now readily available in supermarkets). They add a tangy contrast to the sweet tomatoes. Caponata, by the way freezes beautifully.

caponata

sicilian eggplant appetizer

Caponata hails from Sicily but is found throughout Italy. I like to serve it slightly warm with crostini topped with melted Parmigiano-Reggiano.

2	LARGE EGGPLANTS
	COARSE SEA SALT
¼	CUP EXTRA-VIRGIN OLIVE OIL
1	ONION, CHOPPED
3	CLOVES GARLIC, SLICED
3	THIN STALKS CELERY, CUT INTO ½-INCH-THICK SLICES
1	CAN (14 TO 16 OUNCES) PEELED WHOLE TOMATOES (PREFERABLY SAN MARZANO), CHOPPED
1	CUP PITTED SICILIAN GREEN OLIVES
1	TABLESPOON SUGAR
	FINE SEA SALT
	FRESHLY GROUND BLACK PEPPER
	LIGHTLY TOASTED ITALIAN BREAD SLICES

Peel the eggplant and cut it into large cubes, approximately 1 inch square. Transfer it to a colander, generously sprinkling it with coarse salt in layers. Set the colander in a sink or over a bowl and let the eggplant drain for 30 minutes to remove excess water. Rinse the eggplant well.

In a large skillet over medium heat, heat the olive oil. Add the onion and garlic and cook, stirring a few times, until the onion is transparent; don't let the onion or garlic brown. Add the eggplant and cook, stirring, for 10 minutes. Add the celery and cook, stirring occasionally, until the eggplant is soft. If the eggplant begins to stick to the pan, adjust the heat. Add the tomatoes, olives, and sugar, season to taste with the fine sea salt and pepper, and cook another 10 minutes, stirring to prevent sticking.

Transfer to a serving bowl and serve hot or at room temperature accompanied by lightly toasted Italian bread.

torta di maccheroni

macaroni and meat pie

This savory pie of mushrooms and pasta has its roots in Italian peasant country cooking. It contains only a little bit of meat, and the filling gets its smooth, velvety texture from the besciamella.

PIE PASTRY

2	CUPS ALL-PURPOSE FLOUR
1	TEASPOON SEA SALT
10⅔	TABLESPOONS UNSALTED BUTTER, SOFTENED IF MIXING BY HAND; COLD IF USING A FOOD PROCESSOR

FILLING

½	STICK (4 TABLESPOONS) UNSALTED BUTTER
½	POUND PORK LOIN, FINELY CHOPPED
1	ONION, FINELY CHOPPED
½	CUP DRY WHITE WINE
8	OUNCES BUTTON MUSHROOMS, SLICED
1	CAN (28 OUNCES) CRUSHED TOMATOES (PREFERABLY SAN MARZANO)
2	TABLESPOONS CHOPPED FRESH ITALIAN PARSLEY
	SEA SALT
	FRESHLY GROUND BLACK PEPPER

BESCIAMELLA

1	STICK (8 TABLESPOONS) UNSALTED BUTTER
¼	CUP (4 TABLESPOONS) UNBLEACHED FLOUR
3	CUPS WHOLE MILK
½	TEASPOON SEA SALT
¼	TEASPOON BLACK PEPPER

1	POUND MACARONI, SUCH AS RIGATONI OR PENNE
1	LARGE EGG, LIGHTLY BEATEN

Make the pie pastry: In a medium bowl, combine the flour and salt. Add the butter. With your fingertips or a pastry blender, work the butter into the flour until the mixture is crumbly. Place the dough on a lightly floured work surface and work it into 2 balls, one a little larger than the other. Wrap them in plastic wrap and refrigerate for at least 1 hour.

Make the filling: In a large skillet, melt 2 tablespoons of the butter over medium heat. Add the pork and onion and cook, stirring until the pork is no longer pink. Increase the heat to high and add the wine. When the wine has reduced by half, cover the skillet and reduce the heat to medium. Cook for an additional 10 minutes.

In a large skillet, melt the remaining 2 tablespoons of butter over high heat. Add the mushrooms and cook, stirring a few times, until golden, 2 to 3 minutes. Reduce the heat to low. Add the pork mixture, tomatoes, and parsley, season to taste with sea salt and pepper, and simmer for 5 to 10 minutes.

Make the besciamella: Melt the butter in a medium saucepan over medium heat, add the flour and stir until smooth. Slowly add the milk, whisking constantly to keep any lumps from forming. Stir until mixture thickens to the point that it coats the back of a wooden spoon. Season with salt and pepper.

Preheat the oven to 375F. Butter a 10-inch springform pan.

Bring a large pot of salted water to a boil. Add the macaroni and cook until al dente (if using penne, cook for 7 minutes; if using rigatoni, cook for 8 minutes). Drain, pour into a large bowl, and mix with the besciamella and the pork mixture.

Assemble the pie: On a lightly floured work surface, roll out the larger ball of dough to a 14-inch circle. Fit it into the prepared springform pan. Pour the macaroni mixture into the crust and level the top with a spatula.

Roll out the remaining ball of dough to a 10$\frac{1}{2}$-inch circle. Place it on top of the filling. Trim the edges and crimp the bottom and top crusts together to seal. Brush the top crust with the

beaten egg and, using a fork, puncture the crust in 5 or 6 places so steam can escape.

Bake until the crust is golden, 40 to 50 minutes. Let stand 5 to 10 minutes in the pan. Remove the side of the springform. Place the pie on a large round serving platter and cut into wedges.

"fra il dire e il fare, c'è di mezzo il mare."

between saying and doing, there's an ocean.

pesce ripieno
di finocchio

baked whole fish with fennel

*The fennel bulbs and fronds perfume the fish with
their anise flavor.*

1	WHOLE FISH OF YOUR CHOICE (BRANZINO, SEA BASS, TROUT, OR SIMILAR; 3 TO 4 POUNDS), CLEANED
	SEA SALT
	FRESHLY GROUND BLACK PEPPER
2	FENNEL BULBS, WITH PLENTY OF FRONDS
½	RED ONION, THINLY SLICED
3	TABLESPOONS CHOPPED FRESH BASIL
3	BAY LEAVES
	JUICE OF 1 LEMON
4	TABLESPOONS UNSALTED BUTTER, CUT INTO SMALL PIECES
	EXTRA-VIRGIN OLIVE OIL

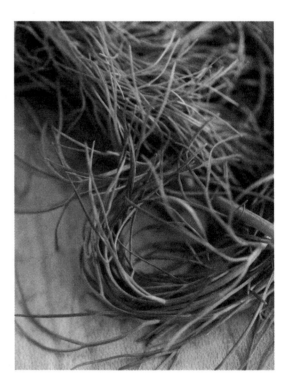

Preheat the oven to 400F.

Place the fish on 2 large pieces of aluminum foil.
Rub it inside and out with sea salt and pepper.

Trim the bottoms of the fennel bulbs. Cut the
fronds from the stalks. Cut off and discard the
heavy stalks. Slice the fennel bulbs.

Place the fennel fronds and sliced fennel, onion,
basil, and bay leaves inside the fish. Pour the
lemon juice over the vegetables and dot with the
butter. Drizzle with a little olive oil.

Wrap the fish tightly in the foil and set on a
baking sheet. Bake until the skin is crisp and
browned (also insert a knife to be sure the flesh
is opaque), about 30 minutes. Transfer to a
platter and serve.

frittata di verdure
vegetable omelet

My maternal grandfather was known for his frittatas. Every Sunday morning we would wait to see what kind he would make. Mushroom? Zucchini? Spinach? It didn't matter—they were all delicious. Frittata di Verdure combines a variety of vegetables and cheese for a hearty contorno.

1	POUND WHOLE SPINACH LEAVES
4	LARGE EGGS
½	CUP MILK
2	TABLESPOONS HEAVY CREAM
1	POUND BUTTON MUSHROOMS, SLICED
1	HOT RED CHILE, CHOPPED
2	CLOVES GARLIC, CRUSHED
2	TABLESPOONS UNSALTED BUTTER
2	TABLESPOONS EXTRA-VIRGIN OLIVE OIL
¼	CUP SHREDDED FONTINA
2	TABLESPOONS GRATED PARMIGIANO-REGGIANO

Add the spinach and 2 teaspoons water to a medium saucepan and cook over medium heat for 5 minutes, until wilted. Drain thoroughly, squeezing out excess water, and chop.

In a large bowl, beat the eggs. Stir in the milk, cream, spinach, mushrooms, red chile and garlic.

In a medium skillet, melt the butter with the olive oil over medium heat. Pour the egg mixture into the skillet and sprinkle evenly with the cheeses. Cook, without stirring, until the underside is golden, 5 to 7 minutes. (The egg mixture will still be liquid but the frittata will be firm underneath.) Flip the frittata onto a plate and slide gently back into the skillet to cook on the other side.

sfogliatelle
ricotta turnovers

Uniquely flaky, with their many layers of light, airy pastry, sfogliatelle are filled with a rich, sweetened ricotta mixture studded with candied fruit.

¾	CUP SEMOLINA FLOUR
	PINCH OF SEA SALT
1	CUP RICOTTA
¾	CUP GRANULATED SUGAR
1	LARGE EGG, BEATEN
¾	CUP CANDIED CITRUS PEEL, CHOPPED
1	TEASPOON VANILLA EXTRACT
1	PACKAGE FROZEN FILO DOUGH, THAWED
	ABOUT 4 TEASPOONS MELTED UNSALTED BUTTER
	CONFECTIONERS' SUGAR

Preheat the oven to 375F.

In a small saucepan, bring 2 cups water to a boil. Stir in the semolina. Add the salt and stir briskly with a wooden spoon for 5 minutes. Transfer to a large bowl and let cool.

In a medium bowl, mix together the ricotta, granulated sugar, beaten egg, candied peel, and vanilla. Add to the semolina and beat until smooth.

On a work surface, stack 8 sheets of filo on top of each other, brushing each sheet with melted butter before adding the next one. Cut the stacked filo into 8 squares. Fill each square with 1 tablespoon of the ricotta mixture. Fold each square over to form a triangle and seal the edges with water. Repeat until all the filo dough is used.

Transfer the triangles to a baking sheet and bake until golden, 10 to 15 minutes. Dust with confectioners' sugar and serve warm or at room temperature.

MENU

panini napolitani
neapolitan anchovy and cheese sandwiches

···

lasagne al forno
real italian lasagne

···

pollo alla vesuvio
chicken vesuvio

···

porri arrostiti
roasted leeks

···

zabaglione con fragole
italian custard with strawberries

My nana's signature dish was her lasagne, the Italian American version with ricotta and mozzarella. It was amazing. But when I moved back to Italy as an adult and ordered lasagne in a trattoria, I realized that the only cheese used there was Parmigiano, and a creamy besciamella made the lasagne velvety and decadent. There is nothing like this real Italian lasagne.

panini napolitani

neapolitan anchovy and cheese sandwiches

Anchovies and mozzarella are hallmarks of Neapolitan cooking, and they are terrific together in this antipasto.

- 16 SLICES THIN WHITE BREAD
- 8 OUNCES MOZZARELLA, THINLY SLICED
- 16 ANCHOVY FILLETS
- 1 STICK (8 TABLESPOONS) UNSALTED BUTTER

Cut the crusts off the bread and cut the slices in half. Place a piece of mozzarella and 2 anchovy fillets on each of 8 half slices of bread. Top with the other half slices to make 16 half sandwiches.

Melt the butter in a large skillet over medium heat. Fry the sandwiches in two batches, about 3 minutes per side. Serve immediately.

lasagne al forno

real italian lasagne

Italian American lasagne is a cheesy affair—layers of ricotta, Parmigiano-Reggiano, and mozzarella. Authentic lasagne al forno gets its velvety texture from besciamella, or white sauce, which is layered with meat sauce and a sprinkling of Parmigiano. This dish can be assembled the day before and refrigerated.

BASIC LASAGNE NOODLES

- 4 CUPS UNBLEACHED ALL-PURPOSE FLOUR
- 3 EXTRA-LARGE EGGS
- 1 TEASPOON SEA SALT
- 4 TEASPOONS EXTRA-VIRGIN OLIVE OIL

BESCIAMELLA

- 2 STICKS (16 TABLESPOONS) UNSALTED BUTTER
- ½ CUP (8 TABLESPOONS) UNBLEACHED FLOUR
- 6 CUPS WHOLE MILK
- 1 TEASPOON SEA SALT
- ½ TEASPOON FRESHLY GROUND BLACK PEPPER
- ½ TEASPOON GRATED NUTMEG

- 5–6 CUPS GRANDMA CAPONIGRI'S RAGU SAUCE (PAGE 66)
- 2 CUPS GRATED PARMIGIANO-REGGIANO

Make the pasta dough: Place the flour in a mound on a pasta board or wooden cutting board. Make a well in the center of the flour and crack the eggs into the well. Add the sea salt and olive oil to the well. Using a fork, begin incorporating the flour into the eggs and oil. After the ingredients are all mixed together, knead the dough with your hands until it develops an elastic consistency.

Break away a small ball of the dough, about the size of your palm, and flatten it. Feed the dough into a pasta machine and continue to run it through the machine until the strips are 4 to 5 inches wide and ⅛ inch thick. As you run the dough through the machine, it will become increasingly more elastic. Cut the strips into 12-inch-long pieces. Repeat this process for the rest of the dough.

Bring a large pot of salted water to a boil. Cook the lasagne noodles in batches, about two pieces at a time, for about 30 seconds. Using silicone-tipped tongs, transfer the pasta to a colander and set under cold running water to stop the cooking. Lay the cooked noodles out flat on a cotton kitchen towel. I also cover them with towels to keep them from drying out.

Meanwhile, make the besciamella: Melt the butter in a medium saucepan over medium heat, add the flour and stir until smooth. Slowly add the milk, whisking constantly to keep any lumps from forming. Stir until the mixture thickens to the point that it coats the back of a wooden spoon. You can add a little more milk if it is too thick. Season with salt, pepper and nutmeg.

Preheat the oven to 400F.

Assemble the lasagne: Into a baking pan at least 13 by 9 by 2½ inches, ladle a little of the ragu and tilt the pan to coat the bottom. Cover with a double or triple layer of lasagne noodles. Spread the noodles with another layer of ragu, a layer of besciamella, and a sprinkling of Parmigiano. Repeat the layers until the pan is full. Top the lasagne with a thick layer of Parmigiano. Bake until bubbly and golden on top, about 30 minutes. Let stand 5 to 10 minutes before serving.

pollo alla vesuvio

chicken vesuvio

This simple stove-top braise is incredibly delicious. Just be sure to brown the chicken and potatoes well before proceeding with the recipe—the caramelization adds lots of flavor and the browned bits stuck to the bottom of the pan become the basis of a fantastic pan sauce.

- ¼ **CUP EXTRA-VIRGIN OLIVE OIL TO COAT THE BOTTOM OF THE PANS**
- 2 **CHICKENS, CUT INTO 8 SERVING PIECES**
  SEA SALT
  FRESHLY GROUND BLACK PEPPER
- 3 **POUNDS SMALL RED POTATOES, CUT IN HALF**
- 4 **LARGE CLOVES GARLIC, SLICED**
- 1 **CUP DRY WHITE WINE**
- 1 **CUP CHICKEN STOCK OR REDUCED-SODIUM CANNED BROTH**
- 1½ **TEASPOONS DRIED OREGANO**
- 1 **TEASPOON DRIED THYME**
- 2 **CANS (14 OUNCES EACH) ARTICHOKE HEARTS PACKED IN WATER (IF MARINATED, RINSE WELL)**
- 2 **TABLESPOONS UNSALTED BUTTER**

Note: Since all the chicken will not cook properly in one vessel, you will need 2 large Dutch ovens or 2 large oven-proof frying pans and you will be dividing the ingredients between the pans. Heat the oil in the Dutch ovens or pans over high heat. Sprinkle the chicken with salt and pepper. In batches, brown the chicken on all sides until golden. Remove the pieces to a plate as they brown. Add the potatoes and cook until the cut sides are golden, about 10 minutes. Add the garlic and stir for 1 minute. Add the wine and scrape up the browned bits from the bottom of the pot and allow to reduce for 3 minutes. Add the stock, oregano, and thyme and return the chicken to the pots. Stir everything gently until the stock mixture boils.

Preheat the oven to 450.

Cover the Dutch ovens and bake the chicken until it is cooked through, about 20 minutes. Transfer the chicken and potatoes to a warm platter and cover with aluminum foil to keep hot.

Add the artichokes to the pot, covered, and simmer until heated through, about 4 minutes. Reduce the heat to low and stir in the butter. Pour the sauce over the chicken, artichokes and potatoes and serve.

"alla famiglia!"

forever family!

porri arrostiti

roasted leeks

Roasting concentrates the sugars in vegetables, and leeks are no exception. The balsamic vinegar provides even more complex flavor.

- 4 **LEEKS**
- 3 **TABLESPOONS EXTRA-VIRGIN OLIVE OIL**
- 2 **TEASPOONS BALSAMIC VINEGAR**
- **SEA SALT**
- **FRESHLY GROUND BLACK PEPPER**

Preheat the oven to 400F.

Trim the roots off the leeks and trim off about 2 inches of the greens. Cut the leeks in half lengthwise, stopping just short of cutting them all the way through at the bulb, so that each one remains held together. Rinse the leeks thoroughly under cold running water to remove all the grit. Dry as thoroughly as you can.

Set the leeks on a baking sheet and brush them liberally with the olive oil. Roast them until knife-tender, about 20 minutes.

Remove the leeks from the oven and brush with the vinegar. Season with sea salt and pepper to taste and serve hot or warm.

zabaglione con fragole

italian custard with strawberries

This fluffy, egg-rich custard is luscious and decadent!

- 8 **LARGE EGG YOLKS**
- ½ **CUP SUGAR**
- ¾ **CUP DRY MARSALA, SHERRY, OR PORT**
- 1 **QUART STRAWBERRIES, WASHED AND CUT IN HALVES**

In a large glass or stainless-steel bowl or in the top of a double boiler, using an electric mixer, beat the egg yolks and sugar together until pale and thick.

Set the bowl or double boiler top over a pan of simmering water (don't let the water touch the bottom of the bowl and don't let the water come to a boil). Add the Marsala slowly, beating constantly. Continue to beat until the mixture triples in volume and is soft and fluffy, 4 to 6 minutes.

Spoon the zabaglione into individual dessert glasses. Top with strawberries and serve immediately.

MENU

23

SERVES 8 TO 10

peperoni arrotolati e ripieni
sicilian rolled peppers

···

zuppa di farro
barley soup

···

dentice alla livornese
red snapper in chunky tomato sauce

···

tortino di patate e prosciutto
potato and prosciutto casserole

···

granita al caffè
coffee ice

Simplicity is one of the hallmarks of Italian cooking, and this menu is a perfect example. Just a few simple, healthy ingredients put together in a delicious manner, and you have an unforgettable meal: grains that are good for you, a fish prepared in a unique and light manner with chunky fresh tomatoes, and simple Italian coffee, frozen for a refreshing dessert. Quintessential Italian.

peperoni arrotolati e ripieni

sicilian rolled peppers

I started roasting peppers when I was very young in my grandmother's kitchen. They were a staple in her refrigerator and made a healthy and tasty snack on a crunchy slice of Italian bread. This preparation elevates the roasted pepper to new heights, the smoky-sweet flavor of the peppers combining with salty tuna and capers for an agrodolce (sweet-savory) partnering.

6   LARGE BELL PEPPERS (2 YELLOW, 2 RED, 2 GREEN)

2   CANS (6 OUNCES EACH) ITALIAN TUNA PACKED IN OLIVE OIL, DRAINED

¼   CUP FRESH LEMON JUICE

¼   CUP EXTRA-VIRGIN OLIVE OIL

½   CUP GREEN SICILIAN OLIVES (ABOUT 12), PITTED AND CHOPPED

6   TABLESPOONS CHOPPED FRESH ITALIAN PARSLEY

3   CLOVES GARLIC, FINELY CHOPPED

2   STALKS CELERY, FINELY CHOPPED

3   TABLESPOONS CAPERS (PREFERABLY SICILIAN), RINSED AND FINELY CHOPPED

SEA SALT

FRESHLY GROUND BLACK PEPPER

Preheat the broiler.

Broil the peppers: Cover a jellyroll pan with aluminum foil. Place the peppers on the pan and broil until their skins bubble up and blacken. Carefully turn the peppers to blacken them on all sides. Remove the peppers from the oven and let cool completely. Peel the black skin from each pepper and remove their stems and seeds. Slice each pepper into 4 pieces lengthwise.

Make the filling: In a medium bowl, mix together the tuna, lemon juice, olive oil, olives, parsley, garlic, celery, and capers. Season to taste with sea salt and pepper.

Place a tablespoon of the tuna mixture on each pepper slice and roll up the slice. Place on a tray and serve.

zuppa di farro
barley soup

Though the grain farro is still unfamiliar to many Americans, it has a long history in Italy, where there is a tradition of preparing it in soups. This version is rich and satisfying, perfect for a cold winter's evening. "Farro" is actually spelt, but if you cannot find spelt, barley works beautifully.

- 1 POUND (500 GRAMS) IMPORTED FARRO (PREFERABLY FROM THE GARFAGNANA REGION OF TUSCANY)
- 1 WHITE ONION, CHOPPED
- 1 CARROT, CHOPPED
- 1 STALK CELERY, CHOPPED
- 3 CLOVES GARLIC, PEELED
- ½ CUP EXTRA-VIRGIN OLIVE OIL, PLUS ADDITIONAL FOR DRIZZLING
- 4 CUPS VEGETABLE STOCK OR REDUCED-SODIUM CANNED BROTH
- ½ TEASPOON GROUND THYME
- SEA SALT
- FRESHLY GROUND BLACK PEPPER
- ½ CUP GRATED PECORINO ROMANO

Rinse the farro in a colander under cold running water and pick over until no sand or small pebbles remain. Drain and transfer the farro to a large pot. Cover generously with water and let soak for 8 hours. Drain well.

In a large frying pan, cook the onion, carrot, celery, and garlic in the olive oil over medium heat, stirring, until soft. (Remove and discard the garlic cloves when they turn brown.)

Stir in the drained farro and cook, stirring, for 2 to 3 minutes. Add the broth and thyme and season with sea salt and pepper. Cook over medium low heat until the farro is al dente, slightly firm and a bit chewy, about 1 hour.

Serve in soup bowls, garnished with the cheese and a drizzle of extra-virgin olive oil.

dentice alla livornese
red snapper in chunky tomato sauce

This dish is my brother's favorite. "Livorno style" means the fish is prepared with a chunky sauce of tomatoes and capers. I love this sauce with red snapper, but cod and flounder also work well.

- ABOUT ¾ CUP ALL-PURPOSE FLOUR
- SEA SALT
- FRESHLY GROUND BLACK PEPPER
- 8–10 RED SNAPPER FILLETS
- ½ CUP EXTRA-VIRGIN OLIVE OIL
- 2 CLOVES GARLIC, CHOPPED
- ¼ CUP CAPERS
- 1 CAN (28 OUNCES) CRUSHED TOMATOES (PREFERABLY SAN MARZANO)
- ½ CUP WHITE WINE

Preheat the oven to 350F.

On a flat plate, season the flour with sea salt and pepper. Dredge the snapper fillets in the flour on both sides, shaking off any excess.

In a large sauté pan, heat the olive oil over medium heat. Cook the garlic and capers in the oil for about 2 minutes, stirring. Add the snapper fillets, 3 or 4 at a time, and cook until golden on both sides, 2 to 3 minutes per side. As the fillets finish cooking, place them in a large baking dish.

When all of the fillets have been transferred to the baking dish, pour the crushed tomatoes and wine into the frying pan and cook over medium heat for 10 minutes.

Pour the tomato sauce over the fillets and bake for 10 minutes, until the sauce bubbles.

tortino di patate
e prosciutto

potato and prosciutto casserole

This dish finds its roots in Emilia-Romagna. Rich and creamy, it provides a perfect counterpoint to the snapper.

> 2 POUNDS YUKON GOLD OR RED-SKINNED POTATOES

BESCIAMELLA

> ½ STICK (4 TABLESPOONS) UNSALTED BUTTER
>
> ⅛ CUP (2 TABLESPOONS) UNBLEACHED FLOUR
>
> 1½ CUPS WHOLE MILK, PLUS ADDITIONAL AS NEEDED
>
> ¼ TEASPOON SEA SALT
>
> ⅛ TEASPOON FRESHLY GROUND BLACK PEPPER

> 2 TABLESPOONS UNSALTED BUTTER FOR COATING THE BAKING DISH, PLUS 1 STICK (8 TABLESPOONS) CUT INTO CUBES
>
> ¼ POUND THINLY SLICED PROSCIUTTO DI PARMA
>
> ½ CUP GRATED PARMIGIANO-REGGIANO
>
> ½ CUP GRATED EMMENTHALER

Peel the potatoes, put them in a large pot of cold water, and boil until just soft but not crumbly, approximately 20 minutes. Drain the potatoes and let them cool.

Meanwhile, make the besciamella: Melt the butter in a medium saucepan over medium heat, add the flour and stir until smooth. Slowly add the milk, whisking constantly to keep any lumps from forming. Stir until the mixture thickens to the point that it coats the back of a wooden spoon. You can add a little more milk if it is too thick. Season with salt and pepper.

Preheat the oven to 300F and butter a large baking dish with 2 tablespoons of the butter. Cut the cooled potatoes into slices and arrange half of them in a layer over the bottom of the

dish. Layer half the prosciutto slices over the potatoes. Sprinkle with half the Parmigiano and half the Emmenthaler. Repeat the layers. Pour the besciamella evenly over the casserole. Top with the remaining butter cubes and bake for 30 minutes, or until golden and bubbly.

granita al caffè

coffee ice

Because it can be made entirely ahead of time, this is a wonderful dessert choice for entertaining.

> 1 CUP SUGAR
>
> 1 CUP FRESHLY BREWED ESPRESSO
>
> SWEETENED WHIPPED CREAM FOR GARNISH

Have ready a 9- by 13-inch metal pan.

In a medium saucepan, stir together the sugar and 2½ cups water. Bring to a boil over medium heat, stirring constantly until the sugar is dissolved.

Remove from the heat, stir in the espresso, and let cool completely.

Pour the espresso mixture into the metal pan and place in the freezer until ice crystals begin to form around the edges of the pan, approximately 15 to 20 minutes. With a fork, stir the crystals back into the liquid and return the pan to the freezer.

Repeat this procedure every 20 minutes or so until the granita is completely frozen and slushy. This should take about 2 hours.

Serve the granita in individual cups topped with a dollop of whipped cream.

MENU

24

SERVES 8 TO 10

rotolo di mozzarella con prosciutto
mozzarella roll with prosciutto

....

farfalle con prosciutto, panna e piselli
bow-tie pasta with prosciutto, cream and peas

....

petti di pollo alla panna
chicken breasts in cream

....

spinaci saltati
sautéed spinach

....

panna cotta con lamponi
cooked cream with berries

When I studied in Urbino, in the Marche region of Italy, I lived with a delightful family, the Dorsis. The mother was an outstanding cook and frequently made the dishes in this menu. At first, since I grew up with the tomato sauces of southern Italy, it took a bit of adjustment to eat a white sauce with prosciutto and cream! But I fell in love with it and have made it ever since my daughter, Felicia, was born.

rotolo di mozzarella con prosciutto

mozzarella roll with prosciutto

Mozzarella and prosciutto are a natural combination; the salty, toothsome prosciutto pairing beautifully with the creaminess of the cheese.

- 3   **LARGE FRESH MOZZARELLA BALLS**
- 12   **THIN SLICES PROSCIUTTO DI PARMA**
- ½   **CUP CHOPPED FRESH ITALIAN PARSLEY**
-     **EXTRA-VIRGIN OLIVE OIL FOR DRIZZLING**
-     **SEA SALT**

Slice the mozzarella balls in half. Gently flatten the halves as much as possible.

Place 2 slices of prosciutto on the mozzarella and scatter some of the parsley on top. Roll up the mozzarella as firmly as possible. If needed, secure each roll with a toothpick.

Refrigerate for 2 hours. Slice before serving.

Drizzle with the oil and sprinkle with sea salt to taste.

farfalle con prosciutto, panna e piselli

bow-tie pasta with prosciutto, cream and peas

I first had this dish as a high-school student studying in Italy. It has since become a favorite of my own family, who love the combination of the salty prosciutto and the sweet peas and cream.

- 2   **POUNDS FARFALLE (BOW-TIE) PASTA**
- ½   **STICK (4 TABLESPOONS) UNSALTED BUTTER**
- ½   **POUND THINLY SLICED PROSCIUTTO DI PARMA, CUT INTO BITE-SIZE PIECES**
- 1   **PACKAGE (12 OUNCES) FROZEN BABY PEAS**
- 2   **CUPS PANNA DA CUCINA OR HEAVY CREAM**
-     **SEA SALT**
-     **FRESHLY GROUND BLACK PEPPER**
- 1   **CUP GRATED PARMIGIANO-REGGIANO**

Bring a large pot of salted water to a boil. Add the pasta and cook until al dente, 10 minutes.

Meanwhile, melt the butter in a large skillet over medium heat. Add the prosciutto and cook, stirring for 1 minute. Add the peas and cook, stirring gently, for 3 to 4 minutes. Add the cream and simmer just until hot, being careful not to allow the mixture to come to a boil. Season to taste with sea salt and pepper.

When the pasta is ready to be drained, transfer the cream mixture to a large warm pasta bowl. Drain the farfalle and add it to the cream mixture. Add the cheese and toss until the pasta is well coated with the cream and cheese. Serve immediately.

petti di pollo alla panna

chicken breasts in cream

This is another dish that was served to me when I was studying and living with a family in the Marche region of Italy on the Adriatic. For an elegant presentation, set a chicken breast on a serving of Spinaci Saltati (recipe follows) and drizzle the cream over the chicken and spinach.

8–10	LARGE BONELESS, SKINLESS CHICKEN BREAST HALVES
1	CUP ALL-PURPOSE FOUR
½	TEASPOON SEA SALT
	FRESHLY GROUND BLACK PEPPER
1	STICK (8 TABLESPOONS) UNSALTED BUTTER
2	CUPS PANNA DA CUCINA OR HEAVY CREAM

Lay a sheet of plastic wrap or waxed paper on your kitchen counter. Place the chicken breasts on top and cover with another sheet of plastic wrap or waxed paper. With a meat mallet, pound the chicken gently until the breasts are about ¼ inch thick.

Pour the flour onto a large flat plate and mix with the sea salt and pepper to taste. Dredge the pounded chicken breasts in the flour, coating them fully, and tap off any excess. Place the dredged breasts on a tray.

Preheat the oven to 350F.

In a large skillet, melt the butter over medium heat. Brown the chicken breasts, 2 or 3 at a time, in the hot butter until golden, 4 to 5 minutes per side.

Once they are all browned, transfer the breasts to a large baking dish, arranging them so they lay flat in a single layer. Pour the panna da cucina over the chicken and bake until golden and bubbly, about 30 minutes.

spinaci saltati

sautéed spinach

The spinach offers a bit of bright green color against the creamy chicken.

4	CLOVES GARLIC, SLICED
½	CUP EXTRA-VIRGIN OLIVE OIL
2	POUNDS FRESH SPINACH, WASHED WELL AND HEAVY STEMS REMOVED, OR FROZEN SPINACH, THAWED AND SQUEEZED DRY
	SEA SALT
	FRESHLY GROUND BLACK PEPPER

In a large skillet, cook the garlic in the olive oil until soft but not brown. Add the spinach and cook until wilted (if using fresh) and heated through. Season to taste with sea salt and pepper.

panna cotta con lamponi

cooked cream with berries

Simple, sinful, and you can make this ahead of time.

2	TABLESPOONS UNFLAVORED GELATIN
4	CUPS HEAVY CREAM
¾	CUP SUGAR
½	QUART BLACKBERRIES
½	QUART RASPBERRIES

In a small bowl, soften the gelatin in ¼ cup warm water. In a large, heavy-bottomed saucepan, heat the cream and sugar over low heat; don't allow it to boil. When the cream is hot, remove the pan from the heat and stir in the softened gelatin. Pour the mixture into 8-ounce ramekins or wine goblets. Let cool. Cover and chill for 4 hours.

Remove from the refrigerator 30 minutes before serving and garnish each with berries.

MENU

25

SERVES 8 TO 10

arancini
rice balls

·······································

pasta alla puttanesca
pasta in tomato sauce with black olives and anchovies

·······································

vitello milanese
veal scallopine in breadcrumbs

·······································

insalata di pere, gorgonzola e nocciole
pear, gorgonzola and hazelnut salad

·······································

torta di grappa e pere
grappa and pear cake

The origin of pasta alla puttanesca is always a source of amusement. Historically, it's known as a dish prepared by "women of the evening" in the port of Naples to provide nourishment and take advantage of the natural heat of the sun to merge the flavors. It has long since taken its place among more respectable dishes and has joined the ranks of classic Italian sauces.

arancini

rice balls

These melt-in-your-mouth bite-size balls of rice bring back memories of enjoying them as a snack with my father at a neighborhood spot when we were living in Rome.

- 3 **CUPS RISOTTO ALLA MILANESE (PAGE 193)**
- 3 **LARGE EGGS**
  PLAIN BREADCRUMBS
- ⅔ **CUP MOZZARELLA, (CUT INTO SMALL CUBES)**
  EXTRA-VIRGIN OLIVE OIL FOR FRYING
- 1 **CUP ALL-PURPOSE FLOUR**

Allow the risotto to cool completely. (The rice balls are even better when made from risotto prepared the day before.)

Beat 2 of the eggs, and mix them well into the cold risotto. Use your hands to form the mixture into balls the size of large eggs. If the mixture is too moist to hold its shape well, stir several tablespoons of breadcrumbs into it.

Poke a hole in the center of each ball, fill it with a few cubes of mozzarella, and close the hole over with the rice mixture.

Heat 3 inches of oil in a deep pan until you see small bubbles forming. (It's best to use enough oil so that the arancini will be submerged when added to the pan.) Spread some flour on a plate. Beat the remaining egg in a shallow bowl. Sprinkle another plate with breadcrumbs.

Roll the rice balls in the flour, then in the egg, and finally in the breadcrumbs. Fry them a few at a time in the hot oil until golden and crisp all over. Using a slotted spoon, remove the arancini from the oil and let drain on paper towels. Serve hot or cold.

pasta alla puttanesca

pasta in tomato sauce with black olives and anchovies

This sauce can be cooked as directed below, but it's equally delicious to mix all the sauce ingredients together, uncooked, then toss with the spaghetti. I like to keep the olives whole, instead of slicing them, for a more rustic presentation.

- 5 **CLOVES GARLIC, SLICED**
- 5 **TABLESPOONS EXTRA-VIRGIN OLIVE OIL**
- 2 **CANS (28 OUNCES EACH) CRUSHED TOMATOES (PREFERABLY SAN MARZANO)**
- ¾ **POUND PITTED BLACK OLIVES**
- 2 **TABLESPOONS SALT-PACKED ITALIAN CAPERS**
- 2 **TEASPOONS RED PEPPER FLAKES**
- ½ **TEASPOON DRIED ITALIAN OREGANO**
- ¼ **TEASPOON FRESHLY GROUND BLACK PEPPER**
- 2 **CANS (2 TO 3 OUNCES EACH) ANCHOVIES, GROUND INTO A PASTE USING A MORTAR AND PESTLE**
- ¼ **CUP CHOPPED FRESH ITALIAN PARSLEY**
  SEA SALT
- 2 **POUNDS SPAGHETTI**

Put a large pot of salted water on to boil.

In a large frying pan over medium heat, cook the garlic in the olive oil until it becomes fragrant. Stir in the crushed tomatoes, olives, capers, red pepper, oregano, and black pepper. Let simmer for about 10 minutes. Stir in the anchovy paste and parsley. Season to taste with sea salt.

Cook the spaghetti in the boiling water until al dente, 5 to 6 minutes. Drain well, add the spaghetti to the frying pan, and let cook with the sauce for 2 minutes.

vitello milanese
veal scallopine in breadcrumbs

Nothing beats the delicious simplicity of Veal Milanese when it's made properly. It was my children's favorite dish growing up in Florence, and the recipe comes from one of our favorite neighborhood trattorie there.

2   CUPS ALL-PURPOSE FLOUR, SEASONED WITH SEA SALT AND FRESHLY GROUND BLACK PEPPER

2   CUPS PLAIN BREADCRUMBS

4   LARGE EGGS, BEATEN

3   POUNDS THINLY SLICED VEAL SCALLOPINE

1   CUP EXTRA-VIRGIN OLIVE OIL

2–3   LEMONS, CUT INTO WEDGES

Preheat the oven to 200F. Place the seasoned flour and breadcrumbs each on its own large flat plate. Pour the beaten eggs into a large shallow dish.

Dredge each piece of scallopine in the flour, tapping off any excess, and then dip in the eggs, making sure to fully coat. Let any excess egg drip off. Dredge the veal in the breadcrumbs, being sure to coat evenly. Set the dipped and dredged cutlets on a large platter.

Heat the olive oil in a large skillet over medium-high heat. Cook a few pieces of veal at a time (don't overcrowd the skillet) until golden brown, about 3 minutes per side. Be careful not to overcook. Transfer the cooked cutlets to a clean ovenproof serving tray and keep warm in the oven as you finish cooking the remaining veal.

Serve the cutlets with the lemon wedges.

"chi si volta,
e chi si gira,
sempre a casa
va a finire."

no matter where you go,
your home
always awaits you.

insalata di pere, gorgonzola e nocciole

pear, gorgonzola and hazelnut salad

This salad features a wonderful interplay of flavors and textures.

- ⅔ **CUP HAZELNUTS**
- ¼ **CUP HAZELNUT OIL**
- 2 **TABLESPOONS RED WINE VINEGAR**
-   **SEA SALT**
-   **FRESHLY GROUND BLACK PEPPER**
- 1 **HEAD RADICCHIO, LEAVES TORN**
- 1 **HEAD BUTTER LETTUCE, LEAVES TORN**
- 1 **ENDIVE, CUT ACROSS INTO 1-INCH-WIDE STRIPS**
- 2 **RIPE PEARS, CORED, EACH CUT INTO 8 WEDGES**
- 4 **OUNCES GORGONZOLA, CRUMBLED**

Preheat oven to 350F. Place the hazelnuts on a cookie sheet and roast for 8-10 minutes. Allow to cool and then with your fingers rub the skins off the hazelnuts. Roughly chop the nuts. Whisk the hazelnut oil and vinegar together well in a small bowl. Season to taste with sea salt and pepper.

Place the radicchio, lettuce, and endive in a large salad bowl. Toss with just enough dressing to coat the greens and add the pear wedges, gorgonzola, and hazelnuts.

torta di grappa e pere

grappa and pear cake

My grandfather, who dearly loved his grappa, never left a crumb on his plate when I served him this grappa-infused cake. My family loves it with pears, but apples and peaches work equally well.

- 3 **CUPS ALL-PURPOSE FLOUR**
- 1½ **TEASPOONS BAKING POWDER**
- ½ **TEASPOON SEA SALT**
- 2 **STICKS (16 TABLESPOONS) UNSALTED BUTTER, SOFTENED**
- 1½ **CUPS GRANULATED SUGAR**
- 3 **LARGE EGGS**
- 3 **TABLESPOONS GRAPPA**
- 1 **TEASPOON VANILLA EXTRACT**
- 4 **LARGE PEARS, CORED, PEELED, AND DICED**
-   **CONFECTIONERS' SUGAR**

Preheat the oven to 350F.

Butter and flour a 10-inch Bundt pan.

In a medium bowl, stir together the flour, baking powder, and salt.

In a large bowl using an electric mixer on medium speed, beat together the butter and granulated sugar until light and fluffy, about 5 minutes. Add the eggs, one at a time, beating well after each addition. Beat in the grappa and vanilla. Reduce the speed to low, add the flour mixture, and beat for 1 minute. Stir in the pears.

Pour the batter into the prepared pan. Bake about 1¼ hours, until the cake is golden. Cool in the pan 10 minutes. Invert the cake onto a rack and remove the pan. Let cool completely. Sprinkle with the confectioners' sugar before serving.

MENU

26

SERVES 8 TO 10

involtini di melanzane
eggplant rollups

....

pasta alla norma
pasta with eggplant

....

pollo alla contadina
farmer's chicken with zucchini and tomatoes

....

cavolfiori gratinati
cauliflower in parmesan sauce

....

torta di mele
apple cake

Eggplant—the prized vegetable of Sicily and everyone in my family—is delicious, and the signature pasta dish there is pasta alla norma, a rich, tomato-based, layered concoction that is one of the most satisfying dishes I have ever eaten. Although it's traditionally made with tomato sauce, I sometimes add a cup of heavy cream to the sauce to make it even more decadent.

involtini di melanzane

eggplant rollups

Eggplant rollups get a Sicilian twist with a breadcrumb filling that includes golden raisins and pine nuts.

2	MEDIUM EGGPLANTS (ABOUT 1 POUND), TRIMMED AND PEELED
	COARSE SEA SALT
2	TABLESPOONS OLIVE OIL, PLUS ADDITIONAL TO MOISTEN SEASONING
2	CLOVES GARLIC, MINCED
2	CUPS PLAIN BREADCRUMBS
¼	CUP SNIPPED FRESH BASIL LEAVES, OR 1 TEASPOON DRIED BASIL, CRUSHED
	PINCH OF FINE SEA SALT
½	TEASPOON FRESHLY GROUND BLACK PEPPER
¼	CUP PINE NUTS
¼	CUP GOLDEN RAISINS

Cut each eggplant lengthwise into 8 slices ¼ inch thick. Layer the slices in a colander, generously salting each layer with coarse sea salt. Place the colander in the sink or over a bowl and let the juices drain for at least 30 minutes to remove excess water. Rinse each slice thoroughly and pat dry with paper towels.

In a 12-inch skillet, heat 2 tablespoons of the olive oil over medium-high heat. Cook the eggplant, 3 or 4 slices at a time, in the hot oil until browned, about 2 minutes per side. As they are cooked, drain the slices on paper towels. Add more of the olive oil as necessary. Let the eggplant cool.

Combine the garlic, breadcrumbs, basil, fine sea salt, pepper, pine nuts, and raisins in a medium bowl. Moisten with olive oil until the mixture has a crumbly texture. Place 1 teaspoon of the mixture at the end of each slice of eggplant. Roll the slices up and place on a platter, seam side down. Serve at room temperature.

"l'amore domina senza regole."

love rules.

pasta alla norma

pasta with eggplant

This is a traditional Sicilian baked pasta that was an integral part of my childhood.

- 4   LARGE EGGPLANTS, TRIMMED, PEELED, AND CUT INTO ROUNDS ⅛ INCH THICK
-     COARSE SEA SALT
- 4   TABLESPOONS EXTRA-VIRGIN OLIVE OIL
- 1½   POUNDS PENNE OR RIGATONI
- 8   CUPS LISA'S CLASSIC TOMATO SAUCE (PAGE 89)
- 1   CUP GRATED PARMIGIANO-REGGIANO

Preheat the oven to 350F.

Layer the eggplant rounds in a colander, generously salting each layer with coarse sea salt. Place the colander in the sink or over a bowl and let the juices drain for at least 30 minutes to remove excess water. Rinse each slice thoroughly and pat dry with paper towels.

In a 12-inch skillet, heat 2 tablespoons of the olive oil over medium-high heat. Cook the eggplant, 3 or 4 slices at a time, in the hot oil until golden, about 2 minutes per side. As they are cooked, drain the slices on paper towels. Add more of the olive oil as necessary.

Bring a large pot of salted water to a boil. Add the pasta and cook 3 to 4 minutes less than you would for al dente (if using penne, cook for 7 minutes; if using rigatoni, cook for 8 minutes). Drain and set aside.

Coat the bottom of a 13 by 9 by 2½-inch baking dish with a thin layer of the tomato sauce. Add a layer of pasta, then sauce, eggplant, and Parmigiano. Repeat the layering until the baking dish is full, ending with a layer of sauce and a final sprinkling of cheese. Bake until bubbly, about 30 minutes.

pollo alla contadina

farmer's chicken with zucchini and tomatoes

This simple dish makes for hearty, satisfying fare.

- 1   STICK (8 TABLESPOONS) UNSALTED BUTTER
- 2   TABLESPOONS EXTRA-VIRGIN OLIVE OIL
- 1   SMALL YELLOW ONION, CHOPPED
- 1   POUND SMALL ZUCCHINI, TRIMMED AND CUT INTO ROUNDS ¼-INCH-THICK
-     SEA SALT
-     FRESHLY GROUND BLACK PEPPER
- 2   CUPS CHOPPED FRESH TOMATOES
- 1   CUP ALL-PURPOSE FLOUR
- 8–10   BONELESS, SKINLESS CHICKEN BREAST HALVES
- ½   CUP GRATED PARMIGIANO-REGGIANO

In a large skillet, melt 2 tablespoons of the butter with the olive oil over medium heat. Add the onion and cook, stirring a few times, until it is transparent. Add the zucchini, season to taste with sea salt and pepper, and cook, stirring occasionally, until the zucchini is soft, about 8 to 10 minutes. Add the fresh tomatoes and let simmer for 15 to 20 minutes.

Preheat the oven to 350F.

Place the flour on a large flat plate. Dredge the chicken breasts in the flour, coating them well and tapping off any excess. Set the dredged chicken on a tray.

Melt the remaining 6 tablespoons butter in another large skillet over medium heat. Add the chicken breasts, 2 or 3 at a time, and cook until golden brown and cooked through, 2 to 3 minutes per side. As the breasts are cooked, transfer them to a serving platter or casserole dish. When they are all cooked, pour the hot zucchini sauce over the top. Sprinkle with the Parmigiano and place in the oven for 5 minutes before serving.

cavolfiori gratinati

cauliflower in parmesan sauce

What's not to love about this creamy, cheesy gratin? Be sure to use only imported Parmigiano-Reggiano—the quality of the cheese makes or breaks the dish.

- 2 TABLESPOONS UNSALTED BUTTER FOR BUTTERING THE DISH
- 2 LARGE HEADS CAULIFLOWER, CUT INTO FLORETS

BESCIAMELLA
- 1 STICK (8 TABLESPOONS) UNSALTED BUTTER
- ¼ CUP (4 TABLESPOONS) UNBLEACHED FLOUR
- 3 CUPS WHOLE MILK, PLUS ADDITIONAL AS NEEDED
- ¾ CUP GRATED PARMIGIANO-REGGIANO
- ½ TEASPOON SEA SALT
- ¼ TEASPOON FRESHLY GROUND BLACK PEPPER
- ¼ TEASPOON GRATED NUTMEG

Preheat the oven to 350F. Butter a large baking dish with 2 tablespoons butter.

Steam or parboil the cauliflower florets for 8 to 10 minutes. Drain and put the florets into the prepared baking dish.

Make the besciamella: Melt the butter in a medium saucepan over medium heat. Add the flour and stir until smooth. Slowly add the milk, whisking constantly to keep any lumps from forming. Stir until the mixture thickens to the point that it coats the back of a wooden spoon. You can add more milk if the sauce gets too thick.

Stir in the Parmigiano and season with sea salt, pepper, and nutmeg. Pour the sauce evenly over the cauliflower and bake for 20 minutes, until bubbly.

torta di mele

apple cake

This rustic apple cake is enjoyed throughout Italy, each region having its own twist. If you like, you can add chopped walnuts or sliced almonds to the batter. Moist and delicious, it is best enjoyed topped with a dollop of fresh whipped cream or gelato.

- 1 TABLESPOON UNSALTED BUTTER FOR GREASING THE PAN
- ¼ CUP PLAIN BREADCRUMBS
- 2 APPLES
- 1 CUP ALL-PURPOSE FLOUR
- ½ CUP SUGAR
- 2 LARGE EGGS, SEPARATED
- ½ CUP MILK
- 1 PACKAGE INSTANT YEAST

Preheat the oven to 375F. Butter the bottom and sides of an 8-inch baking dish. Dust evenly with the breadcrumbs and tap out any excess.

Core, peel, and thinly slice the apples. Arrange the apple slices in a decorative manner in the prepared baking dish.

In a large bowl, place the flour, sugar, egg yolks, milk, and yeast and stir gently to combine.

In a medium bowl with an electric mixer, beat the egg whites until glossy peaks form. Gently fold them into the cake batter and pour the batter over the apples. Bake until golden, 35 to 40 minutes. Transfer the cake to a rack and let it cool for 20 minutes. Invert a plate onto the baking dish and flip the cake onto the plate so the sliced apples are on top.

MENU

27

SERVES 8 TO 10

salumi varie
ANTIPASTO PLATTER OF ITALIAN CURED MEATS

· ·

pasta al boscaiola
WOODMAN'S PASTA WITH MUSHROOM SAUCE

· ·

carne di maiale con finocchio
PORK TENDERLOIN WITH FENNEL

· ·

funghi alla vittoria
MUSHROOMS VICTORIA

· ·

ciliege in chianti
CHERRIES IN CHIANTI

Every autumn weekend when we were in Tuscany, I would pile my children into the car and head for Chianti country. Porcini mushrooms, wild boar sauce, chestnuts roasting over open fires—these are the heavenly scents of the region. Our favorite trattoria was high on the side of a hill, literally in a bosco (forest), hence the name boscaiola (woodman) for the sauce we enjoyed there.

salumi varie

antipasto platter of italian cured meats

I love this antipasto—a plate of thinly sliced cured meats, cheeses piled high, olives piled even higher. It's a starter to linger over, preferably accompanied by a glass of bubbly Prosecco.

- 2 THIN LOAVES ITALIAN BREAD
  EXTRA-VIRGIN OLIVE OIL
- ¼ POUND THINLY SLICED GENOA SALAMI
- ¼ POUND THINLY SLICED PROSCIUTTO DI PARMA
- ¼ POUND THINLY SLICED SOPRESSATTA
- 1 POUND FRESH MOZZARELLA, THINLY SLICED
- 8 OUNCES GORGONZOLA
- 8 OUNCES PROVOLONE, CUT INTO CHUNKS
- 1 POUND MARINATED MIXED GREEN AND BLACK SICILIAN OLIVES
- 8 OUNCES MARINATED ARTICHOKE HEARTS

Preheat the oven to 350F. Cut each loaf of bread on the diagonal into 12 slices. Brush each side with olive oil. Place them in a single layer on large baking sheets and bake for 4 minutes per side.

Meanwhile, roll up the meat slices and arrange them and the cheeses artfully on a large platter. In the middle, pile high the chunks of provolone. Place the olives and artichoke hearts in separate bowls. Serve the toasted bread in a basket alongside the platter.

pasta al boscaiola

woodman's pasta with mushroom sauce

A dish typical of the Chianti region of Tuscany, this pasta features a variety of mushrooms paired with a thick, velvety tomato and cream sauce.

- 6 OUNCES DRIED PORCINI MUSHROOMS
- 2 TABLESPOONS UNSALTED BUTTER
- ¼ CUP EXTRA-VIRGIN OLIVE OIL
- 2 CLOVES GARLIC, FINELY CHOPPED
- 1 LARGE CARROT, FINELY CHOPPED
- 1 STALK CELERY, FINELY CHOPPED
- 8 OUNCES BUTTON MUSHROOMS, SLICED
- 8 OUNCES CREMINI MUSHROOMS, SLICED
  SALT
- 2 POUNDS PENNE OR OTHER LONG TUBULAR PASTA
- 1 CUP LISA'S CLASSIC TOMATO SAUCE (PAGE 89)
- 6 TABLESPOONS HEAVY CREAM OR PANNA DA CUCINA
- 6 OUNCES PARMIGIANO-REGGIANO, GRATED

In a medium bowl, soak the porcini in 1 cup warm water for 30 minutes.

In a large skillet, melt the butter with the olive oil over medium-high heat. Add the garlic, carrot, and celery and cook, stirring, until softened.

Drain the porcini mushrooms, reserving the soaking water. Rinse the porcini and add them to the skillet with the other mushrooms. Cook, stirring, until they lose their liquid, about 5 minutes.

Bring a large pot of salted water to a boil. Add the pasta and cook until al dente (if using penne, cook for 7 minutes).

Meanwhile, pour the reserved porcini soaking water through a fine mesh strainer to remove any sand. Slowly add the porcini water and then the tomato sauce to the mushroom mixture, stirring. Add the cream and stir well. Drain the pasta, add to the sauce, and mix well. Sprinkle with the Parmigiano and serve.

carne di maiale con finocchio

pork tenderloin with fennel

A satisfying choice for an autumn dinner, this dish is nearly effortless to put together.

- 3 **TABLESPOONS FENNEL SEEDS**
- 4 **CLOVES GARLIC, CHOPPED**
- ¼ **CUP EXTRA-VIRGIN OLIVE OIL**
- 2 **TABLESPOONS COARSE SEA SALT**
- 2 **TABLESPOONS FRESHLY GROUND BLACK PEPPER**
- 2 **PORK TENDERLOINS (2 TO 2½ POUNDS EACH; FROM ONE 4- TO 5-POUND PACKAGE)**
- 2 **CUPS DRY WHITE WINE**

Preheat the oven to 325F.

In a small bowl, combine the fennel seeds, garlic, olive oil, sea salt and pepper.

Place the pork in a roasting pan and rub all over with the fennel-seed mixture. Pour the wine over the pork and roast the pork, basting it occasionally with the wine as it roasts, for 1 hour, or until an instant-read thermometer reaches 155F. Let the pork rest 10 minutes before slicing.

"quella destinata a te, nessuno te la prendera."

true love waits.

funghi alla vittoria
mushrooms victoria

You can prepare this with one variety of mushroom or, as in the pasta course, use several different types for a greater depth of flavor.

2 TABLESPOONS UNSALTED BUTTER

2 TABLESPOONS OLIVE OIL

6 LARGE GARLIC CLOVES, FLATTENED

1½ POUNDS LARGE MUSHROOMS OF YOUR CHOICE, CUT IN HALF OR QUARTERED IF VERY LARGE

1 CUP DRY WHITE WINE

SEA SALT

FRESHLY GROUND BLACK PEPPER

CHOPPED FRESH ITALIAN PARSLEY

In a large heavy skillet over medium-high heat, melt the butter with the olive oil. Add the garlic and cook, stirring, just until the cloves begin to brown, about 2 minutes. Using a slotted spoon, remove the garlic and discard.

Add the mushrooms to the skillet and cook until browned and their juices evaporate, stirring a few times, about 15 minutes. Add the wine and reduce until it glazes the mushrooms, stirring a few times, about 10 minutes.

Season to taste with sea salt and pepper, and sprinkle with parsley.

ciliege in chianti
cherries in chianti

This dessert is best when prepared a day or two ahead and allowed to rest, covered, in the refrigerator. Although the cherries are delicious on their own, you can also serve them over vanilla ice cream or with some crisp biscotti or butter cookies.

2 POUNDS RIPE BUT NOT OVERRIPE CHERRIES, STEMS REMOVED AND PITTED

3 CUPS FULL-BODIED CHIANTI

2 TABLESPOONS GRANULATED SUGAR

1 TABLESPOON CONFECTIONERS' SUGAR

2 TABLESPOONS BRANDY OR RUM

FRESH MINT SPRIGS FOR GARNISH

Preheat the oven to 375F.

Place the pitted cherries in a large baking dish. Pour the wine over them (the wine should cover them completely) and sprinkle with the sugars. Bake until the cherries are cooked through but still firm, about 45 minutes.

Add the brandy and bake another 5 minutes.

Transfer the cherries to a serving dish, using a slotted spoon. Pour the liquid into a medium saucepan and simmer over medium heat until it is reduced by half, about 35 minutes. Pour over the cherries and let cool, about 1 hour.

Serve garnished with mint sprigs.

MENU

SERVES 8 TO 10

tortino di funghi e cipolla
onion and mushroom torte

risotto con verdure
arborio rice with sautéed vegetables

manzo marinato
marinated flank steak

insalata siciliana
sicilian coleslaw

torta di frutta secca della nonna
grandma franco's fedora

Mushrooms are plentiful in Tuscany, and the Tuscans are very creative in using them in their recipes. My son Guido ate so many porcini mushrooms when he was little that we used to call him "il porcino." To this day, he devours the torte in this menu. In fact, it is one of my favorite recipes in this cookbook. A typical Tuscan antipasto, it is a unique blend of flavors with a creamy, cheesy texture.

tortino di funghi
e cipolla
mushroom and onion torte

If you can find fresh porcini mushrooms in your market, please use them. If not, feel free to substitute the mushroom of your choice in this savory pie.

FILLING

1	TABLESPOON EXTRA-VIRGIN OLIVE OIL
1	ONION, CUT IN HALF, THEN CUT INTO HALF-MOONS
3	CLOVES GARLIC, CHOPPED
4	CUPS SLICED PORCINI MUSHROOMS OR 16 OUNCES DRIED PORCINI (IF USING DRIED, SOAK IN 1 CUP HOT WATER UNTIL SOFTENED, DRAIN AND RINSE)
4	CUPS SLICED BUTTON MUSHROOMS
1	CUP RED WINE
¼	CUP BALSAMIC VINEGAR
2	TEASPOONS CHOPPED FRESH ROSEMARY
2	TEASPOONS CHOPPED FRESH THYME
	SEA SALT
	FRESHLY GROUND BLACK PEPPER

CRUST

2⅓	CUPS ALL-PURPOSE FLOUR
1	TEASPOON SALT
3	CLOVES GARLIC, MINCED
2	STICKS (16 TABLESPOONS) UNSALTED BUTTER, SOFTENED
½	CUP GRATED FONTINA
1	BEATEN EGG FOR TOP CRUST

Make the filling: In a very large skillet, heat the olive oil over medium heat. Add the onion and garlic and cook, stirring, about 2 minutes, until the onion softens. Add the mushrooms and cook, stirring, for 5 minutes. Add the wine, vinegar, and herbs, reduce the heat to low, and continue to cook until only 1/2 cup liquid remains in the skillet. Season to taste with sea salt and pepper and let cool.

Make the crust: Place the flour, salt, garlic, and butter in a large bowl. Mix together until a coarse dough forms. Drizzle in 1/2 cup cold water and stir gently with a fork until the dough comes together. (It's okay to add a bit more water; it's better to have dough that is slightly wet rather than one that is too dry.) Cover the dough with plastic wrap and let it rest in the refrigerator for 15 to 30 minutes.

Preheat the oven to 425F. Cut the dough in half. On a lightly floured work surface, roll out one half to a 10-inch round. Fit the round into a 9-inch pie pan. Sprinkle the crust with the fontina. Pour the onion-mushroom filling into the crust. Roll out the second piece of dough to a 10-inch circle. Cover the filling with the top crust, crimp the edges to seal, and brush the top with the beaten egg.

Bake the tortino on the center rack for 15 minutes. Reduce the oven temperature to 350F and bake until the crust is golden brown, another 25 to 30 minutes. Remove from the oven and let rest for 5 minutes before cutting into wedges.

risotto con verdure

arborio rice with sautéed vegetables

When we were living in Florence, risotto was an easy way to get my children to eat their vegetables! Have everyone in your family take a turn at stirring the risotto as it cooks.

- ¼ CUP EXTRA-VIRGIN OLIVE OIL
- 2 CUPS ARBORIO RICE
- 1 ONION, FINELY CHOPPED
- 3 STALKS CELERY, FINELY CHOPPED
- 3 CARROTS, FINELY CHOPPED
- 4 CLOVES GARLIC, CRUSHED TO A PASTE OR PUT THROUGH A GARLIC PRESS
- 5 CUPS VEGETABLE STOCK OR REDUCED-SODIUM CANNED BROTH
- 1 CUP WHITE WINE
-   SEA SALT
-   FRESHLY GROUND BLACK PEPPER
- 2 TEASPOONS UNSALTED BUTTER
- 1 CUP GRATED PARMIGIANO-REGGIANO

Heat the olive oil in a large stock pot over medium heat. Add the rice and cook, stirring, for 3 minutes; don't allow the rice to brown. Add the onion, celery, carrots, and garlic and cook over medium heat, stirring, for 3 minutes.

Gradually add the stock, ½ cup at a time, making sure it is all absorbed before adding more. Stir constantly. (This is a great job for the whole family—everyone can take a turn!)

After all the stock has been added and absorbed and the risotto has a creamy texture, add the wine, and salt and pepper to taste. Stir until the wine is absorbed.

Just before serving, stir in the butter and Parmigiano.

manzo marinato

marinated flank steak

Flank steak is such a great cut of meat for entertaining. Put it in a marinade the night before, then pull it out to grill when it's time to eat—so much flavor for so little effort!

MARINADE

- 2 CUPS DRY RED WINE
- 6 TABLESPOONS EXTRA-VIRGIN OLIVE OIL
- ¼ CUP BALSAMIC VINEGAR
- 1 CUP CHOPPED ONION
- 6 CLOVES GARLIC, CHOPPED
- 5 TABLESPOONS SEA SALT
- 1 TABLESPOON FRESHLY GROUND BLACK PEPPER
- 4 TEASPOONS CHOPPED FRESH THYME
- 5 BAY LEAVES

- 2 FLANK STEAKS (2 POUNDS EACH)

Combine the marinade ingredients in a large bowl. Place each flank steak in its own zip-top plastic bag and divide the marinade between the bags. Seal the bags, squish the marinade around to coat the steaks, and let them marinate at room temperature for 1 hour or overnight in the refrigerator.

When ready to cook, remove the steaks from the marinade. You can either broil the steaks for 4 minutes per side or grill them on medium-high heat for 4 minutes per side for medium rare.

Slice the steaks on the diagonal and arrange on a platter.

insalata siciliana
sicilian coleslaw

Instead of using cabbage, this twist on the American classic delivers its crunch using thinly sliced fennel bulb and celery. A refreshing combination of olive oil and lemon juices replaces the traditional creamy dressing.

4 FENNEL BULBS, STALKS REMOVED, BULB CUT INTO ⅛-INCH-THICK SLICES

4 STALKS CELERY, CUT INTO ⅛-INCH-THICK SLICES

LEAVES FROM 1 BUNCH FRESH ITALIAN PARSLEY, CHOPPED

¾ CUP EXTRA-VIRGIN OLIVE OIL

¼ CUP FRESH LEMON JUICE

SEA SALT

FRESHLY GROUND BLACK PEPPER

In a large salad bowl, combine the fennel, celery, and parsley. Add the olive oil and lemon juice, season to taste with sea salt and pepper, and toss to thoroughly mix. Serve at room temperature.

torta di frutta secca della nonna
grandma franco's fedora

This recipe is from my maternal grandfather's mother, who was from a beautiful little town outside of Naples. She raised nine children and was an excellent cook. I feel blessed to have her recipes, written in her own hand. This dessert is typical of Grandma Franco—nutritious, chockfull of dried fruit, and good to the last bite.

2 STICKS (16 TABLESPOONS) UNSALTED BUTTER, SOFTENED, PLUS ADDITIONAL 1 TABLESPOON FOR THE CAKE PAN

4 LARGE EGGS

1 CUP SUGAR

½ CUP RUM (OPTIONAL)

2 CUPS ALL-PURPOSE FLOUR

½ TEASPOON BAKING SODA

½ TEASPOON SALT

1 CUP APPLESAUCE

1½ CUPS GOLDEN RAISINS

1½ CUPS DRIED CHOPPED APRICOTS

1½ CUPS DRIED TART CHERRIES

Preheat the oven to 325F. Butter a 13- by 8-inch baking dish.

In a large bowl, beat together the butter, eggs, sugar, and rum if using. Add the flour, baking soda, salt and applesauce and mix well. Stir in the dried fruit.

Pour the batter into the buttered baking dish and bake for 2 hours, or until a fork comes out clean.

MENU

29

SERVES 8 TO 10

crostini con pesto di ceci
toasts with chickpea paste

··

risotto con zucca e parmigiano
arborio rice with squash and parmesan

··

petti di pollo alla modenese
chicken breasts with mortadella

··

insalata fantasia
fantasy salad

··

uve con mascarpone
grapes in mascarpone cheese

When you make friends with Italians, the first thing they do is invite you to their home for a meal. If you are really lucky, they invite you into their kitchen. This menu comes from years of watching one of my mother's closest friends cook in her Modena kitchen. She's a phenomenal cook, and this menu represents Emilia-Romagna cooking at its best!

crostini con pesto di ceci

toasts with chickpea paste

The blender whips the chickpeas and olive oil into a creamy spread that's delicious on crisp crostini.

- 1   **LOAF THIN ITALIAN BREAD, CUT ON THE DIAGONAL INTO ½-INCH SLICES**
- 5   **TABLESPOONS EXTRA-VIRGIN OLIVE OIL, PLUS ADDITIONAL TO BRUSH ON THE BREAD**
- 1   **CAN (8 OUNCES) ITALIAN CECI (CHICKPEAS)**
-   **SEA SALT**
-   **FRESHLY GROUND BLACK PEPPER**

Preheat the oven to 350F. Arrange the bread slices on a cookie sheet and with a pastry brush lightly brush olive oil on the bread. Bake for 8 minutes.

Place the ceci, 5 tablespoons olive oil, and sea salt and pepper to taste in a blender. Process into a smooth paste and spread over the toasts.

risotto con zucca e parmigiano

arborio rice with squash and parmesan

Any fresh winter squash will work in this tasty autumn twist on risotto. Butternut squash is easy to handle, but fresh pumpkin is very nice too.

- ½   **STICK (4 TABLESPOONS) UNSALTED BUTTER**
- 1   **SMALL WHITE ONION, FINELY CHOPPED**
- 1   **POUND FRESH WINTER SQUASH, PEELED AND CHOPPED**
- 6   **CUPS VEGETABLE STOCK OR REDUCED-SODIUM CANNED BROTH**
-   **SEA SALT**
-   **FRESHLY GROUND BLACK PEPPER**
- 1   **POUND (2 CUPS) ARBORIO RICE**
- 1   **CUP GRATED PARMIGIANO-REGGIANO**
-   **CHOPPED FRESH ITALIAN PARSLEY FOR GARNISH**

In a large heavy saucepan, melt 2 tablespoons of the butter over medium heat. Add the onion and squash and cook until softened, about 7 minutes. Add 1 cup of the stock, season to taste with sea salt and pepper, and simmer over low heat for 10 minutes.

Add the rice to the pan and stir. Once it has absorbed most of the liquid, continue to add the remaining stock a little at a time, letting the rice absorb it before adding more while stirring constantly. Cook until the final addition of broth is absorbed and the rice is al dente.

Stir in the remaining 2 tablespoons butter and the Parmigiano. Garnish the top of the risotto with parsley and serve immediately.

petti di pollo alla modenese

chicken breasts with mortadella

These chicken breasts, cooked in the style of Modena, located in Emilia-Romagna, are topped with a slice of mortadella (a specialty of Bologna) and Parmigiano-Reggiano and finished in a light cream sauce.

8   CHICKEN BREAST HALVES, WITH RIB MEAT AND BONE ATTACHED

1   CUP ALL-PURPOSE FLOUR
    SEA SALT

½   STICK (4 TABLESPOONS) UNSALTED BUTTER

8   VERY THIN SLICES (ABOUT ¼ POUND) IMPORTED MORTADELLA

4   OUNCES PARMIGIANO-REGGIANO, VERY THINLY SLICED

¼   CUP HEAVY CREAM

Place the chicken breasts between 2 sheets of waxed or parchment paper and pound until they are almost flat.

Place the flour on a large flat dish and season with salt.

Melt the butter in 2 skillets over medium heat. Lightly dredge each breast in the flour, coating fully and tapping off any excess. Cook the chicken, in batches, 4 minutes per side.

Just before serving, top each breast with a slice of mortadella and a slice or more of Parmigiano. Add the cream to the pan and let bubble a few minutes.

Serve each breast with the cream sauce spooned over the top.

insalata fantasia

fantasy salad

Dressed in a bright-tasting lemon vinaigrette, this salad is a study in crunchy, peppery, savory, cheesy goodness.

4   OUNCES BUTTON OR CREMINI MUSHROOMS

1   BUNCH RADISHES

1   HEAD ICEBERG LETTUCE

8   OUNCES PARMIGIANO-REGGIANO

½   CUP EXTRA-VIRGIN OLIVE OIL

¼   CUP FRESH LEMON JUICE

1   TABLESPOON DIJON OR WHITE WINE MUSTARD

1   TEASPOON SUGAR

Trim the mushrooms and radishes and thinly slice them. Core lettuce and chop it into pieces. Cut the Parmigiano into long, thin slices.

In a large salad bowl, toss together the mushrooms, radishes, lettuce, and Parmigiano.

In a small bowl, whisk together the olive oil, lemon juice, mustard, and sugar. Pour the dressing over the salad and toss well.

uve con mascarpone

grapes in mascarpone cheese

It's all about the grapes, grappa, and grape juice–infused mascarpone topped with grappa-soaked grapes.

- 4 **CUPS (ABOUT 2 POUNDS) MIXED SEEDLESS RED AND GREEN GRAPES**
- ⅓ **CUP, PLUS 2 TABLESPOONS GRAPPA**
- 1 **CONTAINER (8 OUNCES) MASCARPONE**
- 3 **TABLESPOONS CONFECTIONERS' SUGAR**
- 3½ **TEASPOONS GRATED LEMON ZEST**

Cut 2½ cups of the grapes in half. Place in a bowl, add ⅓ cup of the grappa, and let stand at room temperature for at least 3 hours, stirring occasionally.

In a food processor, purée the remaining 1½ cups grapes. Transfer the purée to a fine mesh strainer set over a bowl. Press on the solids to extract as much juice as possible and discard the solids.

Transfer ½ cup grape juice to a medium bowl. Add the remaining 2 tablespoons grappa, the mascarpone, the confectioners' sugar, and 2½ teaspoons of the lemon zest. Whisk until well blended.

Distribute the mascarpone mixture among 6 dessert glasses. Top with the grappa-marinated grapes. Sprinkle with the remaining 1 teaspoon lemon zest and serve.

"quando
la pera e
matura, casca
da se."

all things happen
in their own
good time.

MENU

30

SERVES 8 TO 10

polenta fritta con funghi e formaggio
fried polenta with mushrooms and cheese

pasta alla checca
pasta with cherry tomatoes, garlic and basil

cappesante ripieni di pesto
scallops stuffed with basil pesto

insalata di arancio, finocchio e cipolla rossa
orange, fennel and red onion salad

limoni ripieni
lemons filled with cream

We southern Italians love our daily bowl of pasta, but the climate during the summer months there is just too hot to let sauces simmer. No-cook sauces like the one for pasta alla checca are a perfect alternative. I would make this on Sunday morning and bring it to the beach for my children to enjoy—it's perfect at room temperature.

polenta fritta con funghi e formaggio

fried polenta with mushrooms and cheese

Fried polenta rounds make a nice change from the usual crostini, and they're no harder to prepare than cutting bread and toasting it when you use store-bought prepared polenta in a tube.

- ½ CUP EXTRA-VIRGIN OLIVE OIL
- 1 ROLL (16 OUNCES) IMPORTED PREPARED POLENTA, CUT INTO ½-INCH-THICK ROUNDS
- ¾ CUP SHREDDED FONTINA
- 1 CUP SAUTÉED MUSHROOMS (PAGE 206)

Preheat the oven to 200F.

In a medium sauté pan, heat the olive oil over medium heat. Fry the polenta rounds until golden on both sides. Let drain on paper towels.

Transfer the still-warm rounds to a baking sheet. Sprinkle them with the fontina and top each with the mushrooms. Place in the oven until the cheese melts, 3 to 4 minutes.

pasta alla checca

pasta with cherry tomatoes, garlic and basil

This recipe was made for the slow pace of summer. Just boil your pasta, drain, and throw it in a big bowl with sweet cherry tomatoes, lots of garlic, fresh-picked basil leaves, and a quality extra-virgin olive oil.

- 2 POUNDS PENNE
- 2 POUNDS CHERRY OR GRAPE TOMATOES, CUT IN HALF
- 1 CUP EXTRA-VIRGIN OLIVE OIL
- 6 CLOVES GARLIC, CHOPPED
- 1 TEASPOON SEA SALT
- 10 LARGE FRESH BASIL LEAVES
  GRATED PARMIGIANO-REGGIANO (OPTIONAL)

Bring a large pot of salted water to a boil. Add the penne and cook until al dente, 7 minutes.

Meanwhile, in a large pasta bowl, toss together the tomatoes, olive oil, garlic, and salt. Pile the basil leaves on top of one another, roll them up into a cigarette shape, and cut them across into 8 strips. Add to the bowl and toss with the other ingredients.

Drain the pasta, add to the bowl, and toss to mix well. Serve sprinkled with Parmigiano, if you like.

cappesante ripieni di pesto

scallops stuffed with basil pesto

These pan-seared scallops make for an impressive presentation on the plate, golden brown on top and bright green with pesto in the center.

- **24 LARGE SEA SCALLOPS**
- **1 CUP PESTO, HOMEMADE (PAGE 98) OR 1 CUP STORE BOUGHT**
- **6 TABLESPOONS EXTRA-VIRGIN OLIVE OIL, PLUS MORE FOR DRIZZLING**

Cut each scallop in half across. Dab the bottom half with pesto. Top with the upper half.

Put the olive oil in a small bowl. Heat a large skillet over high heat until very hot. Dip each scallop, top and bottom, in the oil, then pan sear for 2 minutes per side.

Transfer the scallops to a serving platter and drizzle with a little extra-virgin olive oil.

"chi trova un amico, trova un tesoro."

he who finds a friend, finds a treasure.

175

insalata di arancio, finocchio e cipolla rossa

orange, fennel and red onion salad

This salad is part of my childhood. My aunt Mary loved it and prepared it nearly every day each summer. I never tire of its refreshing mix of piquant citrus, crunchy fennel, and tangy red onion.

- 3 **FENNEL BULBS**
- 1 **RED ONION, PEELED**
- 3 **MEDIUM ORANGES, PEELED**
- 5 **TABLESPOONS EXTRA-VIRGIN OLIVE OIL**
- 3 **TABLESPOONS FRESH LEMON JUICE**
- **SEA SALT**
- **FRESHLY GROUND BLACK PEPPER**

Trim away the stalks from the fennel bulbs. Trim the bottoms and remove any browned outer layers. Slice the fennel, onion, and oranges into pieces 1/4 inch wide. Toss together in a large salad bowl.

In a small bowl, mix together the olive oil, lemon juice, and salt and pepper to taste. Pour over the salad and toss to mix well.

limoni ripieni

lemons filled with cream

On a hot summer day all over Italy, you can walk into any caffè or pasticceria and find a freezer full of these frozen lemons, as well as frozen oranges. In the heat of a Mediterranean afternoon, by the time you stroll to a park to enjoy your confection, the frozen filling will have softened to a delicious creaminess. To create the same effect at home, I recommend you take them out of the freezer 30 minutes before serving.

- 8–10 **MEDIUM LEMONS**
- 2 **CUPS HEAVY CREAM**
- 1/2 **CUP SUGAR**

Wash the lemons well and dry them. Cut off enough of one end of each lemon so that it will stand upright. Cut a "cap" off the other end of each lemon. With a teaspoon or grapefruit spoon, remove all the pulp from inside each lemon. Reserve 3 tablespoons of the pulp, removing any seeds or pith, and squeeze the remaining pulp to get 1/4 cup juice. Set the lemons upright in a dish or pan that can go into the freezer. Reserve the lemon caps.

In a medium bowl with an electric mixer, whip the cream to stiff peaks, adding the sugar gradually. Once the cream is whipped, stir in the lemon juice and pulp. (Note: Don't add the lemon juice while you are whipping the cream or the cream will curdle.)

Immediately spoon the mixture into the lemons. Set them in the freezer to freeze for about 30 minutes.

Remove the lemons from the freezer 30 minutes before serving and top with their caps.

MENU

31

SERVES 8 TO 10

fritelle di melanzane
eggplant fritters

torta di pasta siciliana
sicilian pasta torte

pollo ripieno di finocchio con patate al forno
fennel-stuffed chicken with oven-fried potatoes

i cannoli della nonna
the one, the only, nana's cannoli

This is a great simple menu that usually gets paired with family board games and movies afterward. Italian fun foods—the oven fries, the torta di pasta, the cannoli—all are favorites at our house.

fritelle di melanzane

eggplant fritters

These melt-in-your-mouth eggplant fritters will become an instant family favorite.

1 LARGE EGGPLANT (ABOUT 1½ POUNDS), TRIMMED, PEELED, AND CUT INTO ½-INCH-THICK SLICES

1 CUP EXTRA-VIRGIN OLIVE OIL FOR FRYING, PLUS 2 TABLESPOONS FOR THE FRITTERS

1 LARGE EGG, LIGHTLY BEATEN

2 CLOVES GARLIC, CRUSHED TO A PASTE OR PUT THROUGH A GARLIC CRUSHER

¼ CUP CHOPPED FRESH ITALIAN PARSLEY

2¼ CUPS FRESH WHITE BREADCRUMBS, PLUS ADDITIONAL AS NEEDED

1 CUP GRATED PARMIGIANO-REGGIANO

1 CUP CRUMBLED GOAT CHEESE

SEA SALT

FRESHLY GROUND BLACK PEPPER

8 TABLESPOONS ALL-PURPOSE FLOUR

Preheat the oven to 375F. Brush the eggplant slices with 2 tablespoons of the olive oil, place them on a baking sheet, and bake until golden and tender, about 20 minutes.

When the eggplant is cool enough to handle, finely chop and transfer to a large bowl. Add the egg, garlic, parsley, breadcrumbs, Parmigiano, goat cheese, and sea salt and pepper to taste. Mix well. Let the mixture set for about 20 minutes. If at that point it still looks very sloppy, add more breadcrumbs.

Divide the mixture into 8 balls and flatten them slightly. Place the flour on a flat plate and season with sea salt and pepper. Dredge the fritters in the flour, tapping off any excess.

Heat the remaining 1 cup oil in a large skillet over medium heat. Working in batches, fry the fritters until golden brown, about 1 minute per side, and drain on paper towels. Serve hot.

torta di pasta siciliana

sicilian pasta torte

A spaghetti frittata? That is essentially a torta di pasta. If you've never had it, the combination of eggs and pasta may seem questionable, but, believe me, serve up these golden wedges and there won't be a crumb left.

1 POUND SPAGHETTI

¾ CUP OIL-PACKED SUN-DRIED TOMATOES, CHOPPED

6 LARGE EGGS

2 TEASPOONS SEA SALT

1 TEASPOON FRESHLY GROUND BLACK PEPPER

1 CUP GRATED PARMIGIANO-REGGIANO

1 CUP GRATED FONTINA

2 TABLESPOONS UNSALTED BUTTER

2 TABLESPOONS EXTRA-VIRGIN OLIVE OIL

Bring a large pot of salted water to a boil. Add the spaghetti and cook until al dente, 7 minutes. Drain, return to the pot, and toss with the sun-dried tomatoes.

In a large bowl, whisk together the eggs, sea salt, pepper, and cheeses.

In a large skillet, melt the butter with the olive oil over medium heat. Pour the spaghetti into the pan, flattening it slightly. Cover it with the egg and cheese mixture, and cook until golden on one side, about 4 minutes. Flip onto a large platter, slide back into the pan, and cook the other side until golden.

Flip the torta onto the platter again and cut into wedges to serve.

pollo ripieno di finocchio con patate al forno

fennel-stuffed chicken with oven-fried potatoes

This was absolutely my grandfather's favorite dish—a chicken stuffed with fennel bulbs and roasted until crispy, the fennel perfuming the bird with its anise flavor. The potatoes are seasoned with sage, a common practice all over Italy, which gives them a slightly peppery flavor.

1 **LARGE ROASTING CHICKEN (AT LEAST 5½ TO 6 POUNDS)**

2 **TABLESPOONS EXTRA-VIRGIN OLIVE OIL, PLUS ADDITIONAL FOR DRIZZLING POTATOES**

   SEA SALT

   FRESHLY GROUND BLACK PEPPER

4 **FENNEL BULBS, STALKS REMOVED, BULBS CUT INTO QUARTERS**

2 **CUPS WHITE WINE**

8 **RED OR RUSSET POTATOES**

8 **FRESH SAGE LEAVES, CHOPPED**

6 **CLOVES GARLIC, PEELED**

Preheat the oven to 400F.

Rinse the chicken very well inside and out. Place the chicken in a large roasting pan. Combine the olive oil, sea salt, and pepper in a measuring cup. With a brush or your hands, rub the chicken very well, inside and out, with the seasoned oil. Push as many of the fennel bulb quarters into the cavity of the chicken as you can fit. Set the chicken, breast side up, in the pan. Pour the wine in the pan.

Peel the potatoes and cut them into long, ½-inch-wide strips. Season to taste with salt and pepper. Arrange the potatoes and any remaining fennel quarters around the chicken. Scatter the sage and garlic over the potatoes. Drizzle with some olive oil. Cook until an instant-read thermometer inserted at the thigh registers 160F and the juices run clear, 1½ to 1¾ hours.

Transfer the chicken to a platter, remove the fennel from the chicken, and cover the chicken loosely with foil. Carefully pour the wine sauce from the roasting pan into a saucepan and put the potatoes back in the oven to crisp for about 10 more minutes.

Meanwhile, separate the fat from the wine sauce and reduce the sauce a bit, about 5 minutes.

Carve the chicken and serve on a large platter with the fennel and potatoes.

Serve the wine sauce on the side.

i cannoli della nonna

the one, the only, nana's cannoli

I learned how to make cannoli from my grandmother. We would spend hours in her kitchen, rolling out the dough, frying the shells, mixing the filling, filling the cannoli—but mostly we would laugh. I can still remember my grandfather shouting from the other room, "What are you two laughing about? You're supposed to be making cannoli!"

Metal cannoli cylinders are available at some gourmet stores; however, they remain hot longer than wooden ones and are more difficult to handle. For that reason, I prefer the wooden ones. If you cannot find wooden cannoli cylinders, ask your hardware store to cut a broom handle into 6-inch lengths.

PASTRY

- 2 CUPS ALL-PURPOSE FLOUR
- PINCH OF SEA SALT
- ½ STICK (4 TABLESPOONS) COLD, UNSALTED BUTTER, CUT INTO PIECES
- 2 TEASPOONS GRANULATED SUGAR
- 5–6 TABLESPOONS SWEET MARSALA OR SHERRY

FILLING

- 1 CONTAINER (15 OUNCES) RICOTTA
- 6 TABLESPOONS GRANULATED SUGAR
- 1 TEASPOON VANILLA EXTRACT
- 1 CUP FINELY CHOPPED CANDIED FRUIT

- VEGETABLE OIL FOR FRYING, PLUS EXTRA FOR BRUSHING THE CANNOLI CYLINDERS
- CONFECTIONERS' SUGAR

Make the pastry: Sift the flour and salt into a medium bowl. Add the butter and work it into the flour, using your fingertips. Stir in the granulated sugar and just enough of the Marsala to form a firm dough. Place the ball of dough in a clean bowl, cover with plastic wrap, and chill for 30 minutes.

Make the filling: In another medium bowl, beat together the ricotta and granulated sugar until light and fluffy. Add the vanilla and the chopped fruit, and beat again until evenly mixed. Cover and chill while making the cannoli shells.

Make the cannoli shells: On a lightly floured work surface, roll the dough out until very thin, no more than ⅛ inch thick. Cut the dough into eight 4-inch squares. Brush 8 metal or wooden cannoli cylinders with vegetable oil. Working with one cylinder at a time, place a cylinder diagonally across a pastry square and roll the pastry up around the mold. Brush the end with water and press to seal. Repeat with the remaining cylinders and pastry.

Meanwhile, heat the vegetable oil, about 4-inches deep, in a deep fryer to 375F. Deep-fry the cannoli 1 or 2 at a time until golden and crisp, 2 to 3 minutes. Remove them from the oil with a slotted spoon and carefully remove the molds if they haven't already slipped out. Let the shells drain and cool on paper towels. Finish frying the remaining shells.

Fill and serve the cannoli: When the cannoli shells have completely cooled, carefully spoon in the filling. Arrange the filled cannoli on a serving plate and sprinkle with the confectioners' sugar.

MENU

32

SERVES 8 TO 10

calamari fritti
fried squid

pasta con salmone affumicato e panna
pasta with smoked salmon and cream

involtini di pesce spada
swordfish rollups

finocchio e patate gratinate
fennel and potato cheese casserole

panforte
italian fruit cake

Throughout the summer in Sicily, seafood is plentiful, and the fishermen sell their catch right on the beach. I love buying fresh swordfish and making these delicious rollups on the grill. Have your fishmonger pound the swordfish fillets slightly so they can be rolled up easily.

calamari fritti

fried squid

Lightly breaded and fried crisp in olive oil, this is everyone's favorite. Try it the way it is served in Sicily, with thin slices of lemon that are fried along with the calamari.

- 2 **POUNDS CLEANED CALAMARI (SQUID)**
- 1 **CUP ALL-PURPOSE FLOUR**
- 1 **TEASPOON SEA SALT**
- **FRESHLY GROUND BLACK PEPPER**
- **EXTRA-VIRGIN OLIVE OIL**
- **LEMON WEDGES**

Rinse the calamari thoroughly inside and out. Drain well. Cut the bodies crosswise into 2½-inch-wide rings. Cut the tentacles in half through the base. Pat dry.

Spread the flour on a sheet of waxed paper and season with the salt and pepper to taste.

Preheat the oven to 200F. Pour 2 inches of olive oil into a large, deep, heavy saucepan or deep fryer. Heat the oil to 375F on a deep-frying thermometer, or until a small piece of calamari sizzles and rises to the surface when added to the oil.

When the frying temperature has been reached, lightly roll a few pieces of calamari at a time in the flour, shaking off any excess. Slip the calamari into the oil, without crowding the pan, and cook until a light golden brown, about 3 minutes.

Remove the calamari from the oil with a slotted spoon and drain on paper towels. Put the cooked calamari in the oven to keep warm as you cook the remainder.

Transfer the calamari to a warm platter and serve with lemon wedges.

pasta con salmone affumicato e panna

pasta with smoked salmon and cream

A wonderfully simple pasta with lots of rich flavor.

- 2 **POUNDS FETTUCCINE**
- 1 **POUND THINLY SLICED SMOKED SALMON**
- 1¾ **CUPS HEAVY CREAM OR PANNA DA CUCINA**
- **FRESHLY GROUND BLACK PEPPER**

Bring a large pot of salted water to a boil. Add the fettuccine and cook until al dente, 4 minutes.

Meanwhile, cut the salmon into bite-size pieces. Place in a large pasta bowl, add the cream, and season to taste with pepper.

Drain the pasta, add to the pasta bowl, and toss well to coat with the cream. Mix in the salmon and serve immediately.

involtini di pesce spada

swordfish rollups

Swordfish gets a Sicilian treatment with a stuffing of breadcrumbs, salty capers, anise basil, and the bright, fresh flavor of lemon juice.

4	SWORDFISH STEAKS, ABOUT ½ INCH THICK
6	TABLESPOONS EXTRA-VIRGIN OLIVE OIL
1	CLOVE GARLIC, CHOPPED
½	CUP PLAIN BREADCRUMBS
2	TABLESPOONS CAPERS, RINSED AND CHOPPED
10	FRESH BASIL LEAVES, CHOPPED
¼	CUP FRESH LEMON JUICE
	SEA SALT
	FRESHLY GROUND BLACK PEPPER

Using a very sharp knife, cut the swordfish steaks in half horizontally, removing any bones. Brush the slices on both sides with 2 tablespoons of the olive oil.

Preheat the oven to 400F.

In a small bowl, combine 2 tablespoons of the olive oil and the garlic, breadcrumbs, capers, basil, and lemon juice. Season to taste with sea salt and pepper and mix into a paste.

Lay the swordfish slices flat on a work surface. Divide the filling between the slices and spread it over the center of each. Roll up the slices and secure each with a toothpick.

Heat the remaining 2 tablespoons olive oil over high heat in a flameproof dish large enough to hold the rollups in a single layer. Add the rollups and brown quickly, turning them once or twice.

Place the rollups in the dish in the oven and bake for 10 minutes, basting the rollups with the cooking juices several times (the fish will turn a bright white). Serve warm.

finocchio e patate gratinate

fennel and potato cheese casserole

I am a huge fan of fennel, and here I layer it with potatoes in a rich and hearty casserole. You can assemble the casserole ahead of time and pop it in the oven when needed.

3	FENNEL BULBS
1	TABLESPOON UNSALTED BUTTER
2	TABLESPOONS EXTRA-VIRGIN OLIVE OIL
1	ONION, THINLY SLICED
4	LARGE RUSSET POTATOES
2	CUPS PLUS 2 TABLESPOONS HEAVY CREAM
2½	CUPS GRATED FONTINA
1	TEASPOON SEA SALT
½	TEASPOON FRESHLY GROUND BLACK PEPPER

Preheat the oven to 350F. Butter a 4- or 5-quart shallow baking dish.

Trim any stalks from the fennel bulbs and trim the bottoms. Cut the bulbs lengthwise into ½-inch-wide strips (about 4 cups total).

In a large skillet, melt the butter with the olive oil over medium heat. Add the onion and fennel and cook, stirring occasionally, until tender, about 15 minutes.

Meanwhile, peel the potatoes and thinly slice. In a large bowl, mix together 2 cups of the cream, 2 cups of the fontina, and the salt and pepper. Add the potatoes and toss to combine.

When the fennel and onion have cooked, add them to the bowl and toss to combine. Pour the mixture into the prepared baking dish. Press down on the fennel and potatoes with a spatula to smooth the surface.

In a small bowl, combine the remaining ½ cup fontina and 2 tablespoons cream. Sprinkle the mixture over the top of the fennel and potatoes and bake until browned and tender, about 1½ hours.

panforte
italian fruit cake

A specialty of Siena, Tuscany, that dates back hundreds of years, panforte translates into "strong bread." It might best be described as a dense, delicious fruit cake.

- 4 **OUNCES HAZELNUTS**
- 4 **OUNCES BLANCHED ALMONDS**
- ⅓ **CUP UNSWEETENED COCOA POWDER**
- 1½ **TEASPOONS GROUND CINNAMON**
- ¼ **TEASPOON GROUND ALLSPICE**
- ½ **CUP PASTRY FLOUR**
- ¾ **CUP CANDIED ORANGE PEEL, CUT INTO SMALL PIECES**
- ¾ **CUP CANDIED CITRON PEEL, CUT INTO SMALL PIECES**
- ¾ **CUP CANDIED LEMON PEEL, CUT INTO SMALL PIECES**
- ¾ **CUP HONEY**
- ¾ **CUP GRANULATED SUGAR**
- 2 **TABLESPOONS CONFECTIONERS' SUGAR**

Preheat the oven to 300F. Line the bottom and side of a 9-inch springform pan with well-buttered pieces of parchment paper. Put the hazelnuts on a cookie sheet and toast for 10 minutes in the oven. When cool enough to handle, rub off the skins with your fingers.

In a medium bowl, mix together well the almonds, hazelnuts, cocoa, cinnamon, allspice, flour, and candied citrus peels.

Combine the honey and granulated sugar in a large, heavy saucepan and cook over very low heat until well blended, stirring constantly. Add the nut and fruit mixture and stir to combine. Pour the mixture into the prepared springform pan.

Bake for 30 minutes, until golden brown. Allow the panforte to cool. Remove the sides of the springform pan, then the bottom, and pull away the parchment paper. Sprinkle with the confectioners' sugar.

"il riso fa buon sangue."
laughter is good medicine!

MENU

33

SERVES 8 TO 10

peperoni arrostiti con mozzarella e pesto
roasted peppers with mozzarella and basil pesto

risotto alla milanese
arborio rice with saffron

manzo in barolo
beef in barolo wine

cipolline agrodolce
sweet and savory cipolline onions

pinolata
pine nut cake

I first discovered the small, flat, disk-like cipolline onion in Florence, and luckily they are plentiful in farmers' markets in America, too. Their intense, sweet flavor intensifies when cooked in vinegar. As you may know, all onions, like garlic, are good for your health, but sometimes they are avoided due to their pungency. No need to worry about that with the cipolline!

peperoni arrostiti con mozzarella e pesto

roasted peppers with mozzarella and basil pesto

The mozzarella melts into a decadent creaminess that pairs beautifully with the sweet flavor of the roasted peppers and the brightness of the pesto.

- 4   RED BELL PEPPERS
- 2   LARGE CLOVES GARLIC, THINLY SLICED
- SEA SALT
- FRESHLY GROUND BLACK PEPPER
- ¼   CUP EXTRA-VIRGIN OLIVE OIL
- 3   TABLESPOONS PESTO, HOMEMADE (PAGE 98) OR STORE-BOUGHT
- 8   SLICES FRESH MOZZARELLA CHEESE

Preheat the oven to 350F. Oil a roasting pan.

Cut the peppers in half lengthwise, through their stems. Scrape out and discard the cores and seeds. Wash the peppers and pat dry. Place the peppers, cut side up, in the prepared pan. Divide the garlic slices between them and season to taste with sea salt and pepper. Spoon ½ tablespoon olive oil over each pepper half. Roast for 40 minutes.

Transfer the peppers to individual serving plates and top each with a generous teaspoon of pesto and a slice of mozzarella. Serve warm.

"non tutto il male vien per nuocere."

there is good in everything.

192

risotto alla milanese
arborio rice with saffron

This simple, satisfying classic is a perfect prelude to Beef in Barolo Wine.

- 10 CUPS CHICKEN OR VEGETABLE STOCK OR REDUCED-SODIUM CANNED BROTH
- 2 ENVELOPES SAFFRON POWDER OR 1 LARGE PINCH SAFFRON THREADS
- 1¼ STICKS (10 TABLESPOONS) UNSALTED BUTTER
- 1 ONION, FINELY CHOPPED
- 3 CUPS ARBORIO RICE
- 1 CUP PARMIGIANO REGGIANO, GRATED
- SEA SALT
- FRESHLY GROUND BLACK PEPPER

In a medium saucepan, bring the broth to a simmer and keep warm. In a small bowl, combine 1 ladle of the warm broth with the saffron.

In a large heavy pot, melt 5 tablespoons of the butter. Add the onion and cook until transparent, stirring a few times. Add the rice and cook, stirring, 3 to 4 minutes.

Begin adding the broth, one ladle at a time, and cook, stirring constantly, until the broth is fully absorbed by the rice. Continue adding the warm broth in this way until you've used up the broth. Add the remaining 5 tablespoons butter, the cheese, and the salt and pepper. The risotto will have a creamy consistency but should remain al dente.

manzo in barolo
beef in barolo wine

The rich flavor of beef and full-bodied Barolo are a matchless pairing. It makes for a delicious midwinter indulgence.

- ¼ CUP EXTRA-VIRGIN OLIVE OIL
- 1 BONELESS ROLLED RIB OF BEEF OR BEEF ROUND (2¼ POUNDS)
- 2 CLOVES GARLIC, CRUSHED
- 4 SHALLOTS, SLICED
- 2 STALKS CELERY, THINLY SLICED
- 1 LARGE CARROT, THINLY SLICED
- 1 TEASPOON CHOPPED FRESH ROSEMARY
- 1 TEASPOON CHOPPED FRESH OREGANO
- 2 WHOLE CLOVES
- 1 BOTTLE (750 ML) BAROLO WINE
- BEEF STOCK OR REDUCED-SODIUM CANNED BROTH IF NEEDED
- FRESHLY GRATED NUTMEG
- SEA SALT
- FRESHLY GROUND BLACK PEPPER

Heat the olive oil in a Dutch oven or other large heavy pot over high heat until hot but not smoking and brown the meat on all sides. Remove the meat from the pot.

Add the garlic, shallots, celery, carrot, herbs, and cloves to the pot and cook, stirring, for 5 minutes, until the onion is transparent. Set the meat on top of the vegetables. Pour in the wine, cover, and gently simmer over low heat until the beef is tender, about 2 hours.

Transfer the beef to a serving platter. Using a hand blender or transferring the contents of the pot to a blender, purée the vegetables, adding a little hot beef stock if needed to get the consistency you want. Season to taste with nutmeg, sea salt, and pepper.

Cut the beef into slices and serve with the sauce.

cipolline agrodolce

sweet and savory cipolline onions

The small onions known as cipolline are much sweeter than other onions and are a favorite in Italian cooking. Here I give them a sweet and savory Sicilian treatment.

- ½ STICK (4 TABLESPOONS) UNSALTED BUTTER
- 5 TABLESPOONS SUGAR
- ½ CUP WHITE WINE VINEGAR
- 2 TABLESPOONS BALSAMIC VINEGAR
- 1½ POUNDS CIPOLLINE, PEELED
   SEA SALT
   FRESHLY GROUND BLACK PEPPER

In a large saucepan over low heat, melt the butter. Add the sugar and heat until it dissolves, stirring constantly. Add the vinegars and onions and stir until well combined and the onions are coated with the butter-vinegar mixture. Season to taste with sea salt and pepper.

Cover the saucepan, increase the heat to medium, and cook for 20 minutes. Uncover the pan and cook another 10 minutes, stirring frequently, until the onions are golden and soft when pierced with a knife and the liquid is reduced to a syrupy glaze. Serve hot.

pinolata

pine nut cake

Sweet and crunchy, these pine nut squares couldn't be easier to whip together.

- 2 STICKS (16 TABLESPOONS) UNSALTED BUTTER
- 4 LARGE EGGS
- 1½ CUPS GRANULATED SUGAR
- 2¼ CUPS ALL-PURPOSE FLOUR
- 1 TEASPOON BAKING POWDER
- ¾ CUP MILK
- 1 TABLESPOON FRESH LEMON JUICE
- ½ CUP PINE NUTS
   CONFECTIONERS' SUGAR

Preheat the oven to 350F. Butter a 13- by 9-inch baking dish.

In a large bowl, beat together the butter, eggs, and granulated sugar. Add the flour all at once. Add the baking powder and mix together. Add the milk and lemon juice and mix together well. Stir in the pine nuts.

Pour the batter into the prepared baking dish. Bake for 25 minutes (the top will be golden). Allow to cool completely (30 minutes). Sprinkle with confectioners' sugar and cut into squares.

MENU

34

SERVES 8 TO 10

crostini di melanzane arrostite
toasts with roasted eggplant

gnudi di spinaci alla ricotta e parmigiano
spinach and cheese dumplings

baccalà all'italiano
cod, italian style

*insalata mista con noce, pomodori secchi
e gorgonzola*
mixed greens with walnuts, sun-dried tomatoes and gorgonzola

mele al forno
baked apples in filo dough

My distant cousin Nadia and I both grew up with a love
for cooking Italian food. I always leaned toward the primi
and secondi, while the desserts were Nadia's specialty. She
taught me how to make the wonderful mele al forno in this
menu. Nadia's mother hails from Tuscany, where apples
play a larger role in the cooking than in southern Italy.

crostini di melanzane arrostite

toasts with roasted eggplant

Roasting eggplant gives it a smoky creaminess that is wonderful when spread on crisp crostini.

1	**LARGE EGGPLANT**
	SEA SALT
	FRESHLY GROUND BLACK PEPPER
1	**TABLESPOON EXTRA-VIRGIN OLIVE OIL**
1–2	**LOAVES OF THIN ITALIAN BREAD, CUT INTO SLICES ¼ INCH THICK**

Preheat the oven to 400F.

Place the eggplant on a baking sheet, pierce a couple of times with a skewer, and bake until the entire eggplant collapses, about 20 minutes.

When the eggplant is cool enough to handle, slice it down the middle and scoop out the flesh, placing it in a small bowl. Season to taste with sea salt and pepper and stir in the olive oil.

Place the bread slices on a cookie sheet and toast in the oven for 10 minutes. Spread with the eggplant mixture and serve.

gnudi di spinaci alla ricotta e parmigiano

spinach and cheese dumplings

Looking a little like gnocchi, these lighter-than-air dumplings are thought of as ravioli without the pasta. They're usually made with ricotta cheese, and here I prepare them with the addition of spinach and Parmigiano.

1	**POUND FRESH OR FROZEN SPINACH**
2	**CUPS RICOTTA**
6	**LARGE EGGS**
2	**CUPS SEMOLINA FLOUR, 1 CUP TO BE ADDED TO THE DOUGH AND 1 CUP TO BE SPRINKLED ON THE TRAY**
	SEA SALT
	FRESHLY GROUND BLACK PEPPER
1	**TABLESPOON FRESHLY GRATED NUTMEG**
6	**OUNCES PARMIGIANO-REGGIANO, GRATED, PLUS EXTRA GRATED CHEESE FOR SERVING**
	EXTRA-VIRGIN OLIVE OIL

Cook the spinach by either steaming it or cooking it "dry" in a frying pan (no liquid should be added). Drain. Let cool, and finely chop.

In a large bowl, beat the ricotta with a fork. Add 5 of the eggs, one at a time, beating well after each addition. Separate the last egg, discarding the white. Add the yolk to the ricotta and beat well. Stir in 1 cup of the semolina. Season to taste with sea salt and pepper. Stir in the nutmeg, Parmigiano, and spinach.

Spread the remaining 1 cup of semolina over a large flat tray.

Shape the spinach mixture into oblong football shapes about 2 inches by 1½ inches. As you shape them, place them on the semolina-covered tray. (The semolina keeps them from sticking.) Chill in refrigerator for 2 hours.

To cook the gnudi, bring a large pot of salted water to a boil. Carefully drop the gnudi, in three batches so the pot is not too crowded, into the boiling water and cook until they float to the surface, about 3 minutes. Using a slotted spoon, transfer the gnudi to a warm serving dish.

Serve the gnudi with more Parmigiano and a drizzle of olive oil.

baccalà all'italiano

cod, italian style

Hazelnuts add crunch to the breadcrumb topping for flaky cod fillets; the hazelnut oil, garlic, and lemon juice mixture provides big flavor.

½ **STICK (4 TABLESPOONS) UNSALTED BUTTER**

1 **CUP PLAIN BREADCRUMBS**

¼ **CUP CHOPPED HAZELNUTS**

FINELY GRATED ZEST AND JUICE OF 3 LEMONS, PLUS AN ADDITIONAL ¼ CUP JUICE FOR THE GARLIC-AND-OIL DRIZZLING MIXTURE

LEAVES FROM 4 SPRIGS FRESH ROSEMARY

¼ **CUP CHOPPED FRESH ITALIAN PARSLEY**

8 **COD FILLETS (ABOUT 6 OUNCES EACH)**

2 **CLOVES GARLIC, CRUSHED TO A PASTE**

5 **TABLESPOONS HAZELNUT OIL**

Preheat the oven to 400F. Line a shallow roasting pan with aluminum foil.

In a large saucepan, melt the butter. Remove from the heat, add the breadcrumbs, hazelnuts, lemon zest and juice, rosemary, and parsley, and mix well.

Place the cod in a single layer in the prepared roasting pan. Spread the breadcrumb mixture evenly over the top of the cod. Bake for 20 minutes, until golden and bubbly.

Meanwhile, in a small bowl mix together the garlic, ¼ cup lemon juice, and hazelnut oil.

When the cod has cooked, drizzle the oil mixture over the top and serve.

"chi cerca, trova"

he who seeks, finds.

insalata mista con noce, pomodori secchi e gorgonzola

mixed greens with walnuts, sun-dried tomatoes and gorgonzola

Walnuts and blue cheese are a natural combination in this palate-pleasing salad. Toasting the nuts adds even more flavor.

- 1 **CUP WALNUTS**
- 2 **POUNDS MIXED GREENS, INCLUDING RADICCHIO, ENDIVE, AND FRISÉE, TORN OR CUT INTO BITE-SIZE PIECES, AS NEEDED**
- 2 **TABLESPOONS, CHOPPED, OIL-PACKED SUN-DRIED TOMATOES**
- ¼ **CUP CRUMBLED GORGONZOLA**
- ¼ **CUP EXTRA-VIRGIN OLIVE OIL**
- **SEA SALT**

Preheat the oven to 300F. Put the walnuts on a baking sheet and toast for 10 minutes. Allow to cool.

Place the walnuts, greens, sun-dried tomatoes, and gorgonzola in a large salad bowl. Add the olive oil and toss to coat. Season to taste with sea salt and toss again.

mele al forno

baked apples in filo dough

This recipe was given to me by a cousin who loves to cook just as much as I do. It's heavenly.

- ½ **CUP FIRMLY PACKED LIGHT BROWN SUGAR**
- ¼ **CUP GRANULATED SUGAR**
- 1 **TEASPOON GROUND CINNAMON**
- 1 **TEASPOON FRESHLY GRATED NUTMEG**
- 2 **TABLESPOONS FINELY GRATED LEMON ZEST**
- 8–10 **LARGE TART APPLES**
- 8–10 **SHEETS THAWED FILO DOUGH**
- ½ **STICK (4 TABLESPOONS) UNSALTED BUTTER, MELTED**
- **WHIPPED CREAM FOR GARNISH**

Preheat the oven to 350F.

In a small bowl, mix together both sugars and the cinnamon, nutmeg, and lemon zest.

Leaving the skin on, core each apple from stem to bottom. When you're done, you ought to be able to see through the center of the apple.

Fold a sheet of filo in half. Using a pastry brush, butter the edges well with the melted butter. Place an apple in the middle of the folded filo sheet. Fill the center of the apple with the sugar mixture. Wrap the filo around the apple and butter the top. (Note: The seam of the filo dough can be on top of the apple or underneath—it doesn't matter. Butter the seam well so it doesn't open during baking.) Set the apple on a jelly roll pan. Sprinkle ½ teaspoon of the sugar mixture on top of the folded filo dough. Repeat with the remaining apples, filo, melted butter, and sugar mixture.

Bake the apples until the filo is golden, about 40 minutes. Serve each topped with a dollop of whipped cream.

MENU

35

SERVES 8 TO 10

crostini fiorentini
florentine toasts with chicken liver paste

⋯⋯⋯⋯⋯⋯⋯⋯⋯⋯⋯⋯⋯⋯⋯⋯⋯⋯⋯⋯⋯⋯

tagliatelle al porcino
egg pasta with porcini mushrooms

⋯⋯⋯⋯⋯⋯⋯⋯⋯⋯⋯⋯⋯⋯⋯⋯⋯⋯⋯⋯⋯⋯

bistecca alla fiorentina
florentine t-bone steak

⋯⋯⋯⋯⋯⋯⋯⋯⋯⋯⋯⋯⋯⋯⋯⋯⋯⋯⋯⋯⋯⋯

funghi trifolati
sautéed mushrooms

⋯⋯⋯⋯⋯⋯⋯⋯⋯⋯⋯⋯⋯⋯⋯⋯⋯⋯⋯⋯⋯⋯

zuccotto
dome-shaped chocolate mousse cake

La Sostanza, a trattoria in Florence, is known for its bistecca alla Fiorentina, and it is featured in this menu. One of our family's enduring memories dates back to when my son Guido was two years old and he dropped all the trattoria's silverware from an antique drawer. Even now, when Guido walks into Sostanza, they shout in unison: "Terremoto!" (Earthquake!)

crostini fiorentini

florentine toasts with chicken liver paste

These are the best crostini I have ever eaten. The topping can be prepared the day before. Let it cool completely, cover, and refrigerate. It should come to room temperature before serving.

- 2 TABLESPOONS EXTRA-VIRGIN OLIVE OIL
- ½ ONION, FINELY CHOPPED
- 1 POUND CHICKEN LIVERS, TRIMMED OF MEMBRANES AND RINSED
- ½ CUP VIN SANTO (ITALIAN DESSERT WINE)
- 2 TABLESPOONS UNSALTED BUTTER
- 1 TABLESPOON CAPERS
- 2 ANCHOVY FILLETS
- ¾ TO 1 CUP CHICKEN OR VEGETABLE STOCK OR REDUCED-SODIUM CANNED BROTH
  SEA SALT
  FRESHLY GROUND BLACK PEPPER
  ITALIAN BREAD, THINLY SLICED

In a large skillet, heat the olive oil over medium heat. Add the onion and cook, stirring a few times, until golden. Add the chicken livers and cook for 15 minutes, stirring regularly and slowly adding the vin santo, letting it cook off before adding more.

Add the butter, capers, and anchovies and cook for another 15 minutes over moderate heat, wetting the mixture with a little of the stock at a time and cooking it off before adding more, and mashing it with the back of a wooden spoon. Season to taste with sea salt and pepper.

Let the mixture cool slightly, transfer to a food processor, and pulse until it becomes very smooth and velvety.

Preheat the oven to 350F. Put the bread slices on a cookie sheet and toast for 10 minutes. Spread the paste on the bread and serve.

tagliatelle al porcino

egg pasta with porcini mushrooms

No other pasta dish I have ever experienced (except tagliatelle with truffles) comes close to the deep layers of flavor in this recipe.

- 16 OUNCES DRIED PORCINI MUSHROOMS
- 2 TABLESPOONS EXTRA-VIRGIN OLIVE OIL
- 1 CLOVE GARLIC, MINCED
- 2 TABLESPOONS CHOPPED FRESH ITALIAN PARSLEY OR OTHER FRESH HERBS TO TASTE
  SEA SALT
  FRESHLY GROUND BLACK PEPPER
- 2 POUNDS TAGLIATELLE
- 1 CUP HEAVY CREAM
  GRATED PARMIGIANO-REGGIANO FOR SERVING

In a small saucepan, combine the porcini and ½ cup water. Bring to a simmer, remove from the heat, cover, and let stand for 15 minutes. Drain the mushrooms through a fine-mesh sieve lined with paper towels to remove the grit from the soaking water. Reserve the soaking water. Rinse the mushrooms of any grit, and chop.

In a medium skillet, heat the olive oil over medium-high heat. Add the garlic and cook, stirring, 1 minute. Add the porcini and soaking water and bring to a boil. Reduce the heat to medium and simmer until the sauce has thickened, about 10 minutes. Stir in the parsley and season to taste with sea salt and pepper.

Meanwhile, bring a large pot of salted water to a boil. Add the tagliatelle and cook until al dente, 4 minutes.

Stir the cream into the mushroom sauce. Drain the pasta and toss with the mushroom sauce in the skillet. Serve with the cheese, if desired.

bistecca alla fiorentina

florentine t-bone steak

This recipe is simplicity itself. It's all about the natural flavor of the beef, so be sure to buy the best-quality steaks you can afford.

2   **PORTERHOUSE STEAKS (2 POUNDS EACH), ABOUT 1½ INCHES THICK**

     SEA SALT

     FRESHLY GROUND BLACK PEPPER

     EXTRA-VIRGIN OLIVE OIL

     LEMON WEDGES

Preheat your gas grill to direct high heat or preheat a broiler. Set the grill rack or broiler pan 4 inches away from the heat.

Rub the steaks all over with salt and pepper. Grill or broil the steaks for 4 to 5 minutes per side (depending on their thickness) for rare. Make a small cut in the thickest part to check for doneness. An instant-read meat thermometer should read 145F. For longer cooking, move the steaks to a cooler part of the grill or move the broiler rack away from the heat element.

Let the steaks rest for 5 minutes before cutting into thin slices. Arrange the slices on a platter, sprinkle with salt, drizzle with olive oil, and serve with lemon wedges.

funghi trifolati

sautéed mushrooms

The meaty texture and flavor of mushrooms make them a perfect pairing with beef. Use all of one type of mushroom (your choice) or mix them up.

¼   **CUP EXTRA-VIRGIN OLIVE OIL**

2   **CLOVES GARLIC, PEELED**

1½   **POUNDS BUTTON MUSHROOMS, THINLY SLICED**

1   **TEASPOON SEA SALT**

1   **TEASPOON FRESHLY GROUND BLACK PEPPER**

2   **TABLESPOONS UNSALTED BUTTER**

4   **ANCHOVY FILLETS, CHOPPED**

1   **TABLESPOON CHOPPED FRESH ITALIAN PARSLEY**

     JUICE OF ½ LEMON

In a large skillet, heat the olive oil and garlic together over medium heat until the garlic is browned on all sides. Discard the garlic.

Add the mushrooms, salt, and pepper to the skillet and cook over medium heat, stirring occasionally, until all the water from the mushrooms has evaporated. Add the butter, anchovies, and parsley, stir to combine, and cook for 5 minutes.

Remove from the heat and stir in the lemon juice.

zuccotto

dome-shaped chocolate mousse cake

Keeping with the overall Florentine theme of this menu, we end with the chocolate mousse– and whipped cream–stuffed Zuccotto, whose dome shape is said to resemble Brunelleschi's Duomo at the beautiful Cathedral of Santa Maria del Fiore in the heart of Florence.

2   POUND CAKES
¼   CUP BRANDY
8   OUNCES BITTERSWEET CHOCOLATE, MELTED
2   CUPS HEAVY CREAM
¼   CUP CONFECTIONERS' SUGAR

Line a large glass or stainless-steel bowl with plastic wrap. Cut the pound cakes into ½-inch-thick slices and cut the slices on the diagonal into triangles. Line the bowl with pound cake so that the tips of the triangles touch at the bottom of the bowl (like a windmill). Brush the pound cake with some of the brandy.

Melt the bittersweet chocolate over a double boiler. Allow to cool. Whip the cream until stiff peaks form. Add ¾ cup of the whipped cream to the melted chocolate and stir gently until combined. Layer the chocolate whipped cream over the pound cake slices in the cake bowl. Add the confectioners' sugar to the remaining 1¼ cups of whipped cream and layer the sweetened plain whipped cream on top of the chocolate mixture.

Lay the remaining pieces of pound cake across the whipped cream to form a "floor." Cover the bowl with plastic wrap and refrigerate for at least 2 hours.

When ready to serve, carefully flip the bowl over onto a round platter. Remove the plastic wrap and slice into wedges.

"a buon intenditor, poche parole."

a word to the wise is sufficient

MENU

36

SERVES 8 TO 10

verdure marinate
marinated vegetables

linguine con vongole alla nonna
nana's linguine with clam sauce

gamberi marinati alla siciliana
sicilian marinated shrimp

caprese al forno
baked caprese salad with tomato and mozzarella

castanaccio
chestnut cake

Christmas Eve is a very special time for Italians, as important as Christmas Day. Our all-fish menu, served on this night, is known as the Feast of the Seven Fishes, and it is an elaborate feast. Not all families prepare the magic number of seven dishes, however. The two fish dishes in this menu were my nana's favorites, and we wouldn't think of celebrating Christmas Eve without them.

verdure marinate

marinated vegetables

A classic antipasto offering that is completely do-ahead. Prep everything in the morning and let it all marinate at room temperature until it's time for dinner.

PEPPERS

- 3 **RED BELL PEPPERS**
- 3 **YELLOW BELL PEPPERS**
- 4 **CLOVES GARLIC, SLICED**
- ¼ **CUP CHOPPED FRESH BASIL**
- ½ **CUP EXTRA-VIRGIN OLIVE OIL**
  - **SEA SALT**
  - **FRESHLY GROUND BLACK PEPPER**

MUSHROOMS

- 1 **POUND BUTTON MUSHROOMS**
- ¼ **CUP EXTRA-VIRGIN OLIVE OIL**
- 1 **LARGE CLOVE GARLIC, CRUSHED**
- 1 **TABLESPOON CHOPPED FRESH ROSEMARY**
- 1 **CUP DRY WHITE WINE**
  - **FRESH ROSEMARY SPRIGS**

OLIVES

- 1 **DRIED HOT RED PEPPER, CRUSHED**
  - **GRATED ZEST OF 1 LEMON**
- ½ **CUP EXTRA-VIRGIN OLIVE OIL**
- 1⅓ **CUPS PITTED ITALIAN BLACK OLIVES**

- 2 **TABLESPOONS CHOPPED FRESH ITALIAN PARSLEY**
- 1 **LEMON WEDGE**

Make the peppers: Preheat the broiler. Place the peppers on a broiler pan and set under the broiler. Broil until the peppers are blackened and blistered all over, turning them occasionally. Remove from the broiler and, using tongs, transfer the peppers to a paper bag. Close the bag and let stand until the peppers cool. (This steams the peppers, which makes it easier to remove the skins.) Pull the skins from the peppers. Cut the peppers in half and remove the stems and seeds. Cut the peppers into strips and place them in a bowl. Add the garlic, basil, and olive oil and season to taste with sea salt and pepper. Toss to coat well with the oil, cover, and marinate at room temperature for 3 to 4 hours.

Make the mushrooms: Trim and thickly slice the mushrooms and put them in a large bowl. Heat the olive oil in a small saucepan and add the garlic and chopped rosemary. Pour in the wine and bring to a boil. Reduce the heat to a simmer and cook for 3 minutes. Season to taste with salt and pepper. Pour the mixture over the mushrooms and mix to coat the mushrooms well. Cover and marinate at room temperature 2 to 3 hours, stirring occasionally.

Make the olives: Put the dried pepper and lemon zest in a small saucepan with the olive oil. Heat gently over low heat for about 3 minutes. Add the olives and heat for another minute. Let cool.

To serve, place the peppers, mushrooms, and olives in individual serving bowls. Garnish the mushrooms with the sprigs of rosemary. Garnish the olives with the chopped parsley and set a lemon wedge on a small plate beside the bowl.

linguine con vongole alla nonna

nana's linguine with clam sauce

My nana was famous for her linguine with clams. It was her signature dish at Christmas but she also made it frequently throughout the year, lucky for us!

- 2 POUNDS LINGUINE
- ⅓ CUP EXTRA-VIRGIN OLIVE OIL
- 8 CLOVES GARLIC, SLICED PAPER THIN
- 4 JARS (5 OUNCES EACH) ITALIAN CLAMS, RINSED WELL
- ½ CUP BOTTLED CLAM JUICE
- 2 TEASPOONS RED PEPPER FLAKES
- ¼ CUP CHOPPED FRESH ITALIAN PARSLEY
   SEA SALT

Bring a large pot of salted water to a boil. Add the linguine and cook until al dente, 5 minutes.

Meanwhile, heat the olive oil and garlic together over medium heat until the garlic is soft but not brown. Add the clams and cook, stirring, for 1 minute. Add the clam juice and cook 2 to 3 minutes.

Drain the linguine. Toss it in the pan with the clam sauce over low heat until it is well coated. Add the red pepper flakes, parsley, and sea salt to taste, and toss to mix. Transfer to a warm platter and serve immediately.

gamberi marinati alla siciliana

sicilian marinated shrimp

You can also skewer these shrimp and cook them on a grill over medium heat until slightly blackened.

- ½ CUP FRESH LEMON JUICE
- ¼ CUP FRESH ORANGE JUICE
- 3 CLOVES GARLIC, ROUGHLY CHOPPED
- ¼ TEASPOON SEA SALT
- 2 POUNDS SHRIMP, PREFERABLY JUMBO SHRIMP, SHELLS LEFT ON

In a large bowl, combine the lemon and orange juices, the garlic, and the sea salt. Whisk to combine.

Add the shrimp to the marinade, toss to coat, and let marinate for 5 minutes.

Heat a large skillet over medium heat. Using a slotted spoon, remove the shrimp from the marinade and add to the hot skillet. Cook, stirring, until they turn bright pink and transfer to a serving bowl.

caprese al forno

baked caprese salad with tomato and mozzarella

This is a warm, deliciously melty twist on the classic Caprese salad. Be sure to top each stack with a slice of tomato; if the cheese is on top, it becomes too messy, and if the basil is on top, it will turn black in the heat of the broiler.

6	LARGE RIPE TOMATOES
8	OUNCES FRESH MOZZARELLA CHEESE, THINLY SLICED
1	LARGE BUNCH FRESH BASIL
2	TABLESPOONS EXTRA-VIRGIN OLIVE OIL
	SEA SALT
	FRESHLY GROUND BLACK PEPPER

Preheat the oven to 375F. Line a baking sheet with parchment paper.

Cut the tomatoes across into ¼-inch-thick rounds, discarding the top and bottom rounds. Top a slice of tomato with a slice of mozzarella and a basil leaf. Repeat with a slice of tomato, a slice of mozzarella, and a basil leaf. Top with a final slice of tomato. Repeat so that you have 8 to 10 individual stacks. Transfer the stacks to the prepared baking sheet. Sprinkle the stacks with the olive oil, and season to taste with sea salt and pepper.

Bake for 5 minutes. Turn the broiler on and broil until the mozzarella begins to melt, about 2 minutes. Serve immediately.

castanaccio

chestnut cake

This rich, dense cake is baked in a pie plate, with the unique earthy flavor of chestnut flour. Serve it in wedges topped with a dollop of whipped cream.

1½	CUPS CHESTNUT FLOUR (AVAILABLE IN ITALIAN FOOD OR SPECIALTY STORES)
¼	TEASPOON SEA SALT
2	TABLESPOONS EXTRA-VIRGIN OLIVE OIL
2	TABLESPOONS GOLDEN RAISINS
2	TABLESPOONS PINE NUTS
¼	TEASPOON FRESH ROSEMARY (NOT CHOPPED)

Preheat the oven to 375F. Grease a 9-inch pie plate.

In a medium bowl, mix together the flour, salt, olive oil, raisins, and 1½ cups water until smooth. Pour the batter into the prepared pie plate and scatter the pine nuts and rosemary over the top.

Bake until the top is crisp, about 45 minutes. Slice into wedges and serve when still warm.

MENU

37

SERVES 8 TO 10

spiedini di mozzarella
mozzarella on skewers

pasta all'arrabbiata
pasta with spicy tomato sauce

salsicce e peperoni con patate
nana's classic sausage and peppers with potatoes

insalata verde con finocchio
green salad with fennel

crostata di gelato
spumoni pie bombe

At our house, this go-to summer meal is prepared on the grill by my son Guido, our grill man. From the Italian bread with mozzarella to the sausage to the spumoni, it is his favorite menu of all, and one of the most informal ones in this cookbook. And remember, the key to Sunday dinner has nothing to do with formality; it is just being together with the people you love, cooking together, and eating together.

214

spiedini di mozzarella

mozzarella on skewers

This simple antipasto also makes a great merenda, or afternoon snack. Have your children help you assemble the skewers.

- 3 TABLESPOONS EXTRA-VIRGIN OLIVE OIL
  SEA SALT
  FRESHLY GROUND BLACK PEPPER
- 12 SLICES ITALIAN COUNTRY BREAD, EACH ABOUT ½ INCH THICK AND 4 INCHES IN DIAMETER
- 8 OUNCES MOZZARELLA, CUT INTO ¼-INCH-THICK SLICES

Preheat a gas grill on medium-high heat or preheat the oven to 350F.

In a small bowl, mix the olive oil with sea salt and pepper to taste. Brush the oil on both sides of each slice of bread.

Assemble 8 long metal skewers. Begin skewers with a slice of bread, followed by a slice of mozzarella, and continue, alternating, until the skewer is full. Wrap the skewers in aluminum foil and place on the grill or in the oven. Cook until the mozzarella is softened, about 8 minutes.

pasta all'arrabbiata

pasta with spicy tomato sauce

Arrabbiata means angry, and this version of the classic dish is plenty angry—and delicious—with 2 teaspoons of red pepper flakes.

- ½ CUP EXTRA-VIRGIN OLIVE OIL
- 4 TEASPOONS FINELY CHOPPED GARLIC
- 2 TEASPOONS RED PEPPER FLAKES
- 2 CANS (28 OUNCES EACH) CRUSHED TOMATOES (PREFERABLY SAN MARZANO)
  PINCH OF SEA SALT
- ¼ CUP CHOPPED FRESH ITALIAN PARSLEY
- 2 POUNDS PENNE RIGATE

Heat the olive oil in a large skillet over medium heat. Add the garlic and red pepper flakes and cook until the garlic is soft; don't let the garlic burn. Add the tomatoes, adjust the heat to a simmer, and cook for about 30 minutes, until the sauce is thickened slightly. Add the salt and parsley.

Bring a large pot of salted water to a boil. Add the penne and cook until al dente, 7 minutes. Drain the pasta, toss it with the sauce, and let simmer for 2 to 3 minutes before serving.

salsicce e peperoni con patate

nana's classic sausage and peppers with potatoes

Feel free to make this dish with sweet sausage, hot sausage or a combination of the two.

- 2 POUNDS RED POTATOES, CUT INTO CHUNKS
- ¼ CUP PLUS 2 TABLESPOONS EXTRA-VIRGIN OLIVE OIL
  SEA SALT
- 3 BELL PEPPERS (GREEN, RED, YELLOW), SEEDED AND CUT INTO STRIPS
- 3 RED ONIONS, CUT IN HALF, THEN CUT INTO THICK HALF-MOONS
  FRESHLY GROUND BLACK PEPPER
- 1 TEASPOON RED PEPPER FLAKES
- 2 POUNDS SWEET ITALIAN SAUSAGE WITH FENNEL SEEDS

Preheat the oven to 400F.

Toss the potatoes with ¼ cup of the olive oil and season to taste with sea salt. Spread out in a large baking dish or baking sheet. Roast, turning once, until golden and fork tender, 45 to 60 minutes.

Meanwhile, heat the remaining 2 tablespoons olive oil in a large skillet over medium heat. Add the bell peppers and onions, season lightly with salt, black pepper, and the red pepper, and cook, stirring, until softened.

If you would like to grill the sausages, preheat a gas grill on medium heat. Grill the sausages until cooked all the way through, turning them several times, 25 to 30 minutes. (You can also cook the sausages in a large skillet filled with ½ inch water over medium-high heat. It will take about the same amount of time. When the water evaporates, turn the sausages several times to brown them.)

Place the sausage on a large platter. Mix the potatoes, peppers, and onions together and arrange around the sausage.

"a buon intenditor, poche parole."

a word to the wise is sufficient.

insalata verde con finocchio

green salad with fennel

This salad is guaranteed to cool your palate with crispy, crunchy romaine, cucumbers, and fennel bulb.

- 1 **HEAD ROMAINE, CHOPPED**
- 2 **CUCUMBERS, PEELED AND THINLY SLICED**
- 1 **FENNEL BULB, STALKS REMOVED, BULB THINLY SLICED**
- 3 **TABLESPOONS EXTRA-VIRGIN OLIVE OIL**
- 1 **TABLESPOON BALSAMIC VINEGAR**
  SEA SALT
  FRESHLY GROUND BLACK PEPPER

Toss the romaine, cucumbers, and fennel together in a large salad bowl. Sprinkle with the olive oil and vinegar, season to taste with sea salt and pepper, and toss again.

crostata di gelato

spumoni pie bombe

A mixture of chocolate, cherry, and pistachio ice creams, spumoni is a wholly Italian American invention. Here it's given a biscotti crumb topping for a kind of ice-cream pie treatment.

- 1 **GALLON SPUMONI GELATO**
- 8 **OUNCES BISCOTTI OR CANTUCCINI, CHOPPED INTO SMALL PIECES**
  WHIPPED CREAM

Bring the spumoni to room temperature, but don't let it melt completely.

Line a medium aluminum or freezer-proof glass bowl with plastic wrap. With a rubber spatula, spoon the spumoni into the bowl, pushing it down to make sure there are no air pockets. Flatten it across the top. Top with the chopped biscotti, pushing them gently into the ice cream. Cover with plastic wrap and freeze for about 2 hours.

When ready to serve, remove the bombe from the freezer and allow to soften for 15 minutes. Take the plastic off the top. Place a serving platter on top of the bowl and flip (them both) over. Remove the bowl and the plastic.

Slice the bombe like you would a pie, topping each serving with whipped cream.

MENU

38

SERVES 8 TO 10

crostini di olive verdi
toasts with green olive paste

....

peperonata
pepper stew over arborio rice

....

spiedini di manzo
beef on skewers

....

cavolfiori bontempi
grandma franco's cauliflower bontempi

....

crostata di marmellata
marmalade tart

From Milano to Palermo, the crostata—a buttery tart filled
with the rich jam of your choice—is a classic. And it's so
easy to prepare, all members of your family can make it.
In fact, this whole menu is filled with simple favorites, so
you'll want to make it often throughout the year, and not
just on Sundays.

crostini di olive verdi

toasts with green olive paste

This is a big-flavor crostini. The saltiness of the olives and Pecorino and the bite of the garlic are offset by the creamy sweet butter.

- 3 CLOVES GARLIC, CHOPPED
- ½ STICK (4 TABLESPOONS) UNSALTED BUTTER
- 1 CUP CHOPPED PITTED GREEN OLIVES (PREFERABLY SICILIAN)
- ½ CUP GRATED PARMIGIANO-REGGIANO
- ½ CUP GRATED PECORINO ROMANO
- 2 LOAVES THIN ITALIAN BREAD, EACH CUT ON THE DIAGONAL INTO 12 SLICES

Preheat the broiler.

Place the garlic, butter, olives, and cheeses in a blender and process until chunky. Spread the mixture over one side of each of the bread slices.

Transfer the slices to large baking sheets and broil for 2 minutes. Serve immediately.

peperonata

pepper stew over arborio rice

When simmered together, the bell peppers, tomatoes, and onions are reduced to a rich, velvety texture. Peperonata is delicious with pasta, but here I serve it as a primo over rice.

- ½ CUP EXTRA-VIRGIN OLIVE OIL
- 1 POUND BELL PEPPERS OF MIXED COLORS (RED, YELLOW, GREEN, ORANGE), SEEDED AND CUT INTO ½-INCH-WIDE STRIPS
- 1 POUND RIPE TOMATOES, CUT INTO QUARTERS
- 1 POUND YELLOW OR WHITE ONIONS, CUT IN HALF, THEN CUT INTO THIN HALF-MOONS
  SEA SALT
- 1 POUND ARBORIO RICE
  GRATED PARMIGIANO-REGGIANO FOR SERVING (OPTIONAL)

In a large soup pot over medium heat, combine the olive oil, bell pepper strips, tomatoes, and onions. Cook until all the vegetables are soft, stirring occasionally, for about 2 hours. Season to taste with sea salt.

Meanwhile, cook the rice according to the package directions, adding a small amount of extra-virgin olive oil to the rice at the end of cooking.

To serve, transfer the cooked rice to a large serving bowl and pour the peperonata mixture over the top. Serve sprinkled with Parmigiano if you like.

spiedini di manzo

beef on skewers

Chunks of beef cooked to perfection over fire, then served up with a tomato relish spiked with red onion, garlic, and olives—perfect for outdoor cooking.

- 1   **POUND RUMP OR SIRLOIN STEAK**
- 16   **CHERRY TOMATOES**
- 16   **PITTED LARGE GREEN OLIVES**

BASTING LIQUID

- ½   **CUP EXTRA-VIRGIN OLIVE OIL**
- 3   **TABLESPOONS SHERRY VINEGAR OR RED WINE VINEGAR**
- 1   **CLOVE GARLIC, CRUSHED**
-   **SEA SALT**
-   **FRESHLY GROUND BLACK PEPPER**

FRESH TOMATO RELISH

- 1   **TABLESPOON EXTRA-VIRGIN OLIVE OIL**
- ½   **RED ONION, FINELY CHOPPED**
- 1   **CLOVE GARLIC, FINELY CHOPPED**
- 6   **PLUM TOMATOES, CHOPPED**
- 2   **PITTED GREEN OLIVES, SLICED**
- 1   **TABLESPOON CHOPPED FRESH ITALIAN PARSLEY**
- 1   **TABLESPOON FRESH LEMON JUICE**
-   **SEA SALT**
-   **FRESHLY GROUND BLACK PEPPER**

  FOCACCIA BREAD, SLICED

Soak 8 long wooden skewers in water for at least 30 minutes. Trim any fat from the beef and cut the meat into about 24 evenly sized chunks. Thread the pieces onto the wooden skewers, alternating the meat with the tomatoes and olives. Set on a tray.

Make the basting liquid: In a small bowl, combine the olive oil, vinegar, garlic, and sea salt and pepper to taste.

Make the Fresh Tomato Relish: Heat the olive oil in a medium skillet over medium heat. Add the onion and garlic and cook until softened, 3 to 4 minutes, stirring a few times. Add the tomatoes and olives and cook, stirring gently, until the tomatoes soften slightly, 2 to 3 minutes. Stir in the parsley and lemon juice and season to taste with sea salt and pepper. Remove from the heat and keep warm.

Preheat a gas grill on high heat or preheat the oven to 400F. If grilling, set the skewers on an oiled rack and grill, basting and turning them often, 5 to 10 minutes. If roasting, set them on a baking sheet and cook, basting and turning them often, 5 to 10 minutes.

Serve the skewers with the tomato relish and slices of focaccia.

cavolfiori bontempi

grandma franco's cauliflower bontempi

Bontempi translates literally to "good times," which is what you'll have when you tuck into tender florets of cauliflower topped with crumbs and melty mozzarella.

2	HEADS CAULIFLOWER
¼	CUP EXTRA-VIRGIN OLIVE OIL
2	LARGE EGGS
1	ONION, CHOPPED
1	CLOVE GARLIC, CHOPPED
½	CUP CHOPPED FRESH ITALIAN PARSLEY
1	POUND MOZZARELLA, SHREDDED
	SEA SALT
	FRESHLY GROUND BLACK PEPPER

Bring a large pot of water to a boil. Add the heads of cauliflower, cook about 10 minutes, until crisp-tender, and drain. When the cauliflower is cool enough to handle, cut into florets.

Preheat the oven to 350F.

Pour the olive oil into a 12- by 9-inch baking dish and tilt the dish to coat the bottom. Arrange the florets in the baking dish. In a medium bowl, beat the eggs, then stir in the onion, garlic, parsley, cheese, and sea salt and pepper to taste. Pour evenly over the cauliflower. Bake for 30 minutes, until golden and bubbly.

"casa mia, casa mia, pur che tu sei piccina, mi sembri una badia."

our house may be small, but to us it is a castle!

crostata di marmellata

marmalade tart

This is one of the most popular desserts in Italy, and everyone has his or her own version. I prefer to make my crostata with cherry or raspberry jam, as I think it gives the dessert a richer texture, but any flavor you choose will be delicious.

- 1¼ **CUPS ALL-PURPOSE FLOUR**
- ¼ **TEASPOON BAKING POWDER**
- **PINCH OF SALT**
- ⅓ **CUP SUGAR**
- 9 **TABLESPOONS UNSALTED BUTTER, CUT INTO PIECES**
- 1 **LARGE EGG YOLK**
- 1–1¼ **CUPS GOOD-QUALITY CHERRY JAM**

Combine the flour, baking powder, salt, and sugar in a medium bowl. Make a well in the center of the mixture and add the butter and egg yolk. Work the ingredients together with your fingertips or a pastry blender. Knead the mixture into a soft dough, adding a few drops of ice water. (This can also be done in a stand mixer fitted with the paddle attachment on medium speed.)

Divide the dough into 2 balls, one about two-thirds of the dough, the other one-third. On a lightly floured work surface, roll the larger ball out to a 12-inch circle. Fit it into a 9- to 9½-inch fluted tart or quiche pan with a removable bottom. Trim the dough so there is a 1-inch overhang. Prick the bottom of the crust with a fork. Chill for 30 minutes, along with the other ball of dough.

Preheat the oven to 400F.

Spoon the jam into the chilled crust, smoothing it out evenly. On a lightly floured work surface, roll out the second ball of dough into a 10-inch circle and cut into four 1-inch-wide strips with a pastry wheel. Arrange strips in a crisscross (lattice pattern) over the jam, securing the ends to the bottom pastry, first brushing them with a little water.

Bake the crostata until golden, about 30 minutes. Let it cool before removing the side and serving.

MENU

39

SERVES 8 TO 10

torta al formaggio bianco
white cheese torte

....

risotto con funghi
arborio rice with mushrooms

....

branzino in sale
sea bass in salt

....

insalata di rucola, pere e parmigiano
arugula, pear and parmesan salad

....

tiramisu
italian mascarpone cake

Drama plays a role in Italian food. It is who we are. We don't just throw something together, then rush to the table and eat it quickly. Rather, it is the process that enthralls us. The art of making pasta, the time required to make a perfect cup of espresso, and here, the drama of cooking sea bass in salt, is part of our tradition. Imagine an entire sea bass covered in coarse sea salt cooking slowly on your grill.

torta al formaggio bianco

white cheese torte

This rich, savory pie hails from Emilia-Romagna. The crisp crust holds a creamy filling of ricotta, Parmigiano, and eggs.

CRUST

- 1 CUP ALL-PURPOSE FLOUR
- PINCH OF SEA SALT
- 1 STICK (8 TABLESPOONS) COLD UNSALTED BUTTER, CUT INTO PIECES
- 3 TABLESPOONS MILK

FILLING

- 4 OUNCES (½ CUP) RICOTTA
- 4 OUNCES PARMIGIANO-REGGIANO, GRATED
- 3 TABLESPOONS PANNA DA CUCINA OR HEAVY CREAM
- 3 LARGE EGGS
- PINCH OF FRESHLY GRATED NUTMEG
- SEA SALT
- FRESHLY GROUND BLACK PEPPER

Make the crust: In a medium bowl, combine the flour and salt. Add the butter and work it into the flour with your fingertips or a pastry cutter to the consistency of small peas. Stir in the milk until the mixture comes together. Gather it together in a ball, cover with plastic wrap, and refrigerate for 1 hour.

Preheat the oven to 300F. Butter a 10-inch pie plate.

On a lightly floured work surface, roll the dough out to a 12-inch circle. Fit it into the prepared pie plate. Crimp the edge in whatever way you prefer; I like to make an S design.

Make the filling: In a large bowl, beat together the cheeses, panna da cucina, eggs, nutmeg, and sea salt and pepper to taste.

Pour the filling into the pie crust. Bake for 25 minutes, until slightly golden. Transfer to a rack to cool. This torte is excellent served at room temperature.

risotto con funghi

arborio rice with mushrooms

Make this with one kind of mushroom or mix them up. If you can find fresh porcini mushrooms, by all means, use them.

- 2 TABLESPOONS EXTRA-VIRGIN OLIVE OIL
- 2 ONIONS, CHOPPED
- 4 CLOVES GARLIC, CRUSHED WITH THE SIDE OF A KNIFE
- 1 POUND BUTTON MUSHROOMS, SLICED
- 2 CUPS ARBORIO RICE
- 8 CUPS VEGETABLE STOCK OR REDUCED-SODIUM CANNED BROTH
- SEA SALT
- FRESHLY GROUND BLACK PEPPER
- 1 CUP GRATED PARMIGIANO-REGGIANO
- CHOPPED FRESH ITALIAN PARSLEY FOR GARNISH

In a large, heavy saucepan, heat the olive oil over medium heat. Add the onion and garlic and cook until softened and translucent, about 8 minutes. Add the mushrooms and cook over medium-high heat until they give off their liquid and most of it evaporates, 8 to 10 minutes. Add the rice and cook over medium heat, stirring, for about 1 minute. Start adding the stock, ½ cup at a time, stirring constantly, until it has been fully absorbed by the rice. Continue until all the stock has been added and the risotto is creamy. Remove the pan from the heat, find the garlic cloves, and remove them. Season the risotto with sea salt and pepper to taste. Stir in the cheese until combined.

Transfer the risotto to a warm serving bowl, sprinkle with parsley, and serve immediately.

branzino in sale

sea bass in salt

I first had this dish in a trattoria located right on the beach of a seaside town in Tuscany. The fish just melts in your mouth when prepared this way.

- 8   YUKON GOLD POTATOES, PEELED
- ½   CUP EXTRA-VIRGIN OLIVE OIL, PLUS ADDITIONAL FOR DRIZZLING ON PARCHMENT PAPER AND COATING FISH
- 1   BOX (ABOUT 2 POUNDS) COARSE SEA SALT
- 1   WHOLE SEA BASS, CLEANED (6 TO 7 POUNDS)
- 1   CUP WHITE WINE

Put the potatoes in a large saucepan and cover generously with water. Bring to a boil and continue to boil until almost fully cooked. Drain and set aside until they are cool enough to handle.

Preheat the oven to 425F. Line the bottom of a roasting pan with parchment paper and drizzle with a little of the olive oil.

Pour the sea salt out onto a large sheet of parchment paper. Rub the sea bass with some olive oil, and then roll the fish in the sea salt until its skin is fully coated with salt.

Cut the potatoes into ½-inch-thick slices. Arrange the potato slices in the prepared roasting pan and set the fish on top of the potatoes.

Put the roasting pan in the oven for 5 minutes. Pour in the wine and ½ cup of oil and drizzle the fish with more oil. Bake 20 minutes.

Remove and discard the skin with the salt. Remove the fillets from the bone and set on a warm platter. Pour the wine sauce from the pan over the fish and serve with the potatoes.

insalata di rucola, pere e parmigiano

arugula, pear and parmesan salad

A classic combination of greens, fruit and cheese.

- 2   BUNCHES ARUGULA
- 2   TABLESPOONS EXTRA-VIRGIN OLIVE OIL
- 2   TEASPOONS BALSAMIC VINEGAR
-     SEA SALT
-     FRESHLY GROUND BLACK PEPPER
- 5   TART PEARS, CORED, PEELED, AND DICED
- ½   POUND PARMIGIANO-REGGIANO, CUT INTO SMALL CHUNKS

Trim the stems from the arugula. Wash the leaves well and dry. Tear into bite-size pieces.

In a large salad bowl, whisk together the olive oil, vinegar, and sea salt and pepper to taste. Add the arugula and toss well. Add the pears and Parmigiano and toss again. Serve immediately.

tiramisu

italian mascarpone cake

This recipe has been family-perfected. It comes out perfect every time—never mushy, never dry. Be aware, it does contain raw eggs.

- 30   OUNCES (ABOUT 1¼ CUPS) MASCARPONE
- ½   CUP PLUS 1 TABLESPOON SUGAR
- 6   LARGE EGGS, SEPARATED
- 2   TABLESPOONS VANILLA EXTRACT
- 1½   CUPS VERY STRONGLY BREWED ESPRESSO
- 1   CUP KAHLUA LIQUEUR
- 18   SAVOIARDI (LADYFINGER COOKIES)
-    UNSWEETENED COCOA POWDER FOR DUSTING

In a large bowl, combine the mascarpone, sugar, egg yolks, and vanilla and beat together well.

In another large bowl with an electric mixer, beat the egg whites until stiff peaks form. Gently fold the whites into the mascarpone mixture until evenly incorporated.

Cover the bottom of a flat-bottomed serving bowl (preferably a footed bowl) with a few spoonfuls of the mascarpone mixture. Mix the espresso and Kahlua together in a large shallow dish. Dip 1 ladyfinger at a time into the liquid for a few seconds, turning it over so that it is well soaked but still retains its shape. Arrange a layer of 6 soaked ladyfingers side by side in the bottom of the bowl. Cover the ladyfingers with one-third of the mascarpone mixture. Repeat the layers twice, smoothing out the final top layer of mascarpone with an icing spatula. Sift cocoa liberally over the surface. Cover and chill for at least 1 hour, and up to 24.

"non si vive di solo pane"

one does not live by bread alone.

MENU

40

SERVES 8 TO 10

fritelle di zucchini
zucchini fritters

....

gnocchi con burro e salvia
gnocchi with butter and sage

....

baccalà alla siciliana
cod, sicilian style

....

insalata di funghi
mushroom salad

....

torta bassa di cioccolata
flourless chocolate cake

Until I moved back to Italy as an adult, I had never eaten flourless chocolate cake. A pastry shop in my neighborhood is known for this treat, and once I tried it, I was hooked. I must have experimented with the recipe a hundred times before landing on this perfect balance. I guarantee that it will be a fudgy chocolate creation—not too liquidy or too dry—every time.

fritelle di zucchini

zucchini fritters

Light and crispy, these fritters are a tasty way to start the meal.

1	POUND ZUCCHINI, ENDS TRIMMED
1	CUP ALL-PURPOSE FLOUR
2	LARGE EGGS
½	CUP MILK
	SEA SALT
	FRESHLY GROUND BLACK PEPPER
¼	CUP EXTRA-VIRGIN OLIVE OIL

Preheat oven to 200F.

Using the large holes on a box grater, grate the zucchini. In a large bowl, mix the flour and eggs together well. Beat in the milk. Drain any liquid from the grated zucchini. Add the zucchini and sea salt and pepper to taste and stir to combine well.

In a medium skillet, heat the olive oil over medium-high heat. Drop the zucchini mixture by the tablespoonful into the hot oil, taking care not to crowd the pan, and cook the fritters in three or four batches, turning halfway through cooking, until golden, about 4 minutes per side. Adjust heat as necessary between batches to maintain a constant heat level. Transfer the fritters, as cooked, to paper towels to drain and keep them warm in the oven until all are cooked. Serve warm on a platter.

gnocchi con burro e salvia

gnocchi with butter and sage

I find Yukon Gold potatoes yield the richest-tasting potato gnocchi. Here they are served in the simplest, best way, with butter and sage.

8	MEDIUM POTATOES (PREFERABLY YUKON GOLD)
1	LARGE EGG YOLK
1	TABLESPOON SEA SALT
2–2½	CUPS ALL-PURPOSE FLOUR
1	STICK (8 TABLESPOONS) UNSALTED BUTTER
	FRESH SAGE LEAVES, CHOPPED
½	CUP GRATED PARMIGIANO-REGGIANO

Preheat the oven to 350F. Puncture the potatoes with a fork in several places. Bake until tender, about 1 hour. When cool enough to handle, cut the potatoes in half, scoop out the flesh and discard the skins. Run the hot potatoes through a food mill or ricer into a large bowl. Let cool slightly.

Add the egg yolk, salt, and 2 cups of the flour to the potatoes and mix well. Transfer the potato dough to a lightly floured work surface and knead it into a ball with lightly floured hands. The dough should be soft, pliable, and slightly sticky. If it is too sticky, add more of the flour.

Break the dough into pieces the size of large eggs. Shape the pieces into rolls about the thickness of your thumb. Cut the rolls across into 1-inch pieces. Hold a fork with its tines resting on the work surface at a 45-degree angle and the inside curve facing toward you. Take each piece of gnocchi and press it with your index finger against the outside curve of the fork at its tip end. Quickly slide the gnocchi up and along the tines of the fork, pressing with your index finger. At the top of the tines, remove your finger and let the gnocchi fall to the work surface. The grooves will absorb the sauce served with the gnocchi. Arrange the finished gnocchi on a lightly floured tray or plate until ready to cook.

Melt the butter in a saucepan over low heat until it foams. Add the sage leaves and cook until fragrant. Add the Parmigiano and stir to combine.

Fill a large pot two-thirds full of salted water, bring to a boil and add the gnocchi. When they float to the surface, using a slotted spoon, remove them to a warm serving dish. Pour the butter and sage sauce over the gnocchi and toss gently to coat. Serve immediately.

"amici e vini sonno meglio vecchie."

friends and wine are better old.

baccalà alla siciliana
cod, sicilian style

Italians have a soft spot in their hearts for baccalà, the dried salt cod that sustained them for hundreds of years. Prepared here in the Sicilian style, the rehydrated cod is simmered with tomatoes and olives and spiked with red pepper flakes.

2	POUNDS BACCALÀ
2	TABLESPOONS EXTRA-VIRGIN OLIVE OIL
½	WHITE ONION, FINELY CHOPPED
1	CLOVE GARLIC, MINCED
12–16	PITTED WHOLE SICILIAN GREEN OR BLACK OLIVES
2	BAY LEAVES
⅛	CUP RED PEPPER FLAKES
4	FRESH BASIL LEAVES, CHOPPED
2	CUPS FISH OR VEGETABLE STOCK OR REDUCED-SODIUM CANNED BROTH
2	RIPE TOMATOES, PEELED, SEEDED, AND EVENLY DICED
	SEA SALT
	FRESHLY GROUND BLACK PEPPER

Put the baccalà (cod) in a large bowl of cold water for 24 hours. Change the water a few times during the day until the fish is plump. Rinse the fish in cold water well to rid it of the salt.

In a large skillet, heat the olive oil over medium heat. Add the onion and cook, stirring a few times, for 4 minutes, until it is transparent. Add the garlic and cook, stirring, for 1 minute. Add the olives, bay leaves, red pepper flakes, and basil and cook for 10 minutes.

Add the fish stock, tomatoes, and baccalà and simmer for another 10 to 15 minutes, until slightly thickened. Season to taste with sea salt and black pepper and serve.

insalata di funghi

mushroom salad

Sliced fresh mushrooms dressed with a lemony anchovy vinaigrette offset the heartiness of the baccalà.

- 12 OUNCES FIRM BUTTON MUSHROOMS
- ¼ CUP EXTRA-VIRGIN OLIVE OIL
- 1 TABLESPOON FRESH LEMON JUICE
- 5 ANCHOVY FILLETS, CHOPPED
  FRESHLY GROUND BLACK PEPPER
- 1 TABLESPOON FRESH CHOPPED MARJORAM
  SEA SALT

Gently wipe the mushrooms with a damp cloth to remove any dirt. Trim off the stems and thinly slice the mushrooms with a sharp knife. Place the mushrooms in a medium salad bowl.

In a measuring cup, whisk together the olive oil and lemon juice. Pour it over the mushrooms and toss the mushrooms to coat with the dressing. Stir the anchovies into the mushrooms and season to taste with pepper. Sprinkle the marjoram over the top.

Let the salad stand for about 5 minutes to allow the mushrooms to absorb the flavors and season to taste with sea salt.

torta bassa di cioccolata

flourless chocolate cake

This is a rich, dense indulgence that makes for a beautiful presentation at the table.

- ¾ STICK (6 TABLESPOONS) UNSALTED BUTTER,
  PLUS MORE FOR GREASING THE PAN
- 1¼ CUPS GRANULATED SUGAR
- 6 LARGE EGGS, SEPARATED
- 5 TABLESPOONS INSTANT ESPRESSO GRANULES
- 6 TABLESPOONS UNSWEETENED COCOA POWDER
- 6 TABLESPOONS DARK RUM
- 1½ CUPS GROUND TOASTED BLANCHED ALMONDS
  CONFECTIONERS' SUGAR

Preheat the oven to 375F. Butter and flour a 9-inch springform pan.

Melt the butter in a glass or stainless-steel bowl or the top of a double boiler set over simmering water. Whisk in the granulated sugar and egg yolks and cook for 5 minutes, whisking constantly. Whisk in the espresso, cocoa, rum, and almonds and cook, stirring constantly, until the mixture is smooth and creamy. Transfer the mixture to a large bowl.

In another large bowl, using an electric mixer, beat the egg whites until stiff peaks form. Gently fold them into the chocolate mixture. Pour the batter into the prepared pan. Bake until firm, about 30 minutes.

Let the cake cool 30 minutes. Remove the pan and dust the cake with confectioners' sugar.

MENU

41

SERVES 8 TO 10

crostini ai tre funghi
three-mushroom toasts

....

spaghetti con pesto alla trapanese
spaghetti with pesto, trapani style

....

arista al limone
roast pork with lemon

....

insalata del fattore
farmer's salad

....

cassata siciliana
sicilian sponge cake with ricotta

I loved stuffed anything: stuffed pastas, stuffed meats, stuffed vegetables, stuffed desserts. It's like a surprise package on your plate. Have the youngest members of your family try their hand at stuffing shells or cannoli from the other menus in this book; or here, have them help you stuff the roast pork. Not only is this a unique and delicious dish, but it's fun to prepare.

crostini ai tre funghi

three-mushroom toasts

Using a variety of mushrooms gives a layering of flavors and texture, but feel free to use all of one type or substitute others that are available in your area.

- 8 OUNCES CREMINI MUSHROOMS
- 8 OUNCES FRESH PORCINI MUSHROOMS
- 8 OUNCES BUTTON MUSHROOMS
- 3 TABLESPOONS UNSALTED BUTTER
- 3 TABLESPOONS EXTRA-VIRGIN OLIVE OIL, PLUS ADDITIONAL FOR DRIZZLING ON THE BREAD
- 4 CLOVES GARLIC, CHOPPED, PLUS SLICED GARLIC FOR RUBBING THE BREAD

  LISA'S RUSTIC ITALIAN BREAD (PAGE 78) OR OTHER THICK BRUSCHETTA, SLICED ½ INCH THICK

Trim the stems off the mushrooms and slice the mushrooms thinly.

In a large skillet, melt the butter with the olive oil over medium heat. Add the mushrooms and chopped garlic and cook, stirring a few times, until they are soft. Remove from the heat and let cool. Drain all the liquid.

Meanwhile, toast the bread slices. Rub the toast slices with fresh garlic cloves and drizzle them with olive oil.

Top the toast slices with the mushroom mixture and serve.

spaghetti con pesto alla trapanese

spaghetti with pesto, trapani style

My grandmother was born and raised in a small seaside town in the province of Trapani on the island of Sicily. When Americans hear the word "pesto," they think of basil pesto. But pesto means "paste" in Italian, and there are all sorts of pestos to be found throughout Italy. Here, in the Trapani style, it is a garlic-almond pesto.

- 2 POUNDS SPAGHETTI
- 6 LARGE CLOVES GARLIC, PEELED
- 1 CUP BLANCHED ALMONDS, ROUGHLY CHOPPED
- 1 CUP EXTRA-VIRGIN OLIVE OIL
- 3 TABLESPOONS (4 OUNCES) CAPERS, DRAINED
- 6 VERY RIPE ROMA TOMATOES, CHOPPED

  SEA SALT

  FRESHLY GROUND BLACK PEPPER
- 1 CUP DRY WHITE WINE

Bring a large pot of salted water to a boil. Add the spaghetti and cook until al dente, 7 minutes.

Meanwhile, using a mortar and pestle or food processor, grind the garlic and almonds together into a fine paste.

In a large skillet, heat the olive oil over medium heat. Add the almond and garlic paste and cook a few minutes, stirring, Add the capers and tomatoes and season to taste with sea salt and pepper. Add the wine. Reduce the heat to a simmer and let cook a few minutes.

Drain the pasta, toss it with the sauce in the pan, and serve.

arista al limone

roast pork with lemon

Pockets cut into the pork are stuffed with a savory mix of prosciutto, garlic, oregano, and toasted almonds. It's then pan-seared for a tasty brown crust, slowly simmered to retain its inner juiciness, and served up with a lemony white-wine reduction sauce.

- 1 PORK LOIN FILLET (4 POUNDS)
- ½ CUP CHOPPED NATURAL ALMONDS (NOT BLANCHED)
- 2 TABLESPOONS EXTRA-VIRGIN OLIVE OIL
- 3½ OUNCES THINLY SLICED PROSCIUTTO, FINELY CHOPPED
- 2 CLOVES GARLIC, CHOPPED
- 1 TABLESPOON FRESH OREGANO LEAVES, CHOPPED
  FINELY GRATED ZEST OF 2 LEMONS
- 4 SHALLOTS, FINELY CHOPPED
- 1 CUP WHITE WINE
- 1 TEASPOON SUGAR

Using a sharp knife, cut the pork fillet across into 4 equal pieces. Place the pieces of pork between sheets of waxed paper and pound with a meat mallet or the end of a rolling pin to flatten to about 1½ inches high. Cut a horizontal slit in each piece to make a pocket. Set aside.

Spread the almonds on a baking sheet and toast under the broiler until golden, 2 to 3 minutes. Don't walk away from the stove while toasting the nuts; they can burn in a heartbeat.

Pour the nuts into a medium bowl. Add 1 tablespoon of the olive oil, the prosciutto, garlic, oregano, and half of the lemon zest. Stir to mix well. Stuff the filling evenly into the pork pockets.

In a skillet, heat the remaining 1 tablespoon olive oil over medium heat. Add the shallots and cook, stirring, for 2 minutes. Add the pork and cook until browned, about 2 minutes per side.

Add the wine and bring to a boil. Reduce the heat to a simmer, cover, and let cook until the pork is tender, about 45 minutes.

Remove the pork to a warm platter and cover with foil. Add the remaining zest and the sugar to the pan, bring to a boil, and continue to boil until the mixture is reduced and syrupy, 3 to 4 minutes. Pour the lemon sauce over the pork and serve. For 8 servings cut the slices into halves.

insalata del fattore

farmer's salad

The richness of the pork is matched with a simple green salad tossed with a creamy gorgonzola dressing spiked with vinegar and fresh herbs.

- 2 LARGE HEADS BIBB OR ROMAINE LETTUCE, TORN INTO BITE-SIZE PIECES
- ½ CUP CRUMBLED GORGONZOLA
- 1 CUP HEAVY CREAM
- ¾ CUP EXTRA-VIRGIN OLIVE OIL
- 3 TABLESPOONS RED WINE VINEGAR
- 2 TABLESPOONS CHOPPED FRESH CHIVES
- 2 TABLESPOONS CHOPPED FRESH TARRAGON
  SEA SALT
  FRESHLY GROUND BLACK PEPPER

Place the lettuce in a large salad bowl.

Place the cheese in a medium bowl. Add the cream slowly, stirring constantly, and continue to stir until the mixture is fairly smooth. Stir in the olive oil very slowly, then the vinegar and herbs. Season to taste with sea salt and pepper.

Pour the dressing over the lettuce and toss until well coated. Serve immediately.

cassata siciliana

sicilian sponge cake with ricotta

In some parts of Sicily, the layered dessert known as cassata is served only at holiday time or for special occasions, but in other areas you can walk into any pasticceria (pastry shop) and find it year-round. Cassata is a delicious indulgence, consisting of layers of orange liqueur–soaked sponge cake and sweetened ricotta studded with candied citrus peel.

- 3 **CUPS RICOTTA CHEESE**
  FINELY GRATED ZEST OF 1 ORANGE
- 2 **TABLESPOONS VANILLA SUGAR**
- 5 **TABLESPOONS ORANGE-FLAVORED LIQUEUR**
- 4 **OUNCES MIXED CANDIED CITRUS PEELS, FINELY CHOPPED**
- 8 **STORE-BOUGHT SPONGE CAKES (EACH 4 INCHES IN DIAMETER)**
- ¼ **CUP FRESH ORANGE JUICE**
  CANDIED CITRUS PEEL FOR GARNISH

In a large bowl, beat together the ricotta, orange zest, vanilla sugar, and 1 tablespoon of the liqueur. Transfer about one-third of the mixture to another bowl, cover, and chill until you are ready to serve.

Beat the candied citrus peel into the remaining ricotta until evenly mixed. Set aside while you prepare the pan.

Line the bottom of a 5-cup loaf pan with parchment paper. Cut the sponge cakes horizontally in half. Arrange 4 pieces of the cake side by side in the bottom of the pan and sprinkle with 1 tablespoon each of the liqueur and orange juice. Evenly spread one-third of the ricotta-and-fruit mixture over the sponge cake layer. Cover with 4 more pieces of sponge cake, sprinkle with 1 tablespoon each of the liqueur and orange juice, and spread with half of the remaining ricotta-and-fruit mixture. Repeat

the layering one more time. Top with the final 4 pieces of cake and sprinkle with the remaining liqueur and orange juice.

Cut a piece of parchment paper and a piece of cardboard to fit inside the top of the loaf pan. Set the parchment on top, then the cardboard. Place weights evenly on top of the cardboard. (I use pie weights in a zip-top plastic bag.) Chill the loaf pan for 2 hours.

Remove the weights, cardboard, and parchment from the loaf pan. Run a thin metal spatula along the sides of the pan. Invert a serving plate over the top of the cassata, and then flip the pan and plate over so the cassata is sitting upside down on the plate. Remove the pan and peel away the parchment paper. Spread the chilled reserved ricotta mixture over the top and sides of the cassata. Decorate the top with candied citrus peel cut into fancy shapes. Serve chilled. You can make this cake up to 24 hours ahead and refrigerate it until ready to serve.

MENU

42

SERVES 8 TO 10

funghi ripieni
stuffed mushrooms

....

pasta e fagioli
pasta and white beans

....

tagliata con rucola e limone
sliced rib-eye steak with arugula and lemon

....

*pere cotte in vino bianco con
pistachio e mascarpone*
poached pears in white wine with pistachio and mascarpone cream

Pasta e fagioli is a dish from my nana's childhood. Of course, it is a dish from every Italian's childhood. We are raised to believe that it can cure any ailment, and recently even the health experts have come to praise the earthy goodness of this pasta and beans dish. Chockfull of nutrients, it is good for you, and, of course, it is delicious, too.

funghi ripieni

stuffed mushrooms

These mushrooms, filled with a stuffing of breadcrumbs, garlic, and a little Parmigiano, provide a nice, light start to the meal.

- ¼ CUP EXTRA-VIRGIN OLIVE OIL, PLUS MORE FOR THE PAN AND DRIZZLING
- 1 CUP PLAIN BREADCRUMBS
- 3 CLOVES GARLIC, CHOPPED
- ¼ CUP GRATED PARMIGIANO-REGGIANO
- 1 TABLESPOON CHOPPED FRESH ITALIAN PARSLEY
- 24 LARGE MUSHROOM CAPS

Preheat the oven to 350F. Add 1 tablespoon olive oil to a baking dish large enough to hold the mushroom caps in a single layer, and tilt the dish to coat the bottom.

In a small bowl, combine the breadcrumbs, garlic, Parmigiano, parsley, and ¼ cup olive oil. Distribute the stuffing among the mushroom caps.

Arrange the mushroom caps in the prepared baking dish and bake until the mushrooms darken, 15 to 18 minutes. Drizzle with a little olive oil and serve.

"la calma é la virtu dei forti."

calm is the virtue of the strong.

pasta e fagioli
pasta and white beans

This Sicilian version of Pasta e Fagioli, without tomatoes, is thicker than you might expect. For a thinner version add a 28-ounce can of San Marzano chopped tomatoes.

- 1   **POUND (4 CUPS) MEDIUM SHELLS OR ELBOW MACARONI**
- 1   **CUP EXTRA-VIRGIN OLIVE OIL, PLUS MORE FOR DRIZZLING**
- 1   **CUP CHOPPED RED ONION**
- 1   **CUP SLICED (¼-INCH-THICK ROUNDS) CARROTS**
- 1   **CUP SLICED (¼-INCH-THICK) CELERY**
- 4   **CLOVES GARLIC, MINCED**
- 2   **CANS (19 OUNCES EACH) IMPORTED ITALIAN CANNELLINI BEANS, DRAINED AND RINSED**
- 2   **TABLESPOONS CHOPPED FRESH ITALIAN PARSLEY**
- 1   **TEASPOON RED PEPPER FLAKES**
-     **SEA SALT**
-     **FRESHLY GROUND BLACK PEPPER**
- 1   **CUP GRATED PARMIGIANO-REGGIANO**

Bring a large pot of salted water to a boil. Add the pasta and cook for 5 minutes only. Ladle 3 cups of the pasta cooking water out of the pot and reserve. Drain the pasta.

Heat the olive oil in a large skillet over medium heat. Add the onion, carrots, and celery and cook, stirring a few times, until softened but not mushy, for about 5 minutes. Add the garlic and cook, stirring, for 2 minutes. Add the reserved pasta cooking water and cook over medium heat for 15 minutes.

Stir in the reserved pasta water. Stir in the pasta, beans, and parsley, cover, and cook until the pasta is tender and has absorbed enough of the water that you have a thick soup. Season to taste with red pepper flakes, salt, and black pepper.

Right before serving, sprinkle with the Parmigiano and drizzle with olive oil.

tagliata con rucola e limone
sliced rib-eye steak with arugula and lemon

Rib eyes, thinly sliced and served topped with peppery arugula that's been wilted in a pan with olive oil and tossed with lemon juice—perfectly simple and perfectly delicious.

- ¼   **CUP EXTRA-VIRGIN OLIVE OIL, PLUS MORE FOR DRIZZLING**
-     **SEA SALT**
-     **FRESHLY GROUND BLACK PEPPER**
- 3   **OR 4 BONELESS RIB-EYE STEAKS, AT LEAST 2 INCHES THICK**
- 3   **BUNCHES ARUGULA, STEMS TRIMMED**
- 3   **TABLESPOONS FRESH LEMON JUICE**
- 1   **CUP SHAVED PARMIGIANO-REGGIANO**

Season 2 tablespoons of the olive oil generously with sea salt and pepper, and rub the mixture into the steaks. Cook the steaks over medium-high heat on a grill or in a preheated grill pan on the stove over medium-high heat for 6 to 7 minutes per side for medium rare. Let the steaks rest for 5 minutes while you prepare the arugula.

Heat the remaining 2 tablespoons olive oil in a large skillet over medium heat. Add the arugula and cook, stirring a few times, just until it wilts slightly, about 2 minutes. Toss with the lemon juice and transfer to a warm serving platter.

Cut the rib eye into long strips ¼ inch thick. Place on top of the arugula, drizzle with olive oil, and serve with the Parmigiano in a small bowl for sprinkling.

pere cotte in vino bianco con pistachio e mascarpone

poached pears in white wine with pistachio and mascarpone cream

Poached pears make for such an elegant dessert presentation. The pistachios are an unusual addition, but it really works.

8	FIRM, RIPE PEARS
4	CUPS WHITE WINE
¾	CUP SUGAR
	GRATED ZEST AND JUICE OF 1 LEMON
¼	CUP HEAVY CREAM
4	OUNCES (1 CUP) MASCARPONE
¼	CUP SHELLED UNSALTED PISTACHIOS

Peel the pears, leaving the stems attached. Cut a thin slice off the bottom of each pear so that it can stand upright. Stand the pears close together in a large saucepan or Dutch oven tall enough that you can cover the pears with the lid. Add the wine, ½ cup of the sugar, and the lemon zest. Bring the wine to a boil. Reduce the heat to medium and cover the pan. Let simmer until the pears are tender, 25 to 30 minutes, basting the pears with the wine mixture several times.

Transfer the pears to a glass bowl or platter. Let stand at room temperature until ready to serve.

Add the remaining ¼ cup sugar and the lemon juice to the liquid left in the pan. Bring to a boil and reduce until it has a syrup-like consistency, 15 to 20 minutes.

Meanwhile, in a medium bowl, whisk together the cream and mascarpone. Fold in the pistachios.

Place each pear on a dessert plate, spoon a ladle of hot wine sauce over the top, and add a dollop of the mascarpone cream.

"chi mangia solo, crepa solo."

he who eats alone, dies alone.

MENU

43

SERVES 8 TO 10

bruschetta alla rucola
bruschetta with arugula

gnocchi con gorgonzola e pinoli
potato dumplings with gorgonzola and pine nuts

vitello alla marsala
veal scallopine in marsala wine

pomodori alla emiliana
stuffed tomatoes, emilia-romagna style

pere cotte con menta e parmigiano-reggiano
minted poached pears with parmesan

After my nana passed away at the age of ninety-eight, I went back to the town of her birth in Sicily. As I walked down the same streets where she played as a child, I was flooded with memories of being in the kitchen with her, learning not only her recipes, but also her philosophy of life. The sauce of her veal Marsala, made with the sweet wine from her beloved island, is irresistible.

bruschetta alla rucola
bruschetta with arugula

*With the bite of garlic and arugula's pepperiness,
these crostini will perk up your taste buds.*

- 1 LARGE BUNCH ARUGULA, WASHED WELL, STEMS REMOVED
- 4 CLOVES GARLIC, 3 PEELED, 1 PEELED AND SLICED FOR RUBBING THE TOAST
- ¼ CUP EXTRA-VIRGIN OLIVE OIL, PLUS MORE FOR DRIZZLING ON THE TOAST
- 4 TEASPOONS FRESH LEMON JUICE
- SEA SALT
- FRESHLY GROUND BLACK PEPPER
- 1 LOAF ITALIAN COUNTRY BREAD (SEE LISA'S RUSTIC ITALIAN BREAD, PAGE 78), CUT INTO ¾-INCH-THICK SLICES

Put the arugula, 3 whole garlic cloves, olive oil, lemon juice, salt and pepper in a blender and process into a smooth purée.

Meanwhile, toast the bread slices. Rub the toast with fresh garlic slices and drizzle with olive oil.

Spread the arugula purée on the toasted bread and serve.

gnocchi con gorgonzola e pinoli
potato dumplings with gorgonzola and pine nuts

You can buy packaged gnocchi, but they are not anywhere near as good as homemade. Be warned, this dish is not for the calorie conscious!

- 8 MEDIUM POTATOES PREFERABLY YUKON GOLD
- 1 LARGE EGG YOLK
- 1 TABLESPOON SEA SALT
- 2–2½ CUPS ALL-PURPOSE FLOUR

GORGONZOLA AND PINE NUT SAUCE
- 1 STICK (8 TABLESPOONS) UNSALTED BUTTER
- ½ CUP HEAVY CREAM OR PANNA DA CUCINA
- 4 OUNCES GORGONZOLA, CRUMBLED
- ½ CUP PINE NUTS
- SEA SALT
- FRESHLY GROUND BLACK PEPPER

- ⅓ CUP GRATED PARMIGIANO-REGGIANO

Make the gnocchi: Preheat the oven to 350F. With a fork, puncture the potatoes in several places. Bake until tender, about 1 hour. Remove the insides of the baked potatoes and discard the skins. Over a large bowl, put the potato flesh through a ricer or food mill. Let cool slightly. Add the egg yolk, sea salt, and 2 cups of the flour and mix well. Transfer the mixture to a lightly floured work surface and knead into a ball with lightly floured hands. The dough should be soft, pliable, and slightly sticky. If it is too sticky, add as much of the remaining ½ cup flour as needed to attain the proper consistency.

Break the dough into pieces the size of large eggs. Shape each piece into a 6-inch-long log about the thickness of your thumb. Cut the logs across into 1-inch pieces. Hold a fork with its tines resting on the work surface at a 45-degree angle and the inside curve facing you. Take the gnocchi, one at a time, and press it with your index finger against the outside curve of the fork at the tip. Quickly slide the gnocchi up and along the tines of the fork, pressing with your index finger. Remove your finger and let the gnocchi fall onto the work surface. The grooves made by the fork will absorb the sauce. Repeat with the remaining gnocchi. Arrange the finished gnocchi on a lightly floured tray or large plate.

Cook the gnocchi: Bring a large pot of salted water to a boil. Add the gnocchi and let boil until the gnocchi float to the surface.

Meanwhile, make the sauce: Melt the butter in a large skillet. When the butter foams, add the cream and heat it, being careful not to boil the cream. Add the gorgonzola and cook, stirring, over low heat until the cheese melts and the cream begins to thicken, 3 to 4 minutes. Stir in the pine nuts and season to taste with sea salt and pepper.

Using a slotted spoon, remove the gnocchi from the water and transfer to the sauce. Gently stir in the Parmigiano. Let simmer until the gnocchi are coated with sauce, 30 to 40 seconds and serve immediately.

vitello alla marsala
veal scallopine in marsala wine

My grandmother was born and raised in the Trapani region of southwest Sicily, near the town of Marsala, so this dish is particularly dear to my heart.

ABOUT ½	CUP ALL-PURPOSE FLOUR
	SEA SALT
	FRESHLY GROUND BLACK PEPPER
8–10	THINLY SLICED VEAL SCALLOPINE
½	CUP EXTRA-VIRGIN OLIVE OIL
½	STICK (4 TABLESPOONS) UNSALTED BUTTER
1	CUP MARSALA WINE (I PREFER FLORIO SWEET)
1	CUP SLICED BUTTON MUSHROOMS (OPTIONAL)

Put the flour, sea salt and pepper in a flat dish. Pound the sliced veal until very thin, approximately $1/16$ inch. Dredge each piece of veal in the flour, coat well, and tap off any excess. Place the dredged veal on a tray.

In a large skillet, heat the olive oil and butter together over medium heat until the butter foams. Add 2 or 3 pieces of veal at a time to the skillet and cook until lightly golden, no more than 2 minutes per side. Transfer the veal, as cooked, to a warm serving platter.

When all the veal is cooked, add the Marsala to the skillet. Deglaze the pan, scraping up and dissolving any browned bits stuck to the bottom. Cook until the Marsala thickens, 3 to 4 minutes. If using, add the mushrooms and cook for 2 to 3 minutes.

Pour the Marsala sauce over the veal and serve immediately.

pomodori alla emiliana

stuffed tomatoes, emilia-romagna style

Topped with a Parmigiano-enhanced besciamella, these are not your mother's stuffed tomatoes!

BESCIAMELLA

- 1   STICK (8 TABLESPOONS) UNSALTED BUTTER
- ¼   CUP (4 TABLESPOONS) UNBLEACHED FLOUR
- 3   CUPS WHOLE MILK
- 2   LARGE EGG YOLKS
- ¼   TEASPOON SEA SALT
- ½   CUP GRATED PARMIGIANO-REGGIANO

- 8   NICELY ROUNDED TOMATOES (PREFERABLY CAMPARI TOMATOES), ABOUT 2½ INCHES IN DIAMETER
- ¼   CUP PARMIGIANO-REGGIANO FOR SPRINKLING ON THE TOMATOES

Make the besciamella: Melt the butter in a medium saucepan over medium heat. Add the flour and stir until smooth. Slowly add the milk, whisking constantly to keep any lumps from forming. Stir until the sauce is thick enough to coat the back of a wooden spoon. Remove from the heat and let rest for 3 minutes. Add the egg yolks and incorporate them into the besciamella. Add the salt and Parmigiano-Reggiano.

Preheat the oven to 300F. Butter the bottom of a medium baking dish.

Cut the tops off the tomatoes and scoop out all the pulp and seeds with a spoon, being careful not to puncture the skin. Place the tomatoes in the prepared baking dish and evenly distribute the besciamella among the tomatoes, filling the cavity of each one. Sprinkle with the Parmigiano and bake until golden and bubbly, about 30 minutes.

"volere é potere."

where there's a will, there's a way.

pere cotte con menta e parmigiano-reggiano

minted poached pears with parmesan

Spiked with the bright flavor of fresh mint, these red wine–hued pears make a refreshing end to the meal.

- 2 **CUPS RED WINE**
- 1 **CUP SUGAR**
- 1 **LEMON**
- 6–8 **(1-INCH) SPRIGS FRESH MINT OR 1½ TEASPOONS DRIED MINT**
- 8 **FIRM PEARS WITH STEMS**
- 8 **OUNCES PARMIGIANO-REGGIANO, CUT INTO LARGE NUGGETS**
- 8 **SPRIGS FRESH MINT FOR GARNISH**

In a saucepan large enough to hold all the pears standing upright, combine the wine, sugar, and 2 cups water. Bring the mixture to a boil, stirring until the sugar dissolves.

Cut the zest from the lemon in long strips and juice the lemon. Add the lemon juice and peel and mint to the wine mixture and remove the saucepan from the heat.

Leaving the stem attached, peel each pear and cut a thin slice off the bottom so the pear will stand upright. Stand the pears in the wine mixture. Place the pan over medium-high heat and bring the liquid to a gentle simmer. Adjust the heat as necessary to keep the liquid from coming to a boil. Poach the pears, turning them a few times and spooning the poaching liquid over them, until they are tender when tested with a skewer, 15 to 30 minutes. Let the pears cool in the poaching liquid for 30 minutes.

Transfer the pears to a large plate and cover them with foil. Strain the poaching liquid into a small saucepan. Bring it to a boil and reduce the liquid until it's thick enough to coat the back of a spoon, 15 to 20 minutes.

To serve, spoon a small puddle of the warm syrup onto 8 dessert plates. Set a pear upright in the center of the syrup and arrange several pieces of Parmigiano next to the pear. Garnish with a mint sprig and serve.

MENU

44

SERVES 8 TO 10

crostini con gorgonzola
toasts with gorgonzola

lasagne con funghi e formaggi
mushroom and cheese lasagne

stracotto
pot roast, tuscan style

insalata di rucola con parmigiano
arugula salad with parmesan

affogato di caffè
ice cream drowned in coffee

Throughout the winter I can count on my children asking for the same menu every Sunday: the one that contains the straccoto (Italian pot roast). They never tire of this dish. But don't wait for Sunday to make it; this is a great menu for a week night. In fact, both the lasagne with mushrooms and the straccoto can be made ahead and just reheated.

crostini con gorgonzola

toasts with gorgonzola

The combination of walnuts and blue cheese is a natural and makes for a luscious starter.

1	LOAF CIABATTA BREAD, CUT DIAGONALLY INTO ¼-INCH-THICK SLICES
6	OUNCES GORGONZOLA, SOFTENED
¼	CUP HEAVY CREAM
16–24	WALNUT HALVES

Preheat the oven to 350F. Put the bread slices on a cookie sheet and toast for 10 minutes. In a small bowl, cream together the gorgonzola and cream. Spread the mixture over the toast.

Preheat the broiler. Place the crostini on a baking sheet and broil until golden and the cheese is bubbly, 2 to 3 minutes.

Place a walnut half on each crostino, let set for 1 minute, and serve.

lasagne con funghi e formaggi

mushroom and cheese lasagne

This lasagne is from the Piemonte region, in the north of Italy. Instead of tomato sauce and ricotta, it's prepared with mushrooms and besciamella.

BESCIAMELLA

2	STICKS (16 TABLESPOONS) UNSALTED BUTTER
½	CUP (8 TABLESPOONS) UNBLEACHED FLOUR
6	CUPS WHOLE MILK
1	TEASPOON SEA SALT
½	TEASPOON FRESHLY GROUND BLACK PEPPER
½	TEASPOON GRATED NUTMEG

½	STICK (4 TABLESPOONS) UNSALTED BUTTER
4	CUPS SLICED BUTTON MUSHROOMS
	SEA SALT
	FRESHLY GROUND BLACK PEPPER
2	POUNDS LASAGNE NOODLES (OR HOMEMADE PAGE 129)
2	CUPS GRATED PARMIGIANO-REGGIANO

Make the besciamella: Melt the butter in a medium saucepan over medium heat, add the flour, and stir until smooth. Slowly add the milk, whisking constantly to keep any lumps from forming. Stir until the mixture thickens enough to coat the back of a wooden spoon. Season with the sea salt, pepper, and nutmeg.

In a large skillet melt the butter over medium heat. Cook the mushrooms, stirring, for 5 minutes, or until the liquid is evaporated, and season to taste with sea salt and pepper.

Bring a large pot of salted water to a boil. Place clean kitchen towels on your counter. Add the lasagne noodles to the boiling water in batches. As they cook to al dente, not more than two minutes if homemade, remove them from the water using tongs (be careful not to rip the noodles) and lay them flat on the towels to cool.

Preheat the oven to 400F.

Spread a layer of besciamella over the bottom of a large, deep baking dish. Cover with 2 layers of noodles. Cover the noodles with a layer of mushrooms, a layer of besciamella, and a layer of Parmigiano. Repeat the layering (2 layers of noodles, a layer of mushrooms, besciamella, and Parmigiano) until the dish is full. Finish with a single layer of noodles, and cover with the remaining besciamella and Parmigiano.

Bake for 30 minutes, until bubbly. Let stand 10 minutes before cutting.

"chi la dura, la vince."

he who perseveres, wins at last.

stracotto

pot roast, tuscan style

This dish is best when cooked in a slow cooker for 8 to 10 hours. If you don't have one, use a large Dutch oven and cook it in a preheated 350F oven for 4 to 5 hours. Since the dried porcini mushrooms can be quite costly, feel free to just use 1 ounce (you'll still get that wonderful flavor in the dish, which is all that counts).

3–4	OUNCES DRIED PORCINI MUSHROOMS
½	CUP EXTRA-VIRGIN OLIVE OIL
1	CUP ALL-PURPOSE FLOUR
	FRESHLY GROUND BLACK PEPPER
1	BONELESS BEEF CHUCK ROAST (6 POUNDS)
1½	CUPS FULL-BODIED RED WINE, SUCH AS A CHIANTI
2	PORCINI MUSHROOM BOUILLON CUBES (IMPORTED FROM ITALY; IF YOU CAN'T FIND THEM, USE REGULAR BEEF BOUILLON CUBES) DISSOLVED IN 2 CUPS BOILING WATER

In a small bowl, soak the mushrooms in 1 cup of boiling water for 30 minutes. Drain the mushrooms and rinse them well.

In a large skillet, heat the olive oil over medium heat. Place the flour on a platter, grind the pepper over it, and mix well. Dredge the roast completely in the flour, tapping off any excess. Set the roast in the skillet and brown until golden on all sides.

Transfer the roast to a large slow cooker. Pour the wine and dissolved bouillon over the roast. Add the mushrooms. Scrape all the browned bits and remaining olive oil out of the skillet and pour over the roast. Cover and cook on low heat for 8 to 10 hours.

Transfer the roast to a cutting board and cut into 1-inch squares. Serve in a large bowl with the porcini sauce.

insalata di rucola con parmigiano

arugula salad with parmesan

The buttery flavor of the cheese offers a nice counterpoint to the bite of the arugula.

2   BUNCHES ARUGULA, STEMS TRIMMED

1   HEAD RED-LEAF OR BIBB LETTUCE, SEPARATED INTO LEAVES

1   TEASPOON SEA SALT

2   TABLESPOONS BALSAMIC VINEGAR

¼   CUP EXTRA-VIRGIN OLIVE OIL

¼   TEASPOON FRESHLY GROUND BLACK PEPPER

4   OUNCES PARMIGIANO-REGGIANO, CUT INTO THIN, MEDIUM PIECES

Cut the arugula and lettuce into bite-size pieces. Place in a large salad bowl and mix.

Place the sea salt in a large serving or salad spoon. Pour the vinegar into the spoon and stir with a fork until the vinegar begins to absorb the salt. Toss onto the salad. Pour the olive oil over the salad, add pepper to taste, and toss everything together to coat with the vinegar and oil.

Right before serving, add the Parmigiano.

affogato di caffè

ice cream drowned in coffee

The name of this dessert translates literally into "drowned by coffee." Warm espresso is poured over a scoop of gelato, making for a heavenly combination.

2   PINTS ESPRESSO OR CHOCOLATE ITALIAN GELATO

ABOUT 3 CUPS HOT BREWED ESPRESSO

ABOUT 3 TABLESPOONS SLIVERED ALMONDS FOR GARNISH

Place a scoop of gelato in each of 8 ice cream dishes or small dessert bowls. Pour 3 ounces of espresso over each scoop and sprinkle with 1 teaspoon almond slivers. Serve immediately.

MENU

45

SERVES 8 TO 10

crostini con ricotta e pepe nero
toasts with ricotta and black pepper

gnudi bianchi
ricotta dumplings

spiedini di arista con pane
roast pork skewers with bread

patate con rosmarino
rosemary potatoes

budino al cioccolato
italian chocolate pudding

Gnudi Bianchi—yes, the name really does mean "nudes"!
You'll want to remember this versatile dish because it can
be served as a primo, as in this menu, or as a side with a
meat or chicken dish.

crostini con ricotta e pepe nero

toasts with ricotta and black pepper

This is such a simple but satisfying antipasto. The black pepper brings out the subtle flavor and texture of the ricotta.

2 LOAVES THIN ITALIAN BREAD, EACH CUT INTO 12 SLICES ON THE DIAGONAL

1½ CUPS WHOLE-MILK RICOTTA

2 TABLESPOONS HEAVY CREAM

FRESHLY GROUND BLACK PEPPER

Preheat the oven to 350F. Put the bread slices on a cookie sheet and toast for 10 minutes.

In a medium bowl, beat together the ricotta and cream until smooth. Spread the mixture on the toasted bread. Top each with several grindings of fresh pepper and serve.

gnudi bianchi

ricotta dumplings

These airy pillows of ricotta and Parmigiano will melt in your mouth.

2¼ CUPS RICOTTA

2 CUPS SEMOLINA FLOUR, PLUS MORE FOR DUSTING THE TRAY

3½ OUNCES PARMIGIANO-REGGIANO, GRATED, PLUS MORE GRATED CHEESE FOR SERVING

1 TABLESPOON FRESHLY GRATED NUTMEG

1 STICK (8 TABLESPOONS) UNSALTED BUTTER

3 FRESH SAGE LEAVES, CHOPPED

In a large bowl, beat together the ricotta and semolina. Stir in the Parmigiano and nutmeg.

Dust a large flat tray with semolina. Roll the ricotta mixture into 1-inch balls. As you shape the balls, place them on the semolina-covered tray to keep them from sticking. When all the gnudi are formed, add more semolina to the tray so the gnudi are covered with it. Chill in the refrigerator for 2 to 4 hours.

Melt 4 tablespoons butter over medium heat until foamy. Add the sage and cook until it curls and becomes one shade darker in color.

Put the remaining 4 tablespoons butter in a warm serving dish.

Bring a large pot of salted water to a boil. Add the gnudi in 3 or 4 batches, so the pot is not too crowded, and cook until they float to the surface, about 3 minutes. Using a slotted spoon, transfer them to the serving dish.

Pour the sage butter over the gnudi and serve with the extra Parmigiano.

> **"chi la sera
> i pasti
> li ha fatti,
> sta a gli
> altri lavare
> i piatti."**
>
> if one cooks,
> the others
> do the dishes!

spiedini di arista con pane

roast pork skewers with bread

You'll need 16 to 18 long wooden skewers for this recipe. Be sure to soak them in water for 30 minutes so they don't scorch on the grill.

4	POUNDS PORK LOIN, CUT INTO 2- BY 1-INCH CHUNKS
8–10	ROMA TOMATOES, CUT INTO QUARTERS
4	GREEN BELL PEPPERS, SEEDED AND CUT INTO 2-INCH SQUARES
4	YELLOW BELL PEPPERS, SEEDED AND CUT INTO 2-INCH SQUARES
4	WHITE ONIONS, CUT INTO QUARTERS, THEN CUT IN HALF AGAIN
1	CUP EXTRA-VIRGIN OLIVE OIL
	SEA SALT
	FRESHLY GROUND BLACK PEPPER
2	CIABATTA LOAVES, CUT INTO ½-INCH CUBES

Place the pork and vegetables in a large bowl. Pour the olive oil over the mixture and season to taste with sea salt and pepper.

Preheat a gas grill to medium-high.

On each skewer, begin with a piece of bread, followed by a chunk of pork, a square of pepper, a piece of tomato, and a piece of onion. Repeat the order, ending with a piece of bread.

When all the skewers are loaded, place them on the grill and cook for 15 to 20 minutes, turning them every 5 minutes. The pork should be cooked through and the vegetables charred. If you like, you can baste the spiedini with the olive oil as they grill, but make sure your last basting is at least 5 minutes before the skewers come off the grill so any raw pork juices in the oil have a chance to get hit with the high temperature of the grill.

Serve the skewers on a platter.

patate con rosmarino

rosemary potatoes

The piney flavor of these crisp-roasted potatoes stands up to the charred flavor of the spiedini.

- ½ **CUP EXTRA-VIRGIN OLIVE OIL**
- 2 **TABLESPOONS FRESH ROSEMARY LEAVES**
  COARSE SEA SALT
- 1 **POUND RED OR YUKON GOLD POTATOES**

Preheat the oven to 350F.

Combine the olive oil, rosemary, and sea salt in a large baking dish. Cut the potatoes into quarters and toss them with the mixture to coat. Bake until golden and crispy, about 35 minutes.

budino al cioccolato

italian chocolate pudding

Rich and creamy, this honey-laced chocolate pudding can be made ahead of time. Serve it topped with whipped cream, or perhaps a final garnish of fresh raspberries.

- 3 **CUPS HEAVY CREAM**
- 16 **OUNCES BITTERSWEET CHOCOLATE, CHOPPED**
- 7 **TABLESPOONS HONEY**

In a large, heavy saucepan over low heat, stir ³/₄ cup of the cream, the chocolate, and the honey together until the chocolate melts and the mixture is smooth. Remove from the heat and let cool, stirring occasionally.

In a large bowl using an electric mixer, beat the remaining 2¼ cups cream until soft peaks form. Fold 1³/₄ cups of the beaten cream into the cooled chocolate mixture in 2 batches. Distribute the budino among 10 dessert glasses and refrigerate until set, about 2 hours.

Whip the remaining cream until firm peaks form. When ready to serve, top each budino with a dollop of whipped cream.

MENU

46

SERVES 8 TO 10

panini di bietola
swiss chard stem sandwiches

....

gnocchi alla romana
baked potato dumplings with polenta and cheese

....

agnello scottaditto marinato
della nonna franco
grandma franco's marinated lamb chops

....

pomodori arrostiti con aglio
roasted plum tomatoes with garlic

....

crostata di ricotta
ricotta pie

Frequently, we discard the stems of our vegetables, not realizing that we are losing the nutrients found there. Swiss chard, very commonly used throughout Italy and easily found in the States, has a long and nutritious stem. Instead of throwing the stems away, the ingenious Italians stuff them for a healthy, delicious antipasto.

panini di bietola

swiss chard stem sandwiches

A delightfully different antipasto of little fried sandwiches with a garlic and caper crumb filling, Swiss chard stems serving as the "bread."

24	SWISS CHARD STEMS (LEAF PART REMOVED), CUT INTO 2-INCH PIECES
½	CUP ITALIAN BREADCRUMBS
2	CLOVES GARLIC, CHOPPED
2	TABLESPOONS CAPERS
1	CUP PLUS 2 TABLESPOONS EXTRA-VIRGIN OLIVE OIL
1	CUP ALL-PURPOSE FLOUR
	SEA SALT
	FRESHLY GROUND BLACK PEPPER

Steam the Swiss chard stems for 4 to 5 minutes (stems will become slightly translucent). Remove from the steamer and let cool.

Meanwhile, in a small bowl, combine the breadcrumbs, garlic, capers, and 2 tablespoons of the olive oil.

Season the flour with the sea salt and pepper and pour into a shallow bowl.

Make a little sandwich with 2 pieces of the Swiss chard stems by stuffing them with some of the filling. Dredge the stems in the flour, tapping off any excess and set them on a tray. Repeat with the remaining stems and filling.

In a large skillet, heat the remaining 1 cup olive oil over medium-high heat. Fry the little sandwiches in the hot oil, in batches, turning once, until golden on each side, about 2 to 3 minutes per side. Transfer them with a slotted spoon, as cooked, to paper towels to drain. Serve immediately.

gnocchi alla romana

baked potato dumplings with polenta and cheese

Italian comfort food at the highest level, egg-rich gnocchi dough is chilled, cut into rounds, then layered with Parmigiano-Reggiano and baked into gooey goodness.

1	QUART MILK
1	CUP SEMOLINA FLOUR
½	STICK (4 TABLESPOONS) UNSALTED BUTTER, MELTED
1	TEASPOON SEA SALT
	PINCH OF FRESHLY GRATED NUTMEG
	FRESHLY GROUND BLACK PEPPER
1	CUP GRATED PARMIGIANO-REGGIANO
3	LARGE EGG YOLKS, BEATEN WITH 1 TABLESPOON MILK
1	STICK (8 TABLESPOONS) UNSALTED BUTTER, CUT INTO PIECES AND SOFTENED

In a medium, heavy saucepan over medium heat, bring the milk to a boil. Add the semolina slowly, stirring constantly. Stir in the melted butter, sea salt, nutmeg, and pepper to taste. Reduce the heat and simmer, stirring constantly, for 20 minutes. Remove from the heat and stir in 2 tablespoons of the Parmigiano and the egg yolks. Pour the mixture into a 13- by 9-inch baking dish and smooth the top with a butter knife. Refrigerate until it solidifies, about 1 hour.

Preheat the oven to 400F. Butter a 9- by 9-inch baking dish.

Using a glass or a cookie cutter, cut out 1½-inch-diameter rounds as close as possible to one another.

Place a layer of gnocchi rounds in the prepared baking dish, top with dots of softened butter, and sprinkle with some of the remaining cheese. Repeat for 3 or 4 layers. (Stagger the gnocchi rounds so there are no spaces between the layers.)

Bake until golden, about 15 minutes.

agnello scottaditto marinato della nonna franco

grandma franco's marinated lamb chops

This recipe was handed down from my great-grandmother. Lamb stands up beautifully to the robust flavors of lemon, anchovy, and oregano.

- ¼ **CUP PLUS 2 TABLESPOONS EXTRA-VIRGIN OLIVE OIL**
- **JUICE OF 1 LEMON**
- 3 **OUNCES (6 TABLESPOONS) ANCHOVY PASTE**
- 1 **TABLESPOON DRIED OREGANO**
- 8 **LAMB LOIN CHOPS**

In a small bowl, whisk together ¼ cup olive oil, lemon juice, anchovy paste, and oregano. Rub the lamb chops with the mixture. Place in a glass baking dish and let marinate in the refrigerator for 2 hours.

Preheat the oven to 400F.

Heat the remaining 2 tablespoons olive oil in a large ovenproof skillet over high heat. When the pan is very hot and the oil is smoking slightly, add the lamb chops and sear until golden brown on each side.

Transfer the pan to the oven and roast for 6 to 8 minutes for medium-rare meat. Remove from the oven and let the chops rest for 2 to 3 minutes before serving.

"detto fatto!"

no sooner said than done.

pomodori arrostiti con aglio

roasted plum tomatoes with garlic

Like the lamb chops, this dish is all about fresh flavors—ripe tomatoes, garlic, oregano, bay, and olive oil. Roasting accentuates the sweetness of the tomatoes and transforms the garlic cloves into savory softness—diners squeeze the cloves out onto slices of bread to spread.

- 8 PLUM TOMATOES, CUT IN HALF
- 12 CLOVES GARLIC, LEFT UNPEELED
- ¼ CUP EXTRA-VIRGIN OLIVE OIL
- 3 BAY LEAVES
  FRESHLY GROUND BLACK PEPPER
  SEA SALT
- 3 TABLESPOONS FRESH OREGANO LEAVES
  ITALIAN BREAD FOR SERVING

Preheat the oven to 450F.

Select a baking dish that will hold all the tomatoes snugly in a single layer. Place the tomatoes, cut side up, in the dish and push the garlic cloves between them. Brush the tomatoes with the olive oil, add the bay leaves, and sprinkle pepper over the top. Bake until the tomatoes have softened and are sizzling in the pan; they should be charred around the edges.

Season the tomatoes with sea salt and a little more pepper, if you like. Sprinkle with the oregano and serve with bread (your guests and family squeeze the roasted garlic cloves out of their wrappers onto the bread for spreading).

crostata di ricotta

ricotta pie

An Italian American classic, this pie is delicious topped with fresh cherries, strawberries, or crushed pineapple.

- 2 TABLESPOONS UNSALTED BUTTER, MELTED
- 1 CUP VERY FINELY CRUSHED ALMOND BISCOTTI
- 1 CONTAINER (15 OUNCES) WHOLE-MILK RICOTTA
- ½ CUP SUGAR
- 2 LARGE EGGS
- ½ CUP HEAVY CREAM

Preheat the oven to 350F.

In a small bowl, mix together the melted butter and biscotti crumbs, using your fingertips to create a paste. Spread the buttered crumbs evenly in a 9-inch pie plate all the way up to the rim of the plate.

In a medium bowl, beat together the ricotta, sugar, eggs, and cream until smooth. Pour into the crust and smooth the top.

Bake for 40 minutes. The top of the pie should be firm, not golden. Let cool completely before slicing.

MENU

47

SERVES 8 TO 10

filo ripieno di formaggio e pomodori
filo dough stuffed with cheese and sun-dried tomatoes

minestra di pasta e ceci
pasta and chickpea soup

polpettone alla siciliana
sicilian meatloaf

cavollini di bruxelles saltati
sautéed brussels sprouts

biscotti italiani varie
cookie tray

Sometimes a classic can use a bit of change, and this is exactly what the Sicilians did to meatloaf. With the addition of pine nuts and golden raisins, both the texture and the taste of this great standby are enhanced. Combined with the other recipes in this menu, you have quite a Sunday meal.

filo ripieno di formaggio e pomodori

filo dough stuffed with cheese and sun-dried tomatoes

Flaky and delicious, these savory pastries are best assembled the day before, then baked right before serving.

- 6 OUNCES MASCARPONE
- 6 OUNCES FONTINA, GRATED
- 6 OUNCES EMMENTHALER, GRATED
- 1 STICK (8 TABLESPOONS) UNSALTED BUTTER
- 1 ONION, CHOPPED
- 2 TABLESPOONS FINELY CHOPPED SUN-DRIED TOMATOES
- 16 SHEETS THAWED FILO DOUGH

In a medium bowl, combine the mascarpone, fontina, and Emmenthaler.

In a medium skillet, melt 1 tablespoon of the butter over medium heat. Add the onion and cook, stirring, until it is transparent. Add the mixture to the cheeses and mix well.

Melt the remaining 7 tablespoons butter in the same pan. Remove from the heat.

With a pastry brush, apply some of the melted butter to each sheet of filo, stacking 4 sheets of butter-brushed filo together at a time. At the long end of a stack of filo sheets, place a thin line of the cheese mixture, approximately 1/2 inch wide, across the edge of the sheet. Place a very thin line of sun-dried tomatoes on top of the cheese mixture. Roll up the stacked sheets, brush with melted butter, and set, seam side down, on a large baking sheet. Repeat with the remaining filo, filling, and melted butter.

Chill the filled and rolled filo for at least 4 hours and up to 24 hours.

Preheat the oven to 375F. Cut the filo rolls into 1- to 2-inch pieces. Bake until golden and flaky, 11 to 12 minutes, and serve immediately.

minestra di pasta e ceci

pasta and chickpea soup

Hearty and filling, this minestra is the perfect primo for Sunday dinner on a cold winter's day.

- 1/4 POUND THINLY SLICED PROSCIUTTO DI PARMA
- 1 SMALL RED ONION, CUT INTO SMALL CHUNKS
- 1 MEDIUM CARROT, CUT INTO SMALL CHUNKS
- 3 CLOVES GARLIC, CRUSHED
- 2 TEASPOONS FRESH OR DRIED ROSEMARY LEAVES
- 1/2 CUP EXTRA-VIRGIN OLIVE OIL
- 2 CANS (15 OUNCES EACH) CECI BEANS (CHICKPEAS), DRAINED AND RINSED
- 4 CUPS VEGETABLE STOCK OR REDUCED-SODIUM CANNED BROTH
- 2 TABLESPOONS TOMATO PASTE
- 1 BAY LEAF
- 1 SQUARE PIECE (4 INCHES) PARMIGIANO-REGGIANO RIND
  SEA SALT
  FRESHLY GROUND BLACK PEPPER
- 1 CUP DITALINI PASTA
- 1 CUP GRATED PARMIGIANO-REGGIANO

Finely chop together the prosciutto, onion, carrot, garlic, and rosemary.

Heat the olive oil in a large soup pot over medium-high heat until hot but not smoking. Add the chopped mixture and cook, stirring a few times, until the vegetables are softened, about 10 minutes. Add the chickpeas, broth, tomato paste, bay leaf, and Parmigiano rind.

Season to taste with sea salt and pepper. Bring the soup to a gentle simmer and cook for 30 minutes, stirring occasionally.

Remove the softened cheese rind, cut it into small pieces, and return it to the soup.

Just before serving, add the ditalini to the soup. When it is cooked al dente, approximately 8 minutes, ladle the soup into bowls and sprinkle generously with the Parmigiano. Serve immediately.

polpettone alla siciliana
sicilian meatloaf

The American classic gets a Sicilian twist with the addition of raisins, pine nuts, and garlic.

1	**POUND GROUND PORK**
1	**POUND GROUND VEAL**
1	**POUND GROUND BEEF SIRLOIN**
2	**LARGE EGGS**
1	**CUP PLAIN BREADCRUMBS**
¼	**CUP GOLDEN RAISINS**
¼	**CUP PINE NUTS**
2	**CLOVES GARLIC, CHOPPED**
	SEA SALT
	FRESHLY GROUND BLACK PEPPER

Preheat the oven to 350F.

Mix all the ingredients together in a large bowl. Transfer to an 8- by 4-inch loaf pan. Bake for 1 hour, or until brown and crunchy on top.

cavollini di bruxelles saltati
sautéed brussels sprouts

The secret to Brussels sprouts is not to overcook them; cook them too long and their cabbage nature comes out. Here they are steamed just until they turn bright green, then sautéed with garlic in olive oil until caramelized. The result is sprouts with a sweet, nutty flavor that no one will be able to resist.

50–60	**BRUSSELS SPROUTS, THE SMALLEST ONES YOU CAN FIND**
½	**CUP EXTRA-VIRGIN OLIVE OIL**
3–4	**CLOVES GARLIC, CHOPPED**
	SEA SALT

Trim the stems and any discolored outer leaves from the sprouts. If they are small, leave them whole. If they are medium-size to large, cut the sprouts in half lengthwise.

Steam the Brussels sprouts until they turn bright green but are still firm. Remove from the heat.

In a large skillet, heat the olive oil over medium heat. Add the garlic and Brussels sprouts and cook, turning them with a wooden spoon, until the sprouts are golden brown and almost caramelized.

Transfer the Brussels sprouts to a warm serving platter and season to taste with salt.

biscotti italiani varie

cookie tray

When I think of cookies, I think of my nana bringing out her cookie tray filled with treats she and I had baked together. Here are two favorites, sesame biscotti and ricotta cookies.

SESAME BISCOTTI (MAKES 3 DOZEN)

- ½   CUP MILK
- 2   CUPS SESAME SEEDS
- 4   CUPS ALL-PURPOSE FLOUR
- 1   CUP SUGAR
- 3½   TEASPOONS BAKING POWDER
- ½   TEASPOON SALT
- 2   STICKS (16 TABLESPOONS) UNSALTED BUTTER, CUT INTO PIECES AND SOFTENED
- 2   LARGE EGGS, AT ROOM TEMPERATURE
- 1   TEASPOON VANILLA EXTRACT
- 1   TEASPOON GRATED ORANGE ZEST

RICOTTA COOKIES (MAKES 4 DOZEN)

- 1   STICK (8 TABLESPOONS) UNSALTED BUTTER, SOFTENED
- ¼   CUP RICOTTA CHEESE
- 1   TEASPOON VANILLA EXTRACT
- 1   CUP SUGAR
- 1   LARGE EGG
- 2   CUPS ALL-PURPOSE FLOUR
- ½   TEASPOON BAKING SODA
- ½   TEASPOON SALT

Make the Sesame Biscotti: Preheat the oven to 375F. Butter and flour 2 large baking sheets. Pour the milk into a shallow bowl. Spread the sesame seeds on a sheet of waxed paper.

In a large bowl, mix together the flour, sugar, baking powder, and salt. With an electric mixer on low speed, gradually beat in the butter a little at a time.

In a medium bowl, whisk together the eggs, vanilla, and orange zest. Stir the egg mixture into the dry mixture until well blended.

Pinch off a piece of dough the size of a golf ball and shape it into a log 2½ inches long and ¾ inch thick. Dip the log in the milk, and roll it in the sesame seeds. Place the seed-studded roll on a prepared baking sheet and flatten slightly. Repeat with the remaining dough, milk, and sesame seeds, setting the cookies about 1 inch apart on the sheets.

Bake until well browned, 25 to 30 minutes. Let cool on the baking sheets for 10 minutes. Transfer to wire racks to cool completely.

Make the Ricotta Cookies: Reduce the oven temperature to 350F. Grease a large baking sheet.

In a large bowl, beat the butter and ricotta together until creamy. Add the vanilla and mix well. Beat in the sugar and egg. Add the flour, baking soda, and salt and mix well.

Drop the cookie dough by scant tablespoons about 2 inches apart onto the prepared baking sheet. Bake until just lightly golden, 10 to 12 minutes. Let cool on the sheet for 1 minute. Transfer to a wire rack to cool completely.

MENU

48

SERVES 8-10

crostini con prosciutto e miele
toasts with prosciutto and honey

conchiglie di pasta ripiene
stuffed pasta shells

petto di vitello ripieno con uvette e pinoli
veal breast stuffed with raisins and pine nuts

patate al forno
oven-roasted potatoes

salame al cioccolato
chocolate salami

Veal is a favorite in the Italian diet. Milk-fed beef veal is plentiful in Italy, and it is a delicate, almost sweet meat that adapts to so many preparations. In a wine sauce, in breadcrumbs, and here, rolled and stuffed, it is always light and delicious.

crostini con prosciutto e miele

toasts with prosciutto and honey

I love the combination of salty and sweet, and crostini topped with a slice of prosciutto and a touch of honey hit the spot. The intensely flavored crystallized honey is from Sicily and can be found in many Italian stores and specialty markets. It's absolutely delicious, so try to find it.

2 LOAVES THIN ITALIAN BREAD (ABOUT 2 INCHES IN DIAMETER)

EXTRA-VIRGIN OLIVE OIL

12 VERY THIN SLICES PROSCIUTTO DI PARMA, EACH CUT IN HALF

6 TEASPOONS HONEY (PREFERABLY CRYSTALLIZED)

Preheat the oven to 350F. Cut the bread on the diagonal into 24 slices and arrange on a cookie sheet. Toast them until golden.

Drizzle olive oil over the toast. Set a half slice of prosciutto on each and drizzle with the honey.

conchiglie di pasta ripiene

stuffed pasta shells

It's an Italian comfort food classic!

2 CUPS LISA'S CLASSIC TOMATO SAUCE (PAGE 89)

2 POUNDS JUMBO PASTA SHELLS

2 POUNDS RICOTTA

2 LARGE EGGS

8 OUNCES MOZZARELLA, SHREDDED

½ CUP GRATED PARMIGIANO-REGGIANO

1 TEASPOON SEA SALT

¼ TEASPOON FRESHLY GROUND BLACK PEPPER

1 TEASPOON CHOPPED FRESH ITALIAN PARSLEY

Preheat the oven to 400F. Pour a little of the tomato sauce into a 13- by 9-inch baking dish and tilt the dish to coat the bottom. Set the rest of the tomato sauce aside.

Bring a large pot of salted water to a boil. Add the pasta shells and cook for 5 minutes, until just soft. Drain and rinse under cold running water. Arrange the shells in a single layer on kitchen towels.

Meanwhile, make the filling: In a large bowl, beat together the ricotta and eggs. Stir in the mozzarella and Parmigiano, then the seasonings.

Using a small spoon, fill the shells with the filling. As you fill the shells, set them in the prepared baking dish. Once all the shells are filled, top them with the remaining tomato sauce. Bake until bubbly, 30 to 40 minutes.

petto di vitello ripieno con uvette e pinoli

veal breast stuffed with raisins and pine nuts

Veal breast gets a Sicilian treatment with a filling of spinach, fresh herbs, raisins, and pine nuts. Be sure to have the butcher pound the breast thin for you.

- 6 **TABLESPOONS CHOPPED FRESH SPINACH**
- 2 **TABLESPOONS CHOPPED FRESH ITALIAN PARSLEY**
- 2 **TABLESPOONS CHOPPED FRESH OREGANO**
- 4 **CLOVES GARLIC, THINLY SLICED**
- ½ **CUP GOLDEN RAISINS**
- ½ **CUP PINE NUTS**
  SEA SALT
  FRESHLY GROUND BLACK PEPPER
- 1 **VEAL BREAST (2 POUNDS), POUNDED THIN BY THE BUTCHER**
- ¼ **CUP EXTRA-VIRGIN OLIVE OIL**
- 1 **LARGE ONION, FINELY CHOPPED**
- 1 **STALK CELERY, FINELY CHOPPED**
- 1 **CARROT, FINELY CHOPPED**
- 1 **CUP DRY WHITE WINE**
- 2 **POUNDS CANNED PEELED WHOLE TOMATOES, WITH THEIR JUICE, CRUSHED BY HAND**

In a medium bowl, combine the spinach, parsley, oregano, garlic, raisins, and pine nuts. Stir until well mixed. Season to taste with sea salt and pepper.

Lay the veal breast out flat and cover evenly with the spinach mixture. Roll the veal up fairly tightly and secure in several places with kitchen string. Season the outside of the veal with salt and pepper.

In a large Dutch oven, heat the olive oil over medium-high heat. Brown the veal roll on all sides, reducing the heat as necessary, and remove from the pan. Add the onion, celery, and carrot and cook over medium heat, stirring a few times, until the onion softens, about 5 minutes. Add the wine and cook, stirring, until it evaporates. Stir in the tomatoes. Return the veal to the pan, season with salt and pepper, and bring the liquid to a boil. Reduce the heat to a simmer, cover the pan, and cook for 1 hour. The sauce will be slightly thickened.

Remove the veal from the pan and cut it into ½-inch-thick slices. Arrange the slices on a warm platter. The sauce can be poured over the slices or served separately.

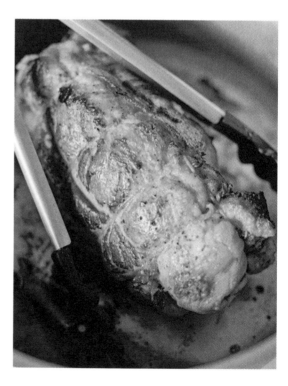

patate al forno

oven-roasted potatoes

So easy to make and so much flavor with the addition of fresh rosemary.

- ¼ CUP EXTRA-VIRGIN OLIVE OIL
- 6 CLOVES GARLIC, CRUSHED TO A PASTE
- 1 TABLESPOON FRESH ROSEMARY LEAVES
- 2 POUNDS VERY SMALL RED OR YELLOW POTATOES

Preheat the oven to 350F.

In a large bowl, combine the olive oil, garlic, and rosemary. Add the potatoes and toss in the oil to coat well.

Pour the potatoes into a large baking dish and arrange them in a single layer. Roast until fork-tender, about 1 hour.

salame al cioccolato

chocolate salami

Chocolate salami is a popular dessert in both Italy and Portugal. Shaped like a salami, it is the perfect combination of creaminess and crunch. Be aware, though, that this contains raw egg yolks.

- 2 LARGE EGG YOLKS
- ½ CUP GRANULATED SUGAR
- 9 TABLESPOONS UNSALTED BUTTER, SOFTENED
- 2 TABLESPOONS UNSWEETENED COCOA POWDER, PLUS MORE FOR ROLLING
- ½ CUP CURAÇAO LIQUEUR
- ½ POUND ALMOND BISCOTTI, CRUSHED (1 GENEROUS CUP)
- CONFECTIONERS' SUGAR

In a medium bowl, whisk the egg yolks and granulated sugar together until yellow and foamy. Whisk in the butter, then the cocoa, mixing each one in completely before adding the next. Stir in the liqueur and crushed biscotti, using a wooden spoon to mix.

Turn the dough onto a work surface (if the dough sticks to the work surface, roll it in a little confectioners' sugar) and form into a log 2 inches wide. Wrap in aluminum foil and refrigerate for 3 to 4 hours.

Before serving, roll the log in cocoa powder and sprinkle with confectioners' sugar. Cut into 1-inch slices and serve cold.

MENU

49

SERVES 8 TO 10

pizzette
small pizzas

maccheroni con ricotta
macaroni with ricotta

petti di pollo con pomodori arrostiti e aglio
chicken breasts with sun-dried tomatoes and garlic crust

bietola alla romana
swiss chard, roman style

crema di amaretto
amaretto decadence

If there's one thing that everyone says about my family when they come over for dinner, it's that we're loud and we're fun! Dinner together should never be a chore, and this menu with its simple pizzette and macaroni is a perfect one to get everybody involved and shouting across the kitchen.

pizzette

small pizzas

My mom always made these pizzette to get the party started. She would pass these delicious and festive starters around as the family was gathering, preparing the table, or working in the kitchen.

1   SMALL SALAMI ROLL

1   LOAF ITALIAN BREAD, CUT INTO ¼-INCH-THICK SLICES

    ABOUT ¼ CUP LISA'S CLASSIC TOMATO SAUCE (PAGE 89)

8   OUNCES FRESH OR STORE-BOUGHT MOZZARELLA, THINLY SLICED

1   TABLESPOON CHOPPED FRESH OREGANO

Preheat the oven to 325F.

Cut thin slices from the salami roll and put a slice on each slice of bread. Spread about ½ teaspoon of the tomato sauce over the salami. Top with a slice of mozzarella and sprinkle with oregano.

Set the pizzette on a large baking sheet and bake until the cheese melts, about 10 minutes. Serve immediately.

maccheroni con ricotta

macaroni with ricotta

This is classic Italian nursery food, prepared anytime someone is feeling under the weather.

2   POUNDS MACARONI, SUCH AS PASTINA OR ELBOW

1   CONTAINER (15 OUNCES) RICOTTA

3   TABLESPOONS SUGAR

1   TEASPOON GROUND CINNAMON

Bring a large pot of salted water to a boil. Add the macaroni and cook until al dente (if using pastina, cook for 6 minutes; if using elbow, cook for 8 minutes).

Meanwhile, in a medium bowl, beat together the ricotta, sugar, and cinnamon.

Drain the macaroni and pour into a warm serving dish. Add the ricotta mixture and stir to mix well. Serve immediately.

petti di pollo con pomodori arrostiti e aglio

chicken breasts with sun-dried tomatoes and garlic crust

The sun-dried tomato coating helps keep the chicken moist as well as providing tons of flavor.

- 4 CUPS FRESH BREADCRUMBS MADE FROM ITALIAN BREAD OR GOOD-QUALITY STORE-BOUGHT BREADCRUMBS
- 1 CUP OIL-PACKED SUN-DRIED TOMATOES, DRAINED
- 6 TABLESPOONS EXTRA-VIRGIN OLIVE OIL
- 4 CLOVES GARLIC, CHOPPED
- SEA SALT
- FRESHLY GROUND BLACK PEPPER
- 8 BONE-IN, SKIN-ON CHICKEN BREAST HALVES

Preheat the oven to 375F.

Combine the breadcrumbs, sun-dried tomatoes, 4½ tablespoons olive oil, and garlic in a food processor or blender. Pulse the mixture until the tomatoes are coarsely chopped. Season to taste with sea salt and pepper.

Heat the remaining 1½ tablespoons olive oil in a large skillet over medium-high heat. Add the chicken, skin side down, and cook until the skin is crisp and golden, about 5 minutes.

Transfer the chicken, skin side up, to a large baking sheet. Spoon the breadcrumb mixture over the breasts, dividing it equally and pressing down to help it adhere to the chicken. Bake until the chicken is cooked through, about 30 minutes. Arrange on a platter and serve.

bietola alla romana

swiss chard, roman style

Sautéed pancetta gives this Swiss chard dish a wonderful crunchy texture.

- 2 BUNCHES SWISS CHARD, STEMS TRIMMED AT LEAST 1 INCH FROM END, AND ALL CHOPPED
- 3 TABLESPOONS EXTRA-VIRGIN OLIVE OIL
- ½ POUND ITALIAN PANCETTA, CHOPPED IN ¼-INCH PIECES
- ½ TEASPOON SEA SALT
- ½ TEASPOON GROUND BLACK PEPPER

Bring 2 cups of water to a boil in a large pot. Add the Swiss chard and boil for 5 minutes. Drain well and set aside.

In a large skillet, heat the olive oil over medium heat until hot but not smoking, then add the chopped pancetta and cook for 4 minutes. Add the Swiss chard and continue to cook until the chard is wilted, about five minutes. Season with salt and pepper.

Transfer to a serving dish and serve.

crema di amaretto

amaretto decadence

What a way to end a meal—an Amaretto-flavored zabaglione folded together with fresh whipped cream!

- 6 **LARGE EGG YOLKS**
- ¼ **CUP SUGAR**
- ½ **CUP AMARETTO LIQUEUR**
- 1 **CUP HEAVY CREAM**
- **SLIVERED ALMONDS, LIGHTLY TOASTED, FOR GARNISH**
- **SHAVED DARK CHOCOLATE FOR GARNISH**

In the top of a double boiler, off the heat, whisk together the egg yolks, sugar, and Amaretto until light colored and frothy. Set the pan over simmering water (don't let the bottom touch the water) and whisk until the mixture thickens to the point that it will coat the back of a spoon, 8 to 10 minutes.

Remove the mixture from the heat and transfer to a bowl. Let it cool a little and refrigerate until thoroughly chilled, at least 30 minutes.

In a large bowl using an electric mixer, whip the cream until stiff peaks form. Fold in the chilled amaretto mixture. Distribute the mixture evenly among long-stemmed wine goblets and keep refrigerated until ready to serve. Right before serving, sprinkle the tops with the toasted almond slivers and chocolate shavings.

"buon vino fa buon sangue!"

good wine makes good blood!

MENU

50

SERVES 8 TO 10

cuore di palmo al balsamico
hearts of palm in balsamic vinegar

minestrone
italian vegetable soup

petti di pollo aglio e olio
chicken in oil and garlic

piselli con prosciutto
peas with prosciutto

crostata di tartufo alla nocciola
hazelnut truffle pie

My father was the thirteenth of thirteen children, and his mother never wasted a thing in the kitchen with so many mouths to feed. A big pot of hearty minestrone (which literally means "big soup") was always on the back burner of her stove. The stalks of vegetables not used in other dishes or leftover meat bones all made it into this soup to flavor the broth.

cuore di palmo al balsamico

hearts of palm in balsamic vinegar

This salad is wonderful served with lightly toasted crostini.

- 2 CANS (8 OUNCES EACH) HEARTS OF PALM
- 1 LEMON, CUT INTO QUARTERS
- 2 TABLESPOONS PLUS 1 TEASPOON BALSAMIC VINEGAR
-   LEAVES FROM 1 SMALL BUNCH FRESH ITALIAN PARSLEY

Rinse the hearts of palm well and pat dry with paper towels. Cut into 1-inch pieces and place in a medium salad bowl. Squeeze the lemon quarters over the hearts of palm and toss with the vinegar. Sprinkle with parsley and serve.

minestrone

italian vegetable soup

Be sure to serve this with a glass of excellent Chianti—it's an excellent accompaniment.

- 3 TABLESPOONS EXTRA-VIRGIN OLIVE OIL
- ¼ POUND PANCETTA, ROUGHLY CHOPPED
- 2–3 STALKS CELERY, FINELY CHOPPED
- 3 MEDIUM CARROTS, FINELY CHOPPED
- 1 MEDIUM ONION, FINELY CHOPPED
- 1 OR 2 CLOVES GARLIC, CRUSHED
- 2 CANS (14 OUNCES EACH) CHOPPED TOMATOES (WITH THEIR JUICE)
- 4 CUPS CHICKEN OR VEGETABLE STOCK OR REDUCED-SODIUM CANNED BROTH
-   SEA SALT
-   FRESHLY GROUND BLACK PEPPER
- 2 CANS (14 OUNCES EACH) CANNELLINI BEANS
- ½ CUP ELBOW MACARONI OR SOUP PASTA
- 2–4 TABLESPOONS CHOPPED FRESH ITALIAN PARSLEY
-   GRATED PARMIGIANO-REGGIANO FOR SERVING

In a large pot, heat the olive oil over medium-low heat. Add the pancetta, celery, carrots, and onion and cook, stirring occasionally, until softened, about 5 minutes.

Add the garlic and tomatoes, breaking the tomatoes up with a wooden spoon. Pour in the stock. Season with sea salt and pepper to taste and bring to a boil. Partially cover the pot, reduce the heat to a gentle simmer, and let cook until the vegetables are soft, about 20 minutes.

Drain the beans and add half of them to the pot. Purée the other half in a blender and add them to the pot. Bring the soup to a boil again. Partially cover, reduce the heat to a gentle simmer, and cook another 20 minutes.

Add the macaroni and let cook until al dente, approximately 8 minutes. Stir in the parsley and taste for salt and pepper.

Serve hot, sprinkled with lots of Parmigiano.

petti di pollo aglio e olio

chicken in oil and garlic

If you love spaghetti aglio e olio, you will love this dish, redolent of garlic and spiked with a generous sprinkling of hot red pepper flakes.

- ¾ CUP EXTRA-VIRGIN OLIVE OIL
- 6 CLOVES GARLIC, THINLY SLICED
- 8–10 BONELESS, SKINLESS CHICKEN BREAST HALVES
- 1 TABLESPOON RED PEPPER FLAKES
  SEA SALT

In a large skillet, heat the olive oil over medium heat. Add the garlic and cook, stirring, 1 to 2 minutes. Add the chicken breasts and cook until golden on both sides and cooked through, about 8 minutes per side. Transfer the chicken to a warm serving platter.

Add a little more olive oil to the skillet. Add the red pepper flakes and salt and cook over medium heat 1 minute. Pour mixture over the chicken and serve.

piselli con prosciutto

peas with prosciutto

Sweet baby peas and salty, savory prosciutto are a perfect combination, and an inspired contorno for Petti di Pollo Aglio e Olio.

- 2 POUNDS FROZEN BABY PEAS
- 10 THIN SLICES PROSCIUTTO DI PARMA
- ¼ CUP EXTRA-VIRGIN OLIVE OIL
  SEA SALT

Steam the peas until tender.

Meanwhile, cut the prosciutto into bite-size squares and place in a medium serving bowl. Drain the peas and add them to the bowl. Add the olive oil and toss to mix. Season to taste with salt, if desired.

crostata di tartufo alla nocciola

hazelnut truffle pie

"Glorious" is the only way to describe this dessert. The hazelnuts give crunch and rich flavor to the crust.

CRUST

- 1¼ STICKS (10 TABLESPOONS) UNSALTED BUTTER, CUT INTO PIECES AND SOFTENED
- ¾ CUP CONFECTIONERS' SUGAR
- 1 LARGE EGG
- 1½ CUPS PLUS 2 TABLESPOONS ALL-PURPOSE FLOUR
- ¼ CUP FINELY GROUND PEELED TOASTED HAZELNUTS

FILLING

- 1 POUND BITTERSWEET CHOCOLATE (70% CACAO), CHOPPED
- 1 CUP HEAVY CREAM
- 2 TEASPOONS VANILLA EXTRACT

Make the crust: In a large bowl using an electric mixer, cream the butter until smooth. Add the confectioners' sugar and beat in well. Add the egg and beat until smooth. Add the flour all at once and, using a wooden spoon (unless you have a stand mixer), mix until almost incorporated. Add the hazelnuts and mix just until smooth, being careful not to overmix the dough. Form the dough into a disk and wrap in plastic wrap. Chill at least 2 hours.

On a lightly floured work surface, roll out the pastry to a 10-inch circle. Fit the crust into a 9-inch pie plate and crimp the edge. Chill the crust while you make the filling.

Preheat the oven to 375F.

Make the filling: Over gently simmering water (in the top of a double boiler or in a glass or stainless-steel bowl), melt the chocolate. Gradually stir in the cream, never allowing the mixture to boil. Stir in the vanilla. Continue to stir until the mixture thickens and pour into the chilled crust.

Bake the pie for 20 minutes. Let cool to room temperature and serve.

MENU

51

SERVES 8 TO 10

grissini con erbe e prosciutto
breadsticks with herbs and prosciutto

....

lasagne verde
spinach lasagne

....

braciole della nonna
nana's braciole

....

cipolline al forno
baked cipolline

....

monte bianco
chestnuts with cream

Rolling out the lasagne pasta with my nana is a warm memory, and it's one of the first dishes I taught my own children to make. I wake them up on Sunday morning to the smell of homemade breakfast rolls and coffee, and before you know it, they are kneading, rolling, and layering the lasagne. Green lasagne, with its delicate taste and texture, is a nice alternative to lasagne with meat sauce.

grissini con erbe e prosciutto

breadsticks with herbs and prosciutto

This is a quick, easy antipasto that also makes a wonderful merenda, or snack.

2	PACKAGES (14 OUNCES EACH) ITALIAN BREAD STICKS
3	TABLESPOONS EXTRA-VIRGIN OLIVE OIL
1	TABLESPOON COARSE SEA SALT
2	TABLESPOONS DRIED ROSEMARY
12–18	VERY THIN SLICES PROSCIUTTO DI PARMA

Rub each breadstick with the olive oil and roll in the salt and rosemary. Wrap each stick with a slice of prosciutto and serve.

lasagne verde

spinach lasagne

Lasagne Verde uses very little tomato sauce in order not to overpower the flavor of the spinach noodles. The besciamella and plenty of Parmigiano-Reggiano make it a creamy delight.

SPINACH PASTA DOUGH

1	POUND FRESH OR FROZEN SPINACH
4	CUPS UNBLEACHED ALL-PURPOSE FLOUR
3	EXTRA-LARGE EGGS
1	TEASPOON SEA SALT
4	TEASPOONS EXTRA-VIRGIN OLIVE OIL

BESCIAMELLA

2	STICKS (16 TABLESPOONS) UNSALTED BUTTER
½	CUP (8 TABLESPOONS) UNBLEACHED FLOUR
6	CUPS WHOLE MILK
1	TEASPOON SEA SALT
½	TEASPOON GROUND BLACK PEPPER

LASAGNE

1	CONTAINER (15 OUNCES) RICOTTA
2	EXTRA-LARGE EGGS
	SEA SALT
	FRESHLY GROUND BLACK PEPPER
2	CUPS LISA'S CLASSIC TOMATO SAUCE (PAGE 89)
2	CUPS GRATED PARMIGIANO-REGGIANO

Make the pasta dough: Wash the fresh spinach thoroughly to remove any dirt, and transfer the leaves, still wet, to a large pot. Cover the pot and steam the spinach over high heat for a few minutes, until the leaves wilt. Drain the spinach, and when it's cool enough to handle, squeeze it dry and finely chop. If using frozen spinach, cook according to package directions, drain, and chop.

Place the flour in a mound on a pasta board or wooden cutting board. Make a well in the center of the flour and crack the eggs into the well. Add the sea salt and olive oil to the well. Using a fork, begin incorporating the flour into the eggs and oil. After it is all mixed together, knead the dough with your hands until it develops an elastic consistency. Add the spinach and continue to knead until the spinach is fully incorporated into the dough.

Break away a small ball of the dough, about the size of your palm, and flatten it. Feed the dough into a pasta machine and continue to run it through the machine until the strips are 4 to 5 inches wide and ⅛ inch thick. As you run the dough through the machine it will become increasingly more elastic. Cut the strips into 12-inch-long pieces.

Make the besciamella: Melt the butter in a medium saucepan over medium heat, add the flour and stir until smooth. Slowly add the milk, whisking constantly to keep lumps from forming. Stir until mixture thickens and coats the back of a wooden spoon. Season with the salt and pepper.

Cook the pasta: Bring a large pot of salted water to a boil. Cook the lasagne noodles in batches, about two pieces at a time, for about 30 seconds. Using silicone-tipped tongs, transfer the pasta to a colander and set under cold running water to stop the cooking. Lay the cooked noodles out flat on a cotton kitchen towel. I also cover them with towels to keep them from drying out.

Preheat the oven to 375F.

Assemble and bake the lasagne: In a medium bowl, combine the ricotta, eggs, and sea salt and pepper to taste.

In a large, deep rectangular baking dish, begin layering the lasagne. Spoon in just enough of the tomato sauce to coat the bottom. Cover with a layer of noodles. Spread the noodles with about ¾ cup tomato sauce, then a layer of ¾ cup besciamella, then about ¾ cup of the ricotta mixture. Sprinkle with Parmigiano and repeat the layering until the pan is full. Finish with a layer of noodles, then tomato sauce, then besciamella, then a final sprinkling of Parmigiano. (Extra pasta can be frozen.) Bake for 30 minutes, until bubbly.

braciole della nonna

nana's braciole

What would an Italian American Sunday dinner be without braciole? I use flank steak and roll it up with my nana's filling of breadcrumbs, lots of garlic, pine nuts, raisins, and oregano, then simmer it for hours in a big pot of tomato sauce until it's fork tender.

- 8 CUPS LISA'S CLASSIC TOMATO SAUCE (PAGE 89)
- 3 FLANK STEAKS (ABOUT 2 POUNDS EACH)
- 1 CUP EXTRA-VIRGIN OLIVE OIL
- 1½ CUPS PLAIN BREADCRUMBS
- 8 CLOVES GARLIC, CHOPPED
- 1 CUP PINE NUTS
- ¾ CUP GOLDEN RAISINS (OPTIONAL)
- 1 TEASPOON DRIED OREGANO
-    SEA SALT
-    FRESHLY GROUND BLACK PEPPER

Bring the sauce to a simmer in a pot.

Place each of the flank steaks between two pieces of plastic wrap or waxed paper and pound gently with a meat mallet until 1/4 to 1/8 inch thick. Rub the steaks with some of the olive oil.

In a medium bowl, combine the breadcrumbs, garlic, pine nuts, raisins if using, oregano, and sea salt and pepper to taste. Add enough of the olive oil to moisten the mixture. Spread the filling in a thin layer across the flank steaks. Roll them up and tie in 3 or 4 places with kitchen string.

In a large skillet, heat the remaining olive oil. Brown the braciole on all sides and transfer to the simmering sauce. Turn the heat down to low, cover the pan, and cook in the sauce for at least 5 to 6 hours.

When ready to serve, remove the braciole from the sauce. Cut into 2- to 3-inch-wide slices and arrange on a platter. Freeze the tomato sauce to use for another meal.

cipolline al forno

baked cipolline

Cipolline are small Italian onions. Once you peel them, they are flat on either side.

- 3 TABLESPOONS EXTRA-VIRGIN OLIVE OIL
- 36 CIPOLLINE, PEELED
-    COARSE SEA SALT

Preheat the oven to 350F.

Pour the olive oil in a medium baking dish and tilt the dish to coat the bottom. Set the cipolline flat in the dish. Place 1 or 2 grains of the salt in the center of each onion.

Bake until the onions are golden and slightly caramelized, about 30 minutes.

monte bianco

chestnuts with cream

Monte Bianco is named for the highest mountain in the Alps (Mont Blanc), as it is shaped to resemble a snow-peaked mountain.

- 2 POUNDS CANNED CHESTNUTS, DRAINED
- 1 CUP GRANULATED SUGAR
- ½ CUP DARK RUM
- 2 CUPS HEAVY CREAM
- ¼ CUP CONFECTIONERS' SUGAR

Place the chestnuts, granulated sugar, and 1/4 cup of the rum in a food processor and process until smooth. Form the mixture into the shape of a mountain on a serving platter.

In a medium bowl using an electric mixer, whip the cream until peaks begin to form. Add the confectioners' sugar and the remaining 1/4 cup rum until stiff peaks form. Spoon the cream over the chestnut mixture.

MENU

52

SERVES 8 TO 10

biscotti di parmigiano
parmesan wheels

timballo
sicilian timbale

filetto di manzo grigliata
grilled beef tenderloin

verdure siciliane arrostiti
roasted sicilian vegetables

strufoli della nonna
nana's strufoli

We all can relate to having unexpected guests. One Sunday, my two grown nephews showed up at my home unannounced to surprise my daughter on her birthday. Fortunately, Felicia had requested Timballo, a dish that is "basta e avanza" (enough and then some) to feed a crowd. This menu is perfect for a Sunday dinner when you are not sure how many people will be around your table.

biscotti di parmigiano
parmesan wheels

These crispy, buttery rounds, each topped with a walnut half, are positively addictive.

- 1 **CUP ALL-PURPOSE FLOUR**
- ¼ **TEASPOON SALT**
- ¼ **TEASPOON CAYENNE PEPPER**
- 1 **STICK (8 TABLESPOONS) COLD UNSALTED BUTTER, CUT INTO ½-INCH-THICK SLICES**
- 1 **CUP GRATED PARMIGIANO-REGGIANO**
- 1 **LARGE EGG, BEATEN**
- 24–36 **WALNUT HALVES**

In a medium bowl, blend the flour, salt, and cayenne, and add the butter slices. Using a pastry cutter or 2 knives, cut the butter into the flour mixture until it resembles coarse peas. Add the Parmigiano. Mix everything together well, and quickly knead the mixture into a ball. Flatten the ball slightly, cover with plastic wrap, and refrigerate for 45 minutes.

Preheat the oven to 400F.

On a lightly floured work surface, roll the dough out to ¼ inch thickness. Cut out circles of dough using an upside-down espresso cup (about 2½ inches in diameter). Place the circles on a large baking sheet and lightly brush each with the beaten egg. Top each with a walnut half, pushing it gently into the dough. Bake 10 to 15 minutes, until golden.

timballo
sicilian timbale

There's no doubt about it—making a timballo is an undertaking. But this is a special menu, the one I serve every year at Christmas, and it's all about family and celebrating the day. Timballo, a layered dome of risotto, pasta, and vegetables, is a traditional dish at Christmas in Sicily, and it makes for a spectacular presentation. You'll need a 5-quart stainless-steel bowl in which to bake it.

- 2 **POUNDS ARBORIO RICE**
- 5 **LARGE EGGS**
- 4½ **CUPS GRATED PECORINO ROMANO**
- 2 **CUPS LISA'S CLASSIC TOMATO SAUCE (PAGE 88)**
- 1 **POUND ZITI**
- 3 **TABLESPOONS EXTRA-VIRGIN OLIVE OIL**
- ½ **ONION, FINELY CHOPPED**
- ¼ **POUND BUTTON MUSHROOMS, SLICED**
  SEA SALT
- ¾ **POUND GROUND VEAL**
- ½ **POUND GROUND PORK**
- 1 **TABLESPOON SUGAR**
  LEAVES FROM 3 SPRIGS FRESH BASIL, CHOPPED
- ⅛ **TEASPOON FRESHLY GRATED NUTMEG**
  FRESHLY GROUND BLACK PEPPER
- 1 **CUP FROZEN PEAS**
  UNSALTED BUTTER AND PLAIN BREADCRUMBS TO PREPARE THE TIMBALLO BOWL

The night before you plan to prepare the timballo, cook the rice according to the package directions. Drain well and let cool. Once it is cool, beat 4 of the eggs and add to the rice along with 2 cups of the cheese, mixing together well. Transfer the mixture to a large shallow bowl and smooth the top with a rubber spatula. Cover with a clean kitchen towel and place in a cool spot (not the refrigerator) to set up overnight.

Also, since Lisa's classic tomato sauce takes 2 to 4 hours to prepare, you may want to make it the night before. Otherwise, prepare the sauce the next day, before you continue with the recipe.

Bring a large pot of salted water to a boil and cook the pasta until al dente, approximately 7 minutes.

Meanwhile, in a medium saucepan, heat the olive oil over medium heat. Add the onion and cook until softened, stirring a few times, taking care not to brown it. Add the mushrooms and salt and turn the heat to high. Cook the mushrooms, stirring. Once they lose their liquid and it begins to evaporate, add the ground meat. Turn the heat down to medium. Add the tomato sauce when the mixture begins to thicken. Stir in the sugar, basil, nutmeg, and salt and pepper to taste.

Drain the pasta and toss it with just enough of the sauce to coat it. Using a slotted spoon, transfer three quarters of the solids (the meat and mushrooms) from the sauce to the pasta. Mix in the remaining 2$\frac{1}{2}$ cups cheese and the peas. (Be careful not to transfer much in the way of liquid or the timballo will get soggy and crack.) Let the mixture cool to room temperature.

Preheat the oven to 400F.

Grease a 5-quart stainless-steel bowl generously with butter. Coat the inside thoroughly with breadcrumbs. Sprinkle an additional tablespoon of crumbs over the bottom of the bowl. Line the bowl with the rice mixture, packing it $\frac{1}{2}$ inch thick against the inside of the bowl. Press the rice gently but firmly with your hand, moistened with water to keep it from sticking. Be sure there are no thin spots. Bring the wall of rice up to the edge of the bowl.

Fill the center of the bowl with the pasta mixture so it reaches 1 inch from the top. Add the remaining rice to create a top layer that is even with the top of the bowl. Smooth the rice into a flat layer and make sure you've got a tight seal all the way around the bowl. (This is important because after the timballo is cooked, it is flipped over, so the top becomes the bottom.)

Beat the 1 remaining egg and brush it over the top of the timballo. Bake on the center rack until the top is a light golden brown, about 1 hour.

Remove the timballo from the oven and immediately run a knife around the edge to release the timballo from the bowl. Let the timballo rest for 10 minutes. Place a serving platter on top of the bowl, flip, and remove the bowl. Let the timballo rest for another 5 minutes, and then bring it to the table to slice there.

filetto di manzo grigliata
grilled beef tenderloin

Beef tenderloin is a delicious indulgence, and here it gets an Italian twist, marinating in red wine. It is then served on a bed of arugula dressed with lemon juice.

- 1 WHOLE BEEF TENDERLOIN (6 POUNDS)
  SEA SALT
  FRESHLY GROUND BLACK PEPPER
- 3 CUPS RED WINE
- 2 BUNCHES ARUGULA, STEMS TRIMMED
  JUICE OF 2 LEMONS

Trim the tenderloin of any fat and silver skin. Season all over with sea salt and pepper and place in a large glass baking dish. Pour the wine over the beef and let it marinate at room temperature for 1 hour, turning it a couple of times.

Preheat the grill or a grill pan on the stove over very high heat. Remove the tenderloin from the marinade and cut across into ½-inch-thick slices. Stretch the pieces out and season with salt and pepper. Brown the slices on the grill or in the grill pan for 2 to 3 minutes per side. As they are cooked, remove them to a warm tray.

In a large bowl, toss the arugula with the lemon juice.

To serve, place a mound of dressed arugula on each plate and top with 3 or 4 slices of tenderloin.

verdure siciliane arrostiti
roasted sicilian vegetables

This earthy combination of red bell peppers, onions, and eggplant is a perfect complement to the beef. Feel free to add potatoes to the mix, if you like.

- 2 MEDIUM EGGPLANTS
  COARSE SEA SALT
- 2 LARGE RED BELL PEPPERS
- 2 RED ONIONS
- 1 CUP EXTRA-VIRGIN OLIVE OIL
- ¼ CUP FRESH LEMON JUICE
  FINE SEA SALT
  FRESHLY GROUND BLACK PEPPER

Cut the eggplant into bite-size cubes, leaving the skin on. Place in a colander and sprinkle generously with coarse sea salt. Let the eggplant drain for at least 30 minutes to remove excess water. Rinse well and pat dry.

Meanwhile, seed the bell peppers and cut into bite-size squares. Peel and cut the red onions into bite-size cubes.

Preheat the oven to 350F.

In a large bowl, combine the olive oil, lemon juice, and fine sea salt and pepper to taste. Add the peppers, eggplant, and onions and toss until well coated. Pour the mixture onto a large baking sheet and spread into a single layer. Bake for 45 minutes, until tender.

strufoli della nonna

nana's strufoli

No Sicilian Christmas is complete without strufoli, bite-size pieces of golden fried dough coated with a honey glaze. My nana added her own personal touch to the recipe by presenting the strufoli in a wreath shape, decorated with brightly colored sprinkles.

4   CUPS ALL-PURPOSE FLOUR

6   LARGE EGGS

½   STICK (4 TABLESPOONS) UNSALTED BUTTER, SOFTENED

    VEGETABLE OIL FOR FRYING

1   CUP HONEY

    FINELY GRATED ZEST OF 1 LEMON

    FINELY GRATED ZEST OF 1 ORANGE

    MULTICOLORED SPRINKLES

Mound the flour on a work surface. Make a well in the center and add the eggs, one at a time, mixing in gently with a fork after each addition. With your hands, add the butter and mix well to form a dough. Knead until the dough is soft and supple, about 10 minutes. Transfer the dough to a large bowl, cover with a damp kitchen towel, and let rest for 30 minutes.

Dust two trays or baking sheets with flour. Pull off a small piece of dough (about the size of a walnut) and roll it out like a pencil. Cut the pencil into ½-inch-wide pieces and transfer to the flour-dusted trays. Repeat with the remaining dough.

Heat about 1 inch of vegetable oil in a wide, deep skillet until very hot. Drop the balls into the hot oil, in batches, and fry until golden, about 3 minutes. Remove from the oil using a slotted spoon and drain on paper towels.

In a large skillet, warm the honey with the citrus zests over medium-low heat for about 5 minutes. Remove from the heat and fold the strufoli into the honey, stirring until they are evenly coated.

Pour the strufoli onto a serving platter to form a wreath shape; you can use two wooden spoons to perfect the shape. Before serving, decorate with the sprinkles.

caponigri family history

My family history is like that of any other Italian-American; it is a story of struggle, triumph, and treasured tradition, the glue that holds all the different generations together. My father's parents, the Caponigris, came to America in the late 19th century from a small town called Ricigliano in the region of Campagna, not far from Naples. The town itself was inhabited by shepherds, and indeed, that is what my grandfather, Nicola, was. His bride, my grandmother Lucia Sarocco Caponigri, was only eighteen years old when they set sail for America a week after their wedding. They settled in Chicago, where my grandfather opened a newspaper stand on the corner of State Street and Congress Parkway. He got up every morning at four to fold and sell the papers, a job my father would help him with as a little boy. My grandmother, on the other hand, barely left the house, except to serve as a midwife. Eventually she gave birth to thirteen children, my father being the thirteenth.

In 1898, my maternal grandmother,

left: *My Caponigri grandparents with my father, Chicago, Illinois*

Catherine Lione Franco, was born in Castelvetrano, on the western coast of Sicily. Her grandfather owned a successful general store, which allowed him some time to enjoy his passion for poetry, and for her father and uncles to enjoy a comfortable life. Unfortunately, when my nana turned twelve, economic difficulty came to Sicily. Suddenly clients were bringing in goods such as chickens to pay for her grandfather's goods, and just as suddenly, her father was unable to pay his own bills. Something had to be done, and the decision was made to move the family to America.

Emigrate they did, in 1910, but upon their arrival at Ellis Island, my nana was quarantined for six months because her severe case of glaucoma was considered to be contagious. Nana often recalled these days to me with great sadness, but would always insist that they made her strong. When she finally joined her family on Christopher Street in New York's Little Italy misfortune struck again. Her mother, Rosa Bacile Lione, died suddenly of pneumonia. As the only girl in a house with four brothers who were attending law school and pharmacy school, my nana soon was forced to quit school in order to cook, clean, and care for them. Occasionally she would venture out to the steps of the brownstone to play with the other neighborhood girls. On one of these occasions she met my grandfather.

My maternal grandfather, Francesco Franco, came to America with his parents from the town of Amorosi outside of Naples. His father, Nicola, opened a tailor shop in Little Italy, which soon became renowned for its quality, servicing clients such as Mayor Fiorello La Guardia and making uniforms for the New York Police Department. My grandfather, eldest of eight boys and one girl, delivered the pack-ages of dresses and suits to the wealthy clients on Fifth Avenue. One day, between deliveries, he spotted my grandmother's bouncing curls, and the rest, as they say, is pure amore. They secretly married at City Hall at ages 18 and 20, but, luckily, someone in the neighborhood told my great-grandfather the news. I think the most beautiful part of this story is that my great-grandparents had also fallen for my grandmother. On Easter in 1918, just one day after my grandparents had secretly wed and the entire Franco family was seated at the Easter table, my great grandfather made the announcement that they could not begin Easter Dinner because a member of the family was missing. He turned to my grandfather and said: "Go get your wife." My grandparents had five children and were married for 78 years; they lived to the ripe old ages of 98 and 101.

My mother, Winifred Filomena Franco, was an ambitious woman who decided that she wanted to go to college, but back then, as in my nana's time, this just wasn't done. Against my grandfather's wishes (he was a traditional male who didn't believe in university education for women), but with my nana's blessing, she defied the odds and earned a scholarship to the University of Iowa. Nervous, but determined,

top left: *Guido and me, Florence, Italy* / top right: *My grandparents, Catherine and Francesco Franco* / bottom: *Felicia, Guido, and me, Forte dei Marmi, Italy*

my mother, at age 17, boarded a train to Iowa and her future.

As fate would have it, my father, A. Robert Caponigri, a very young Professor of Philosophy, arrived at the University of Iowa that same year. My mother walked into my father's class to fulfill a humanities requirement. He took one look at this young Italian girl from New York and decided she needed to be properly fed. After many dinners together and shared family histories, my father proposed. Four years later he and my mother moved to the University of Notre Dame, where they remained for the rest of their lives—my father as a world-renowned philosopher, my mother as a professor of Geology and Chemistry at Holy Cross College of Notre Dame.

My father's life story is quite interesting: When he was only twelve years old, his Jesuit teachers determined that he was incredibly bright, and they sat my grandparents, Nicola and Lucia Caponigri, down in their home in Chicago, to plead the case of sending my father to one of the Jesuit boarding schools in Wisconsin. My grandparents, aware that they could never give my father the opportunities a Jesuit education could, did the unthinkable and sent their young son away from their close-knit Italian family. He never lived at home again. Going on to Loyola University, Harvard for his Master's, and the University of Chicago for his PhD., my father became one of the most recognized authorities on Italian philosophy in the world, writing over 17 books on the subject. Due to his many research projects, he received numerous Fulbright, Rockefeller, and Folger grants, to name just a few, all of which took him abroad to Europe. We would almost always accompany him, and my earliest memories of living in Italy begin at the age of four. My father had visiting professor positions or research positions in Rome, Bologna, Perugia, Padova, and Florence.

Wherever we lived in Italy, my father believed we should live like natives, going to Italian schools and speaking native Italian, respecting the local traditions, learning the local customs. From the ages of six to nine I lived in Madrid, Spain, where my father taught and conducted research at The University of Madrid on the Spanish philosopher Zubiri, and my memories of Spain under Franco remain with me to this day. My father immediately sent me to a Spanish convent school, even though I did not speak one word of Spanish. It is thanks to my father that today I am natively proficient in English, Italian, and Spanish, and fluent in French.

I always felt both American and Italian growing up; much like my father had felt his entire life. Both cultures were home to me. After I completed my education, undergraduate and doctorate, at the University of Notre Dame, I entered the legal and corporate arenas in the United States. But as I began to have my own family, I knew I wanted my children to grow up bi-culturally. I was presented with a wonderful opportunity to work in Italy when my children were very small. Felicia

left: *Caponigri family Chicago, Illinois /* **right:** *Felicia, Roberto and Guido in Tuscany.*

top left: *Me with my parents and grandparents, Notre Dame, Indiana*
bottom right: *Felicia and me*

was entering second grade, Bobby was entering kindergarten, Guido was barely in preschool, and I jumped at the opportunity that changed my children's lives. I implemented the philosophy my father had instilled in me, and Felicia and Guido are both multi-lingual. My son Bobby is autistic and non-verbal.

It was while raising my children abroad that I realized the difference between the hectic American lifestyle and the Italian way of life. Stopping and eating "pranzo" with your family every day, creating meals together with your children, not only creates more quality time with your family but adds in positive ways to their development as people—socially, emotionally, academically and healthfully. Childhood obesity in Italy barely exists. I had grown up with family Sunday Dinner, thanks to my nana and my mother, but raising my own children in Italy for a decade showed me on a daily basis what our American lifestyle lacks.

And then I returned to the United States because Bobby was not progressing in the Special Education Schools in Italy. Felicia entered high school here in the States and Guido, junior

high. Of course, our tradition of Sunday Dinner continued, and frequently my children would ask if their friends could join us because they did not have Sunday Dinner at their homes. Of course, I said yes. These children would ask if we ate like this every week, if I made food from scratch, if I could tell their parents about Sunday Dinner. And frequently, during the week, I would receive phone calls from their mothers asking what I had prepared, how did I get my children to cook with me, and especially how did I create my menus. They would tell me that their children could speak of nothing else. Felicia and I had long discussions about these reactions, and one day she said to me, "Mommy, you have to write a cookbook with your Sunday menus."

And so, here are all the recipes that I prepare for my family, every Sunday, with love—the very same recipes that were handed down to me, as well as those from my years with my children in Italy!

My warmest wish for each of you is for many happy, memorable Sunday Dinners with your family.

Buon Appetito!
Lisa Caponigri

acknowledgments

I WOULD LIKE TO EXPRESS MY PROFOUND APPRECIATION TO THE FOLLOWING PEOPLE:

My agent, Tony Gardner, for his unwavering support, constant guidance and friendship—but for Tony, this book would never have come to fruition;

my attorney, Cathy Frankel, for her wise counsel and ability to see and quantify the present and future;

Marcus Leaver, Jason Prince, and Carlo Devito of Sterling Publishing, who believed in my message of Sunday Dinner and made my dream of taking it nationally a reality;

Diane Abrams of Sterling Publishing, who has worked tirelessly as my editor to create a breathtakingly beautiful book;

everyone at Sterling Publishing in marketing, publicity and sales.

MY FAMILY, WHOSE LEGACY OF LOVE AND LOYALTY SUSTAINS ME:

my grandparents, who lived the belief "sempre famiglia" every day of their lives;

my father, whose quiet and indomitable strength continues to guide me from above;

my mother, for her indelible strength of character, resiliency and unending support;

my siblings, Victoria and Robert, whose love and support, in word and action, is constant;

my three children:

Felicia, my kindred spirit, the embodiment of sunshine, support and love;

Bobby, who through his autism shows me that love is not limited to words;

Guido, "amore della mia vita," who with his huge heart, wit and sensitivity beyond his years, remains my calm eye in the midst of life's storm;

Ricordatevi, bambini miei, che la vostra Mamma vi adora per sempre.

And lastly, but ever so importantly, to every individual who came to meet me at Italian festivals, farmer's markets and book signings, who echoed my sentiment: "Whatever DID happen to Sunday dinner?" and who faithfully bought the first self-published book, keeping our wonderful tradition of Sunday dinner alive, cooking and eating with their families and building incomparable memories. Without each and every one of you this new edition would not have been possible.

index

(Mrs. Bea)

...sugar...
...eggs... less one egg white
...cup milk
1/2 tbsp baking powder
...tsp vanilla
Blend all together
...ke small amo...

Beat one egg
...le water
...en the dough and
...m seeds Bake 350°
cookies - 1 1/2 c crisco - 1/4 c sugar
...avoring. flour
...wich little
...ugh all together with
...he little balls roll...
...grated almonds
...center & bake

Almond Cookies

3 c - flour also use 1/2 rice flour
1 tsp soda - 1/2 tsp Salt
1 c sugar
1 1/2 c of shortning - use 1/2 butter
1 tsp almond extract
1 beaten egg
1 c blanche alm(s)
Seft dry ing
    mix shortning & sugar

2 - eggs - 1 Lemon -
1 cup of Sugar - 1 Cup
1 1/2 tbsp Melted Butt...
- Separate eggs
(add about half of t...
eggs will beat up to a
add other ingredients
Beat egg whites and
Yolk Mixture. Pou...
Pou...

Sausage + Broccoli Rabe

with leaves in
salted water for one minute + then put
in ice water. Cook orecchiette in broccol
water.
Sweet Ital Sausage (out of casing), cook
thoroughly breaking up. Season with
cloves of garlic, mince garlic +
add a few pinches of red pepper.
Add broccoli rabe to sausage + add
to pasta; grate parmigiano on top.

- SALTIMBOCCA -

For 8 Scallopini, you need 8 very thin
slices of Ham (PROSCIUTTO OR) Top each
Scallopini with a slice of Ham, pound
the two together with a meat Mallet
working into the veal side a mixture
of 1 teaspoon grated lemon rind, 1/2 tps
Sage & 1/4 tbs Salt. Roll up with ham inside
Fasten together with picks. Saute in butter till brown
on all sides. Serve immediately - Makes 4 servings

8 scallopini
olive oil + butter
add to the
...til tender
...e. Garnish